ETERNAL WARRIOR

SWORD OF THE WILD

GREG PAK | TREVOR HAIRSINE | CLAYTON CRAIN | DIEGO BERNARD

CONTENTS

Collection Cover Art: Clayton Crain

VALIANT.

Eternal Warrior®: Sword of the Wild. Published by Valiant
Entertainment, LLC. Office of Publication: 424 West 33rd Street,
New York, NY 10001. Compilation copyright © 2014 Valiant
Entertainment, Inc. All rights reserved. Contains materials originally
published in single magazine form as Eternal Warrior #1-4
Copyright ©2013 Valiant Entertainment, Inc. All rights reserved. All
characters, their distinctive likenesses and related indicia featured
in this publication are trademarks of Valiant Entertainment, Inc.
The stories, characters, and incidents featured in this publication
are entirely fictional. Valiant Entertainment does not read or accept
unsolicited submissions of ideas, stories, or artwork.
Printed in the USA. First Printing. ISBN: 9781939346209.

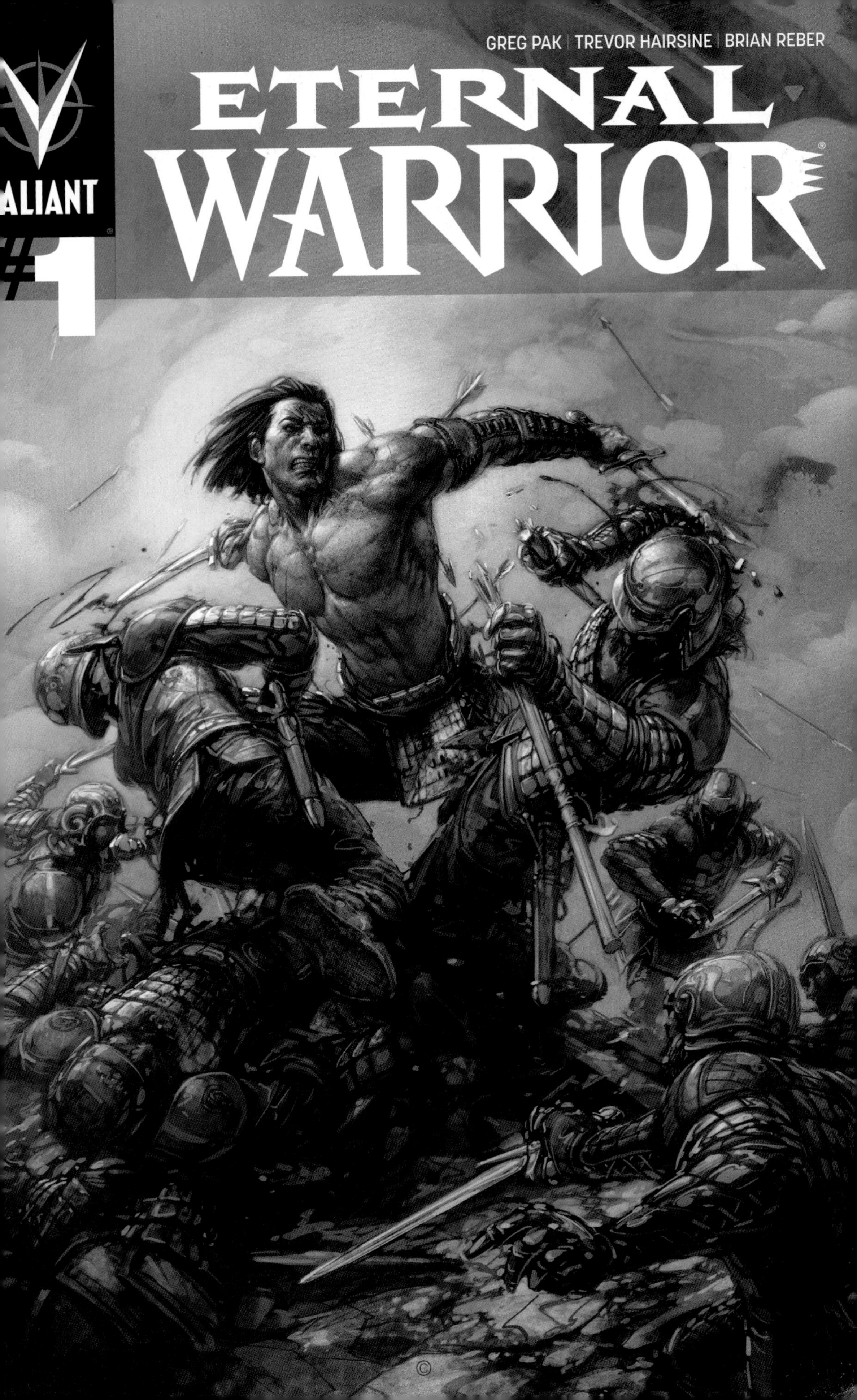
GREG PAK | TREVOR HAIRSINE | BRIAN REBER
ETERNAL WARRIOR
VALIANT
#1

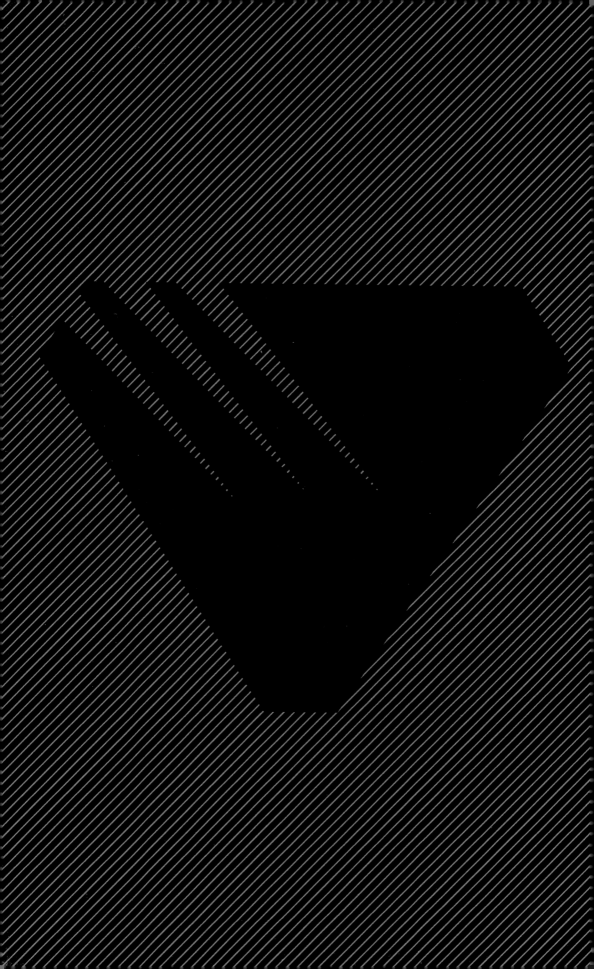

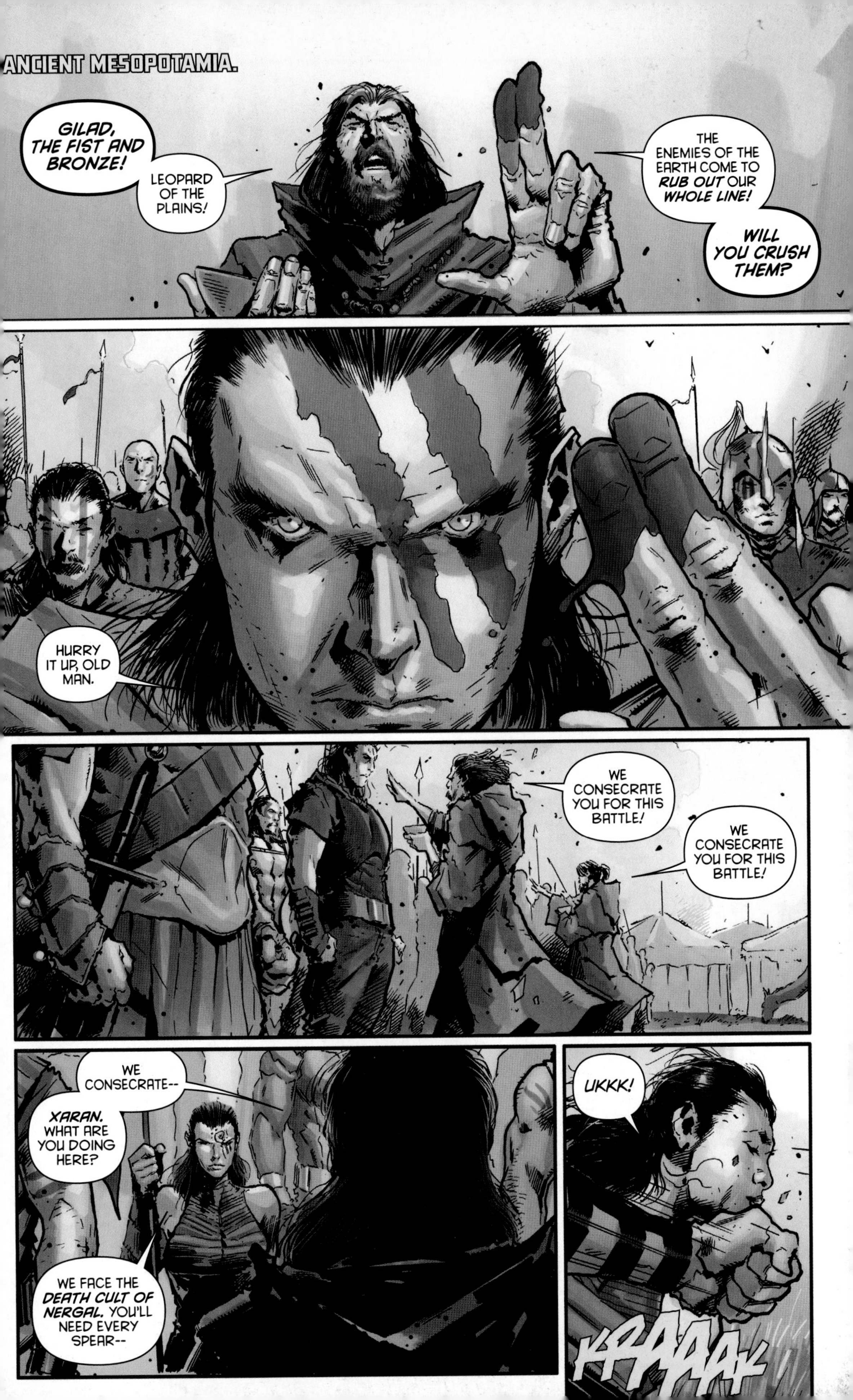
ANCIENT MESOPOTAMIA.
GILAD, THE FIST AND BRONZE!
LEOPARD OF THE PLAINS!
THE ENEMIES OF THE EARTH COME TO RUB OUT OUR WHOLE LINE!
WILL YOU CRUSH THEM?
HURRY IT UP, OLD MAN.
WE CONSECRATE YOU FOR THIS BATTLE!
WE CONSECRATE YOU FOR THIS BATTLE!
WE CONSECRATE--
XARAN. WHAT ARE YOU DOING HERE?
WE FACE THE DEATH CULT OF NERGAL. YOU'LL NEED EVERY SPEAR--
UKKK!
KRAAAK

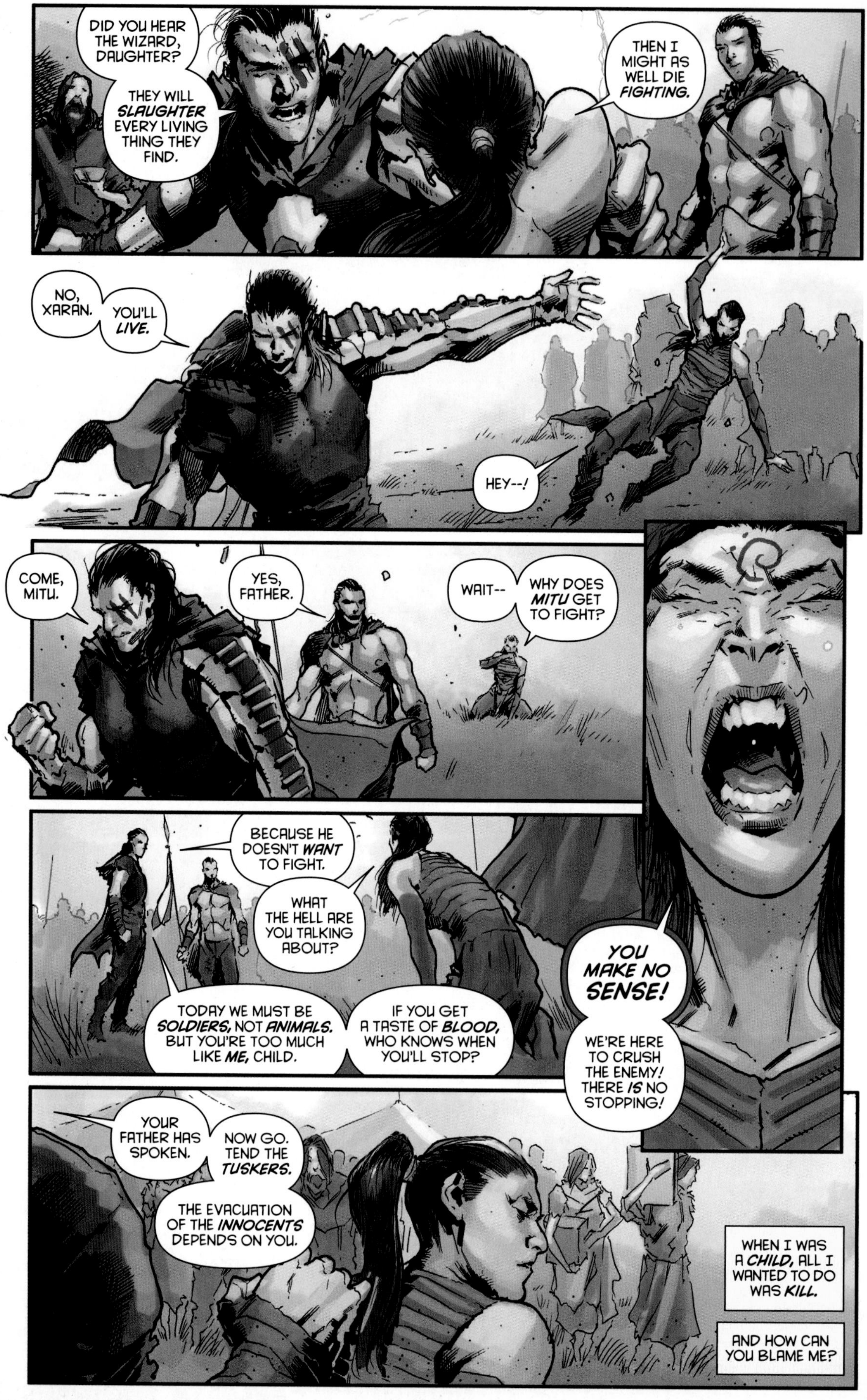

DID YOU HEAR THE WIZARD, DAUGHTER?
THEY WILL SLAUGHTER EVERY LIVING THING THEY FIND.
THEN I MIGHT AS WELL DIE FIGHTING.
NO, XARAN.
YOU'LL LIVE.
HEY--!
COME, MITU.
YES, FATHER.
WAIT--
WHY DOES MITU GET TO FIGHT?
BECAUSE HE DOESN'T WANT TO FIGHT.
WHAT THE HELL ARE YOU TALKING ABOUT?
TODAY WE MUST BE SOLDIERS, NOT ANIMALS. BUT YOU'RE TOO MUCH LIKE ME, CHILD.
IF YOU GET A TASTE OF BLOOD, WHO KNOWS WHEN YOU'LL STOP?
YOU MAKE NO SENSE!
WE'RE HERE TO CRUSH THE ENEMY! THERE IS NO STOPPING!
YOUR FATHER HAS SPOKEN.
NOW GO. TEND THE TUSKERS.
THE EVACUATION OF THE INNOCENTS DEPENDS ON YOU.
WHEN I WAS A CHILD, ALL I WANTED TO DO WAS KILL.
AND HOW CAN YOU BLAME ME?

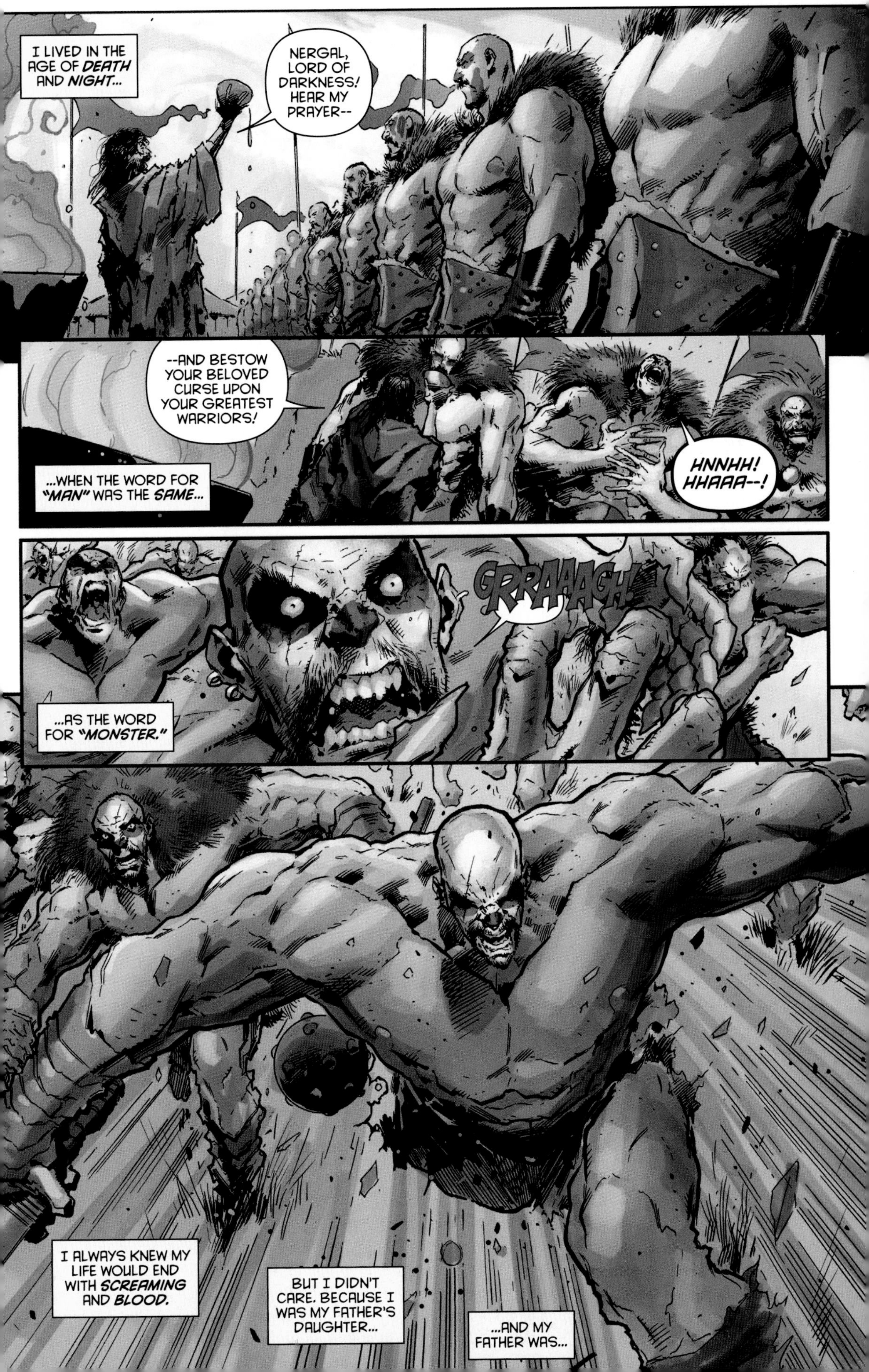
I LIVED IN THE AGE OF DEATH AND NIGHT...
NERGAL, LORD OF DARKNESS! HEAR MY PRAYER--
--AND BESTOW YOUR BELOVED CURSE UPON YOUR GREATEST WARRIORS!
...WHEN THE WORD FOR "MAN" WAS THE SAME...
HNNHH! HHAAA--!
GRRAAAGH!
...AS THE WORD FOR "MONSTER."
I ALWAYS KNEW MY LIFE WOULD END WITH SCREAMING AND BLOOD.
BUT I DIDN'T CARE. BECAUSE I WAS MY FATHER'S DAUGHTER...
...AND MY FATHER WAS...

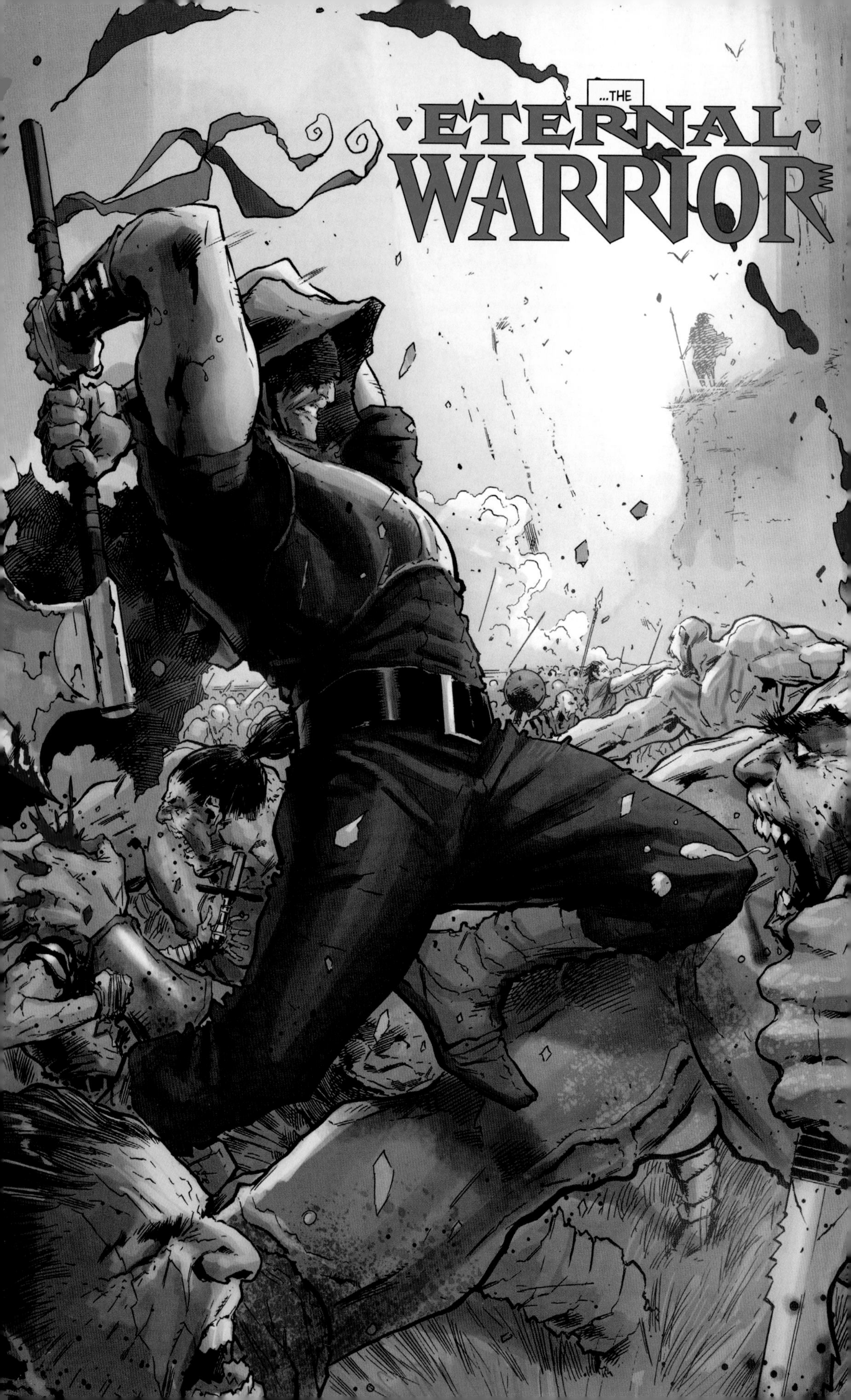
...THE
ETERNAL
WARRIOR

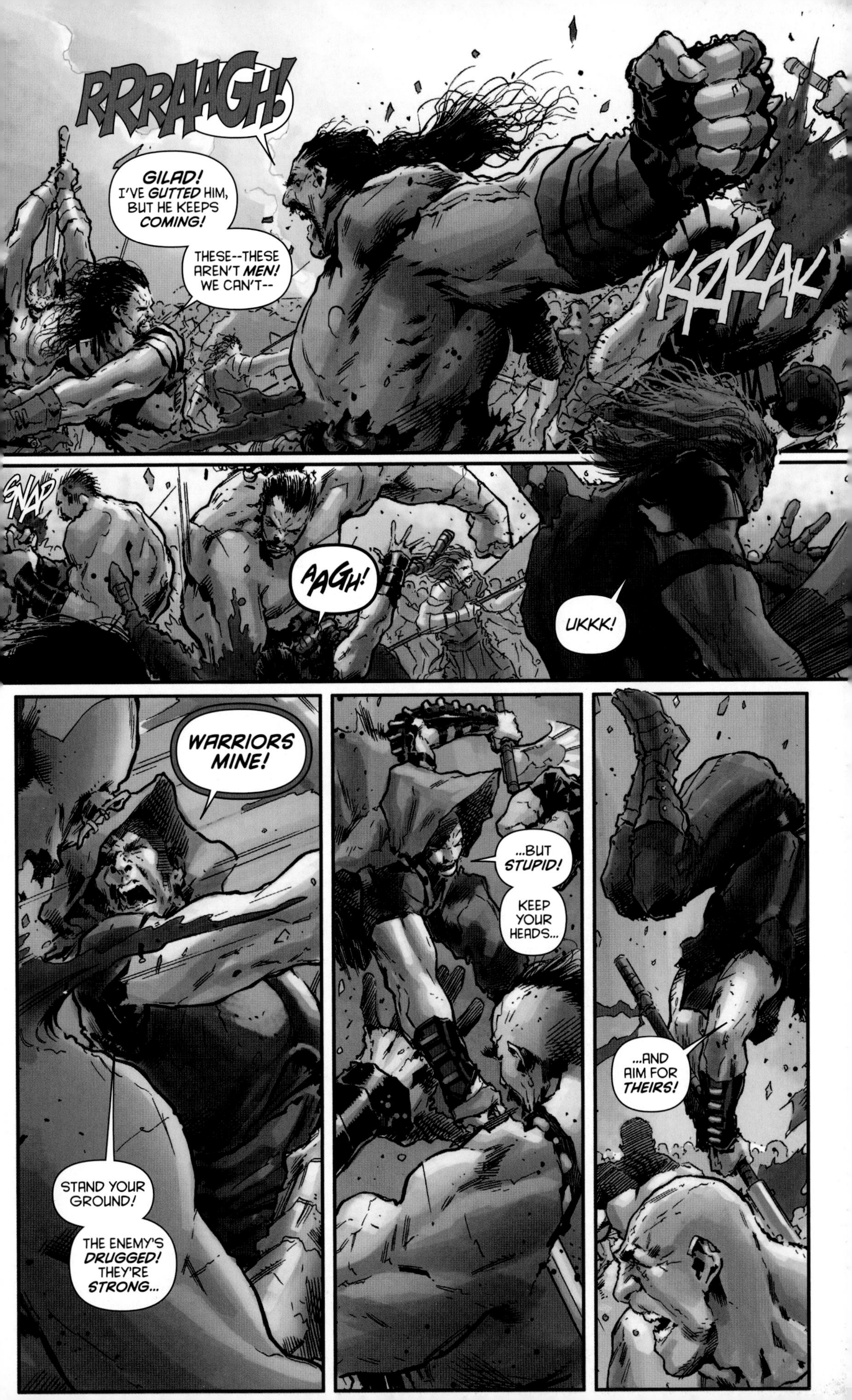
RRRAAGH!
GILAD! I'VE GUTTED HIM, BUT HE KEEPS COMING!
THESE--THESE AREN'T MEN! WE CAN'T--
KRRAK
SNAP
AAGH!
UKKK!
WARRIORS MINE!
STAND YOUR GROUND!
THE ENEMY'S DRUGGED! THEY'RE STRONG...
...BUT STUPID!
KEEP YOUR HEADS...
...AND AIM FOR THEIRS!

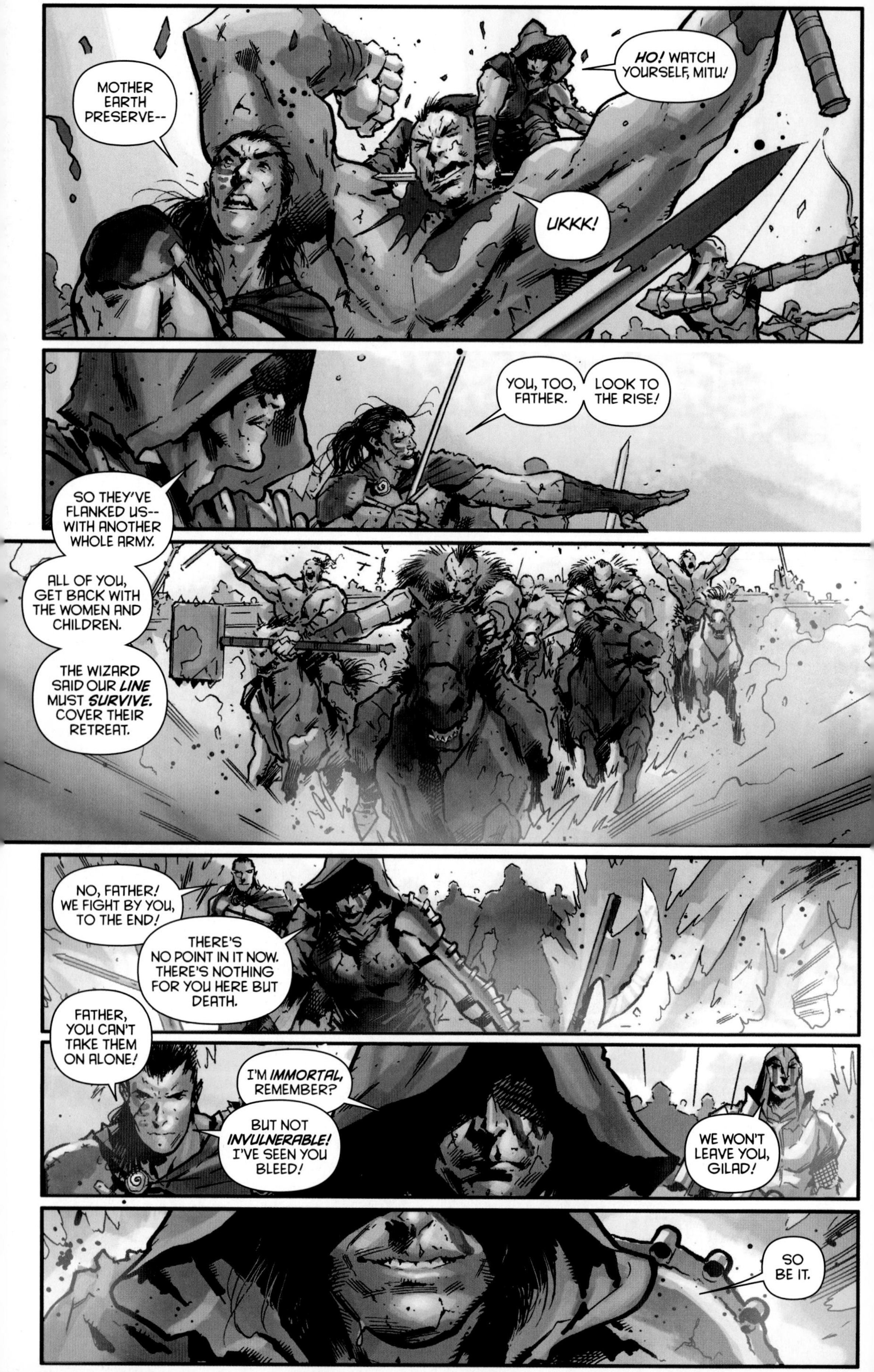
MOTHER EARTH PRESERVE--
HO! WATCH YOURSELF, MITU!
UKKK!
YOU, TOO, FATHER.
LOOK TO THE RISE!
SO THEY'VE FLANKED US-- WITH ANOTHER WHOLE ARMY.
ALL OF YOU, GET BACK WITH THE WOMEN AND CHILDREN.
THE WIZARD SAID OUR LINE MUST SURVIVE. COVER THEIR RETREAT.
NO, FATHER! WE FIGHT BY YOU, TO THE END!
THERE'S NO POINT IN IT NOW. THERE'S NOTHING FOR YOU HERE BUT DEATH.
FATHER, YOU CAN'T TAKE THEM ON ALONE!
I'M IMMORTAL, REMEMBER?
BUT NOT INVULNERABLE! I'VE SEEN YOU BLEED!
WE WON'T LEAVE YOU, GILAD!
SO BE IT.

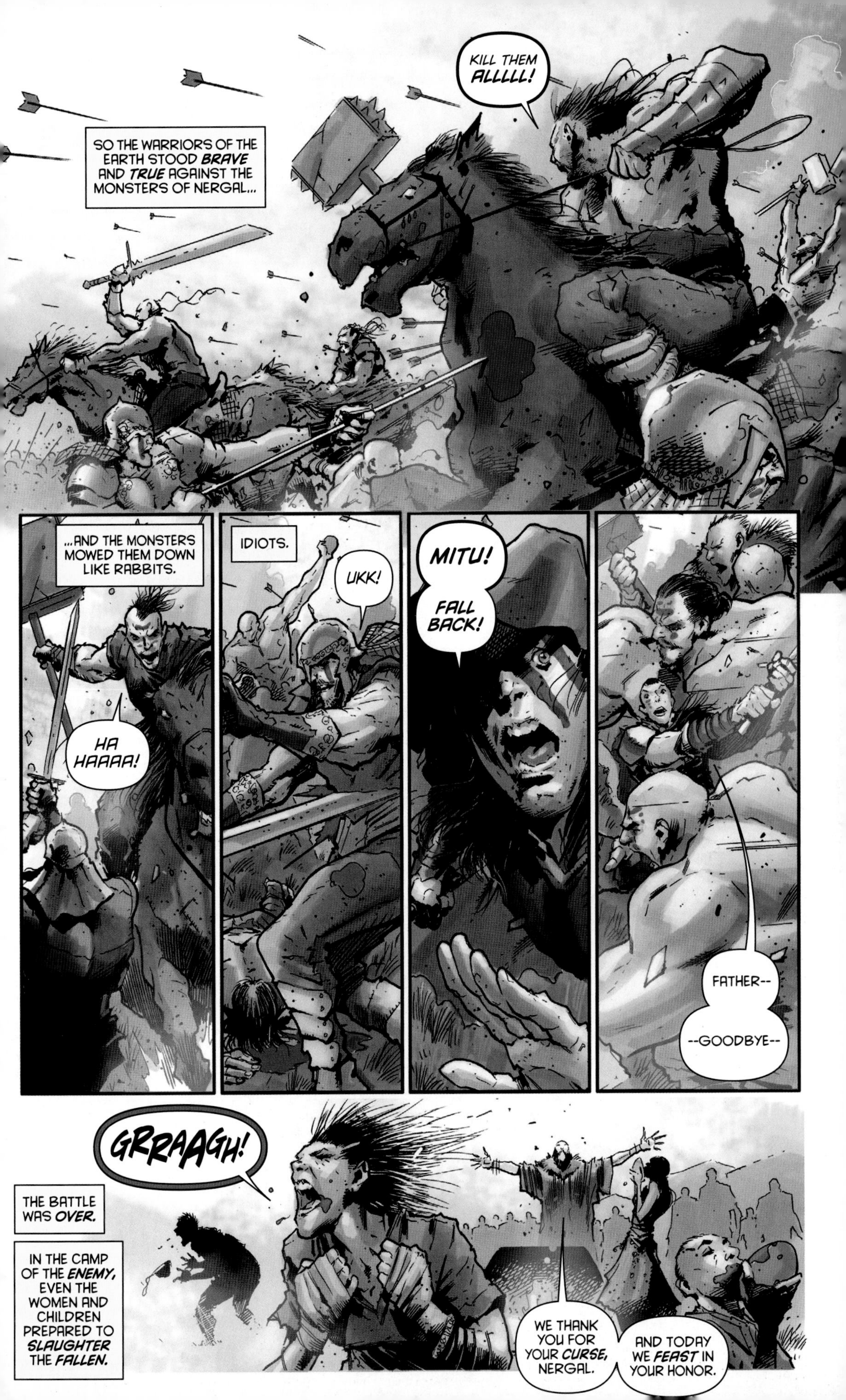

SO THE WARRIORS OF THE EARTH STOOD BRAVE AND TRUE AGAINST THE MONSTERS OF NERGAL...
KILL THEM ALLLLL!
...AND THE MONSTERS MOWED THEM DOWN LIKE RABBITS.
HA HAAAA!
IDIOTS.
UKK!
MITU!
FALL BACK!
FATHER--
--GOODBYE--
GRRAAGH!
THE BATTLE WAS OVER.
IN THE CAMP OF THE ENEMY, EVEN THE WOMEN AND CHILDREN PREPARED TO SLAUGHTER THE FALLEN.
WE THANK YOU FOR YOUR CURSE, NERGAL.
AND TODAY WE FEAST IN YOUR HONOR.

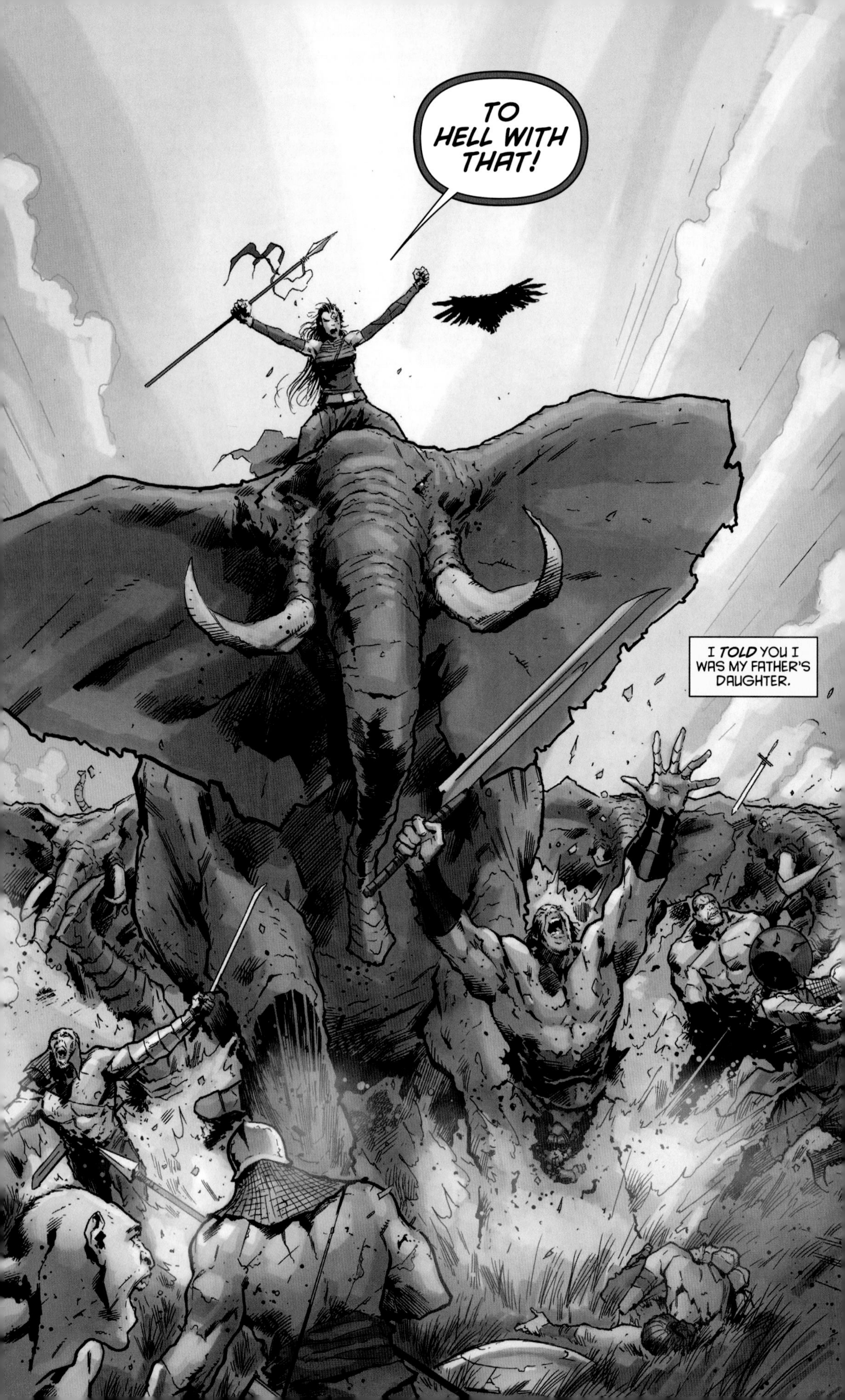
TO HELL WITH THAT!
I TOLD YOU I WAS MY FATHER'S DAUGHTER.

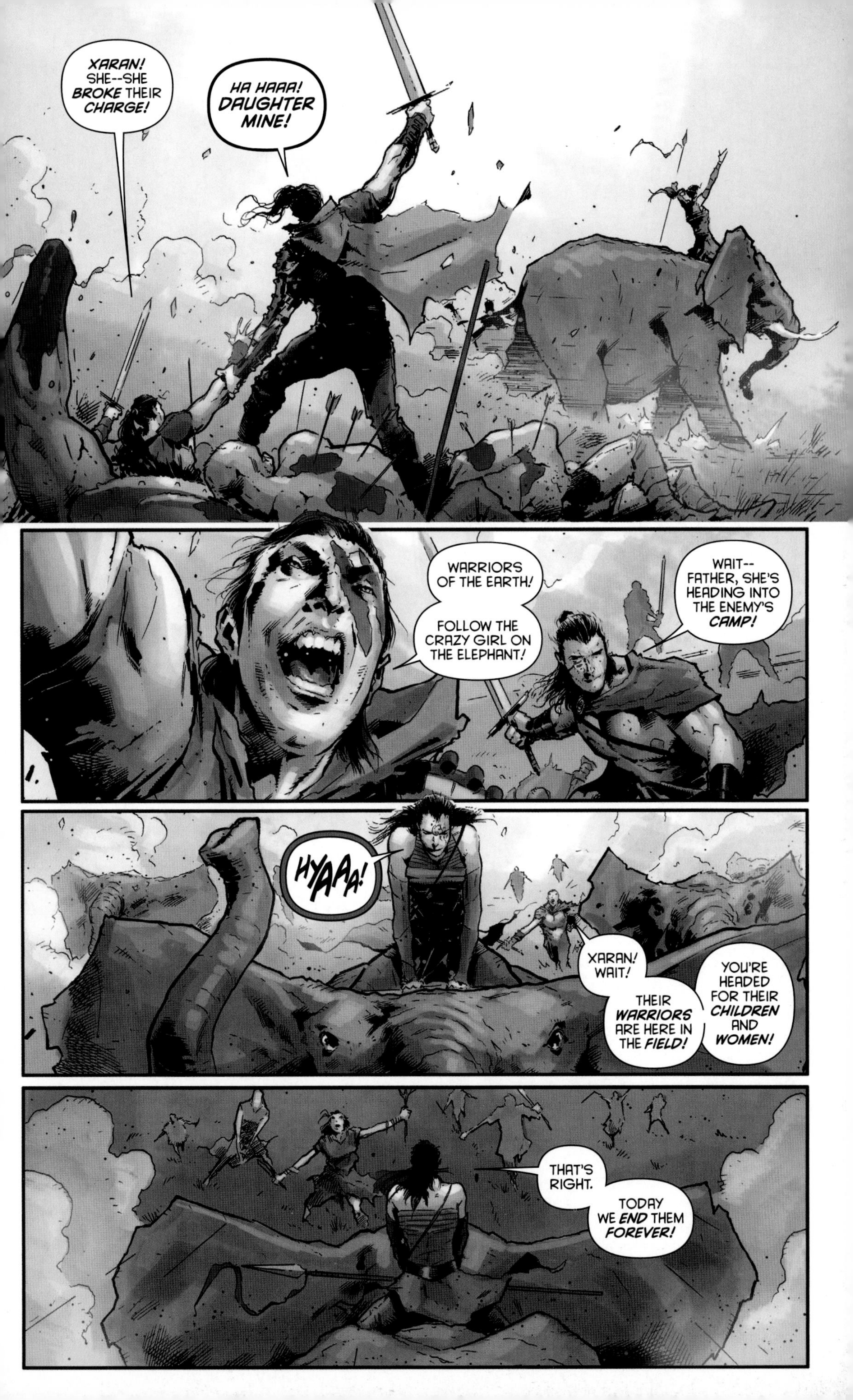
XARAN! SHE--SHE BROKE THEIR CHARGE!
HA HAAA! DAUGHTER MINE!
WARRIORS OF THE EARTH!
FOLLOW THE CRAZY GIRL ON THE ELEPHANT!
WAIT-- FATHER, SHE'S HEADING INTO THE ENEMY'S CAMP!
HYAAA!
XARAN! WAIT!
THEIR WARRIORS ARE HERE IN THE FIELD!
YOU'RE HEADED FOR THEIR CHILDREN AND WOMEN!
THAT'S RIGHT.
TODAY WE END THEM FOREVER!

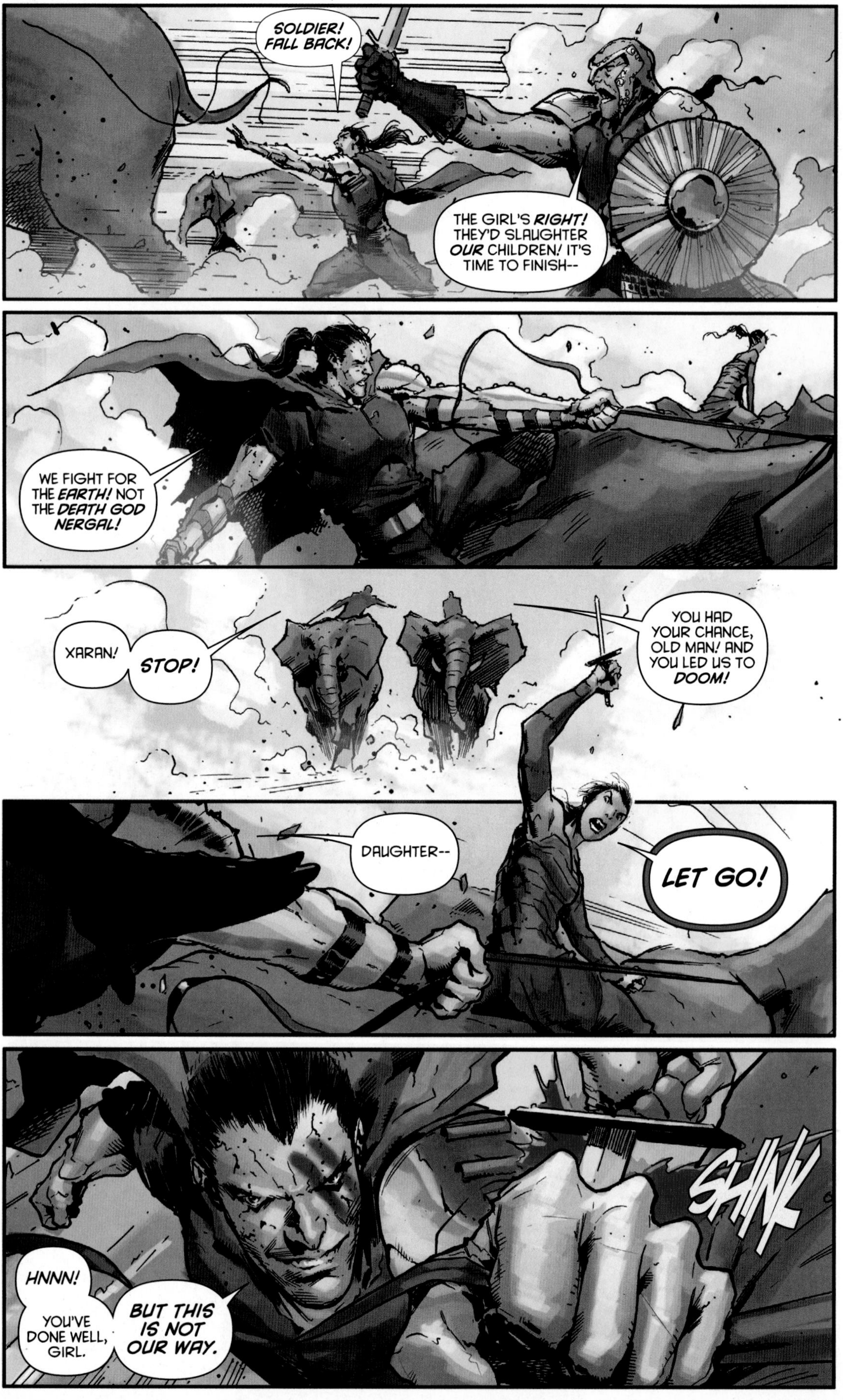

SOLDIER! FALL BACK!
THE GIRL'S RIGHT! THEY'D SLAUGHTER OUR CHILDREN! IT'S TIME TO FINISH--
WE FIGHT FOR THE EARTH! NOT THE DEATH GOD NERGAL!
XARAN!
STOP!
YOU HAD YOUR CHANCE, OLD MAN! AND YOU LED US TO DOOM!
DAUGHTER--
LET GO!
SHINK
HNNN!
YOU'VE DONE WELL, GIRL.
BUT THIS IS NOT OUR WAY.

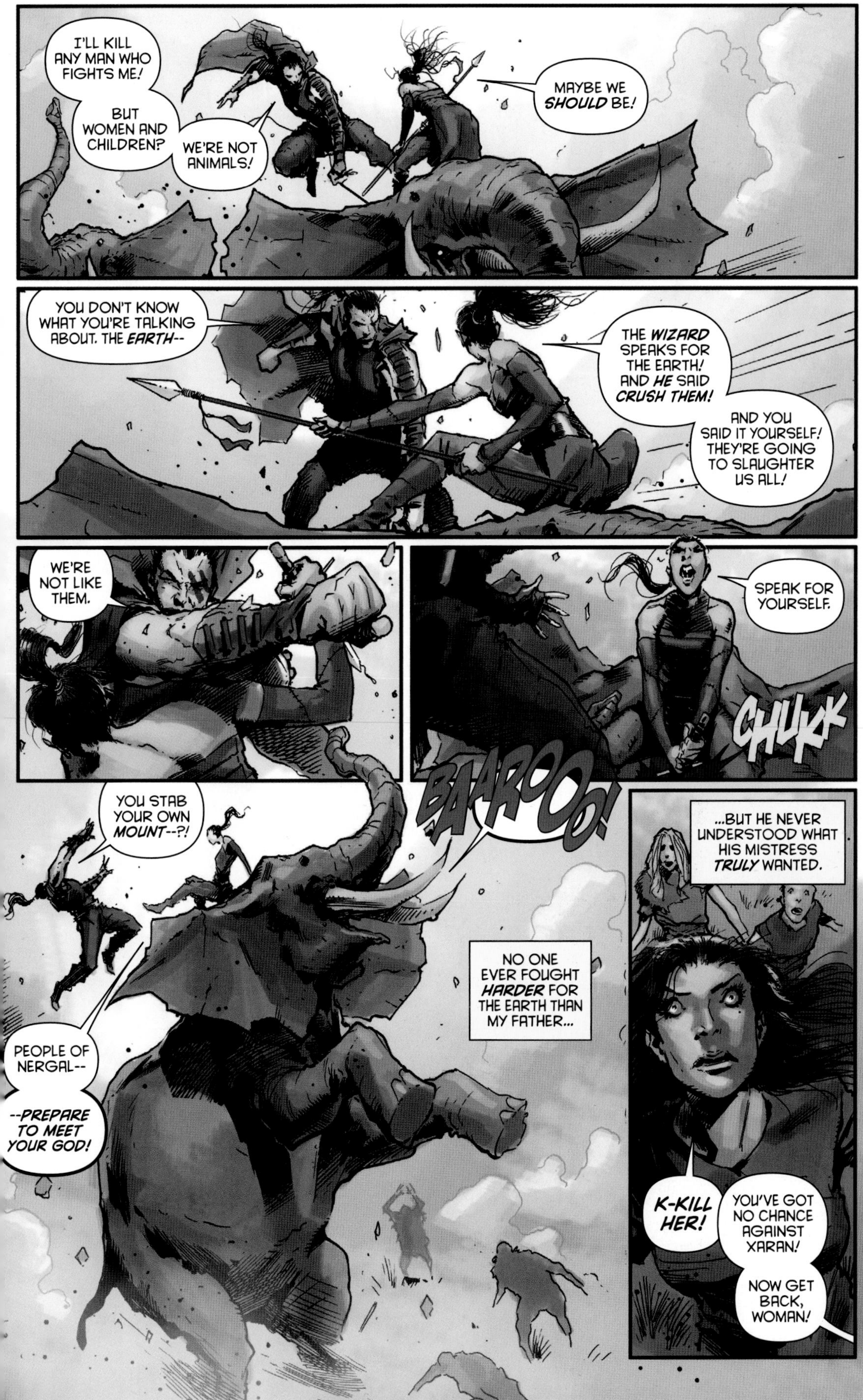
I'LL KILL ANY MAN WHO FIGHTS ME!
BUT WOMEN AND CHILDREN?
WE'RE NOT ANIMALS!
MAYBE WE *SHOULD* BE!
YOU DON'T KNOW WHAT YOU'RE TALKING ABOUT. THE *EARTH*--
THE *WIZARD* SPEAKS FOR THE EARTH! AND *HE* SAID *CRUSH THEM!*
AND YOU SAID IT YOURSELF! THEY'RE GOING TO SLAUGHTER US ALL!
WE'RE NOT LIKE THEM.
SPEAK FOR YOURSELF.
CHUKK
YOU STAB YOUR OWN *MOUNT*--?!
BAAROOOO!
PEOPLE OF NERGAL--
--PREPARE TO MEET YOUR GOD!
NO ONE EVER FOUGHT *HARDER* FOR THE EARTH THAN MY FATHER...
...BUT HE NEVER UNDERSTOOD WHAT HIS MISTRESS *TRULY* WANTED.
K-KILL HER!
YOU'VE GOT NO CHANCE AGAINST XARAN!
NOW GET BACK, WOMAN!

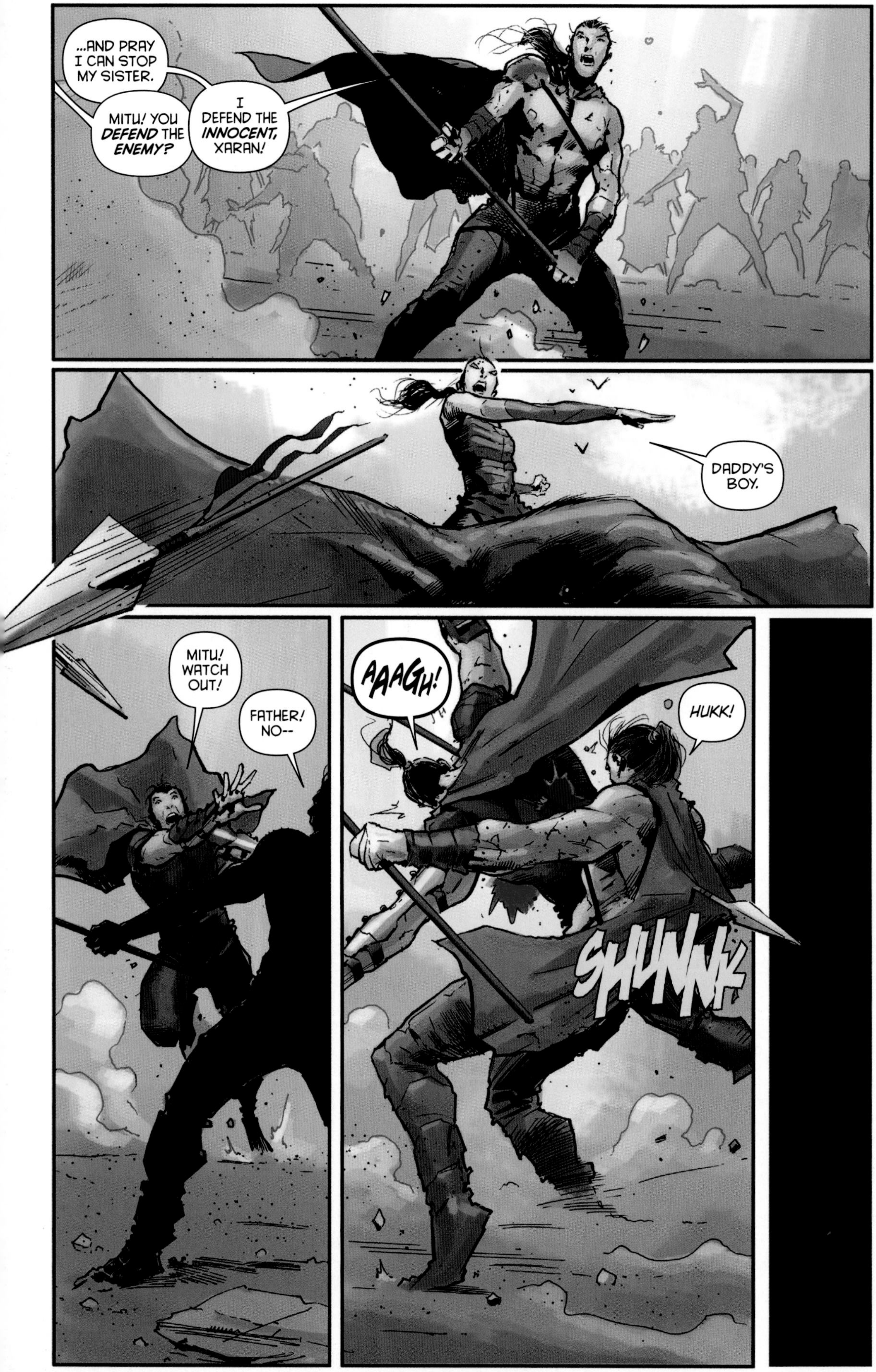
...AND PRAY I CAN STOP MY SISTER.
MITU! YOU *DEFEND* THE *ENEMY?*
I DEFEND THE *INNOCENT,* XARAN!
DADDY'S BOY.
MITU! WATCH OUT!
FATHER! NO--
AAAGH!
HUKK!
SHUNNK

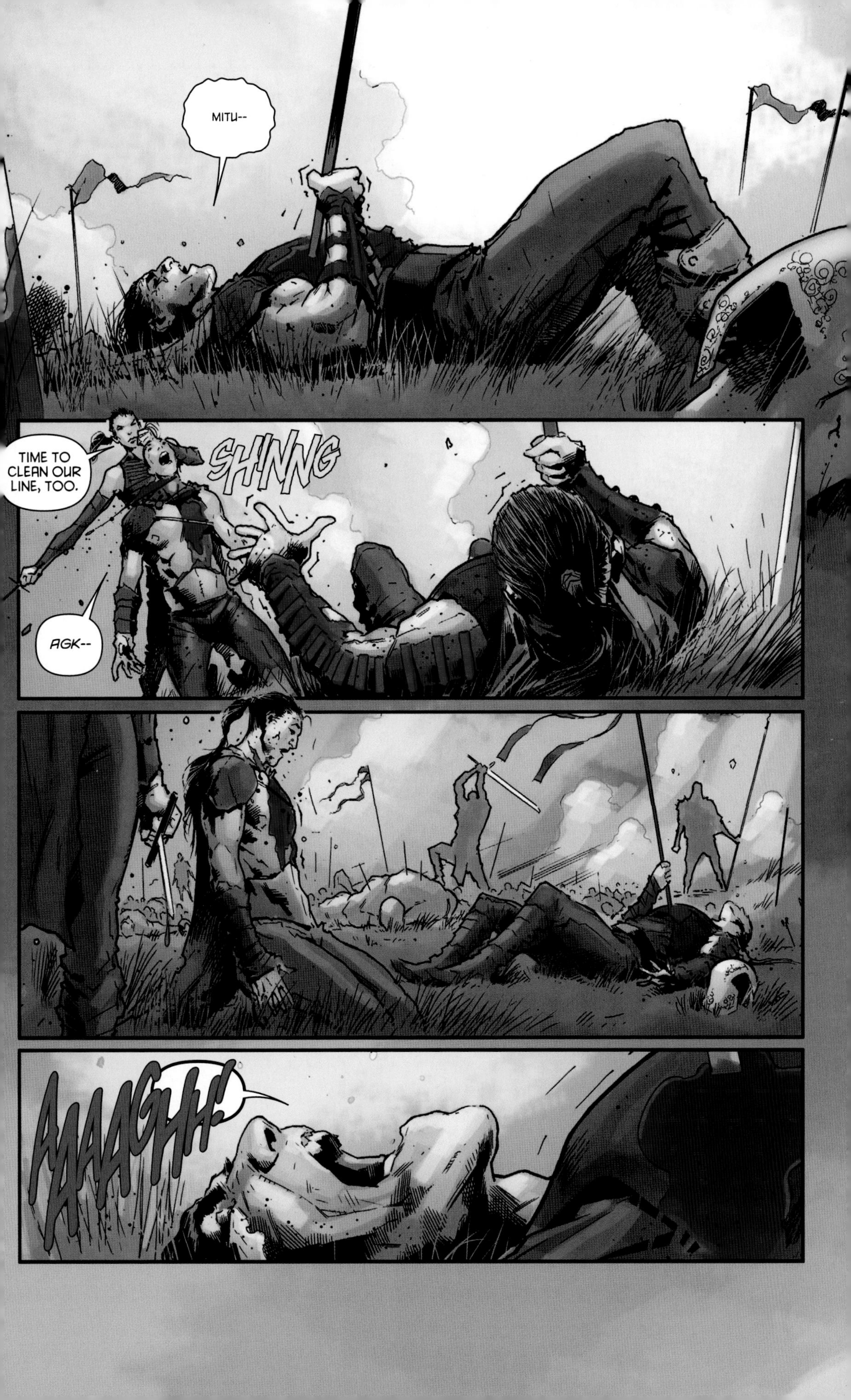
MITU--
TIME TO CLEAN OUR LINE, TOO.
SHINNG
AGK--
AAAAGHH!

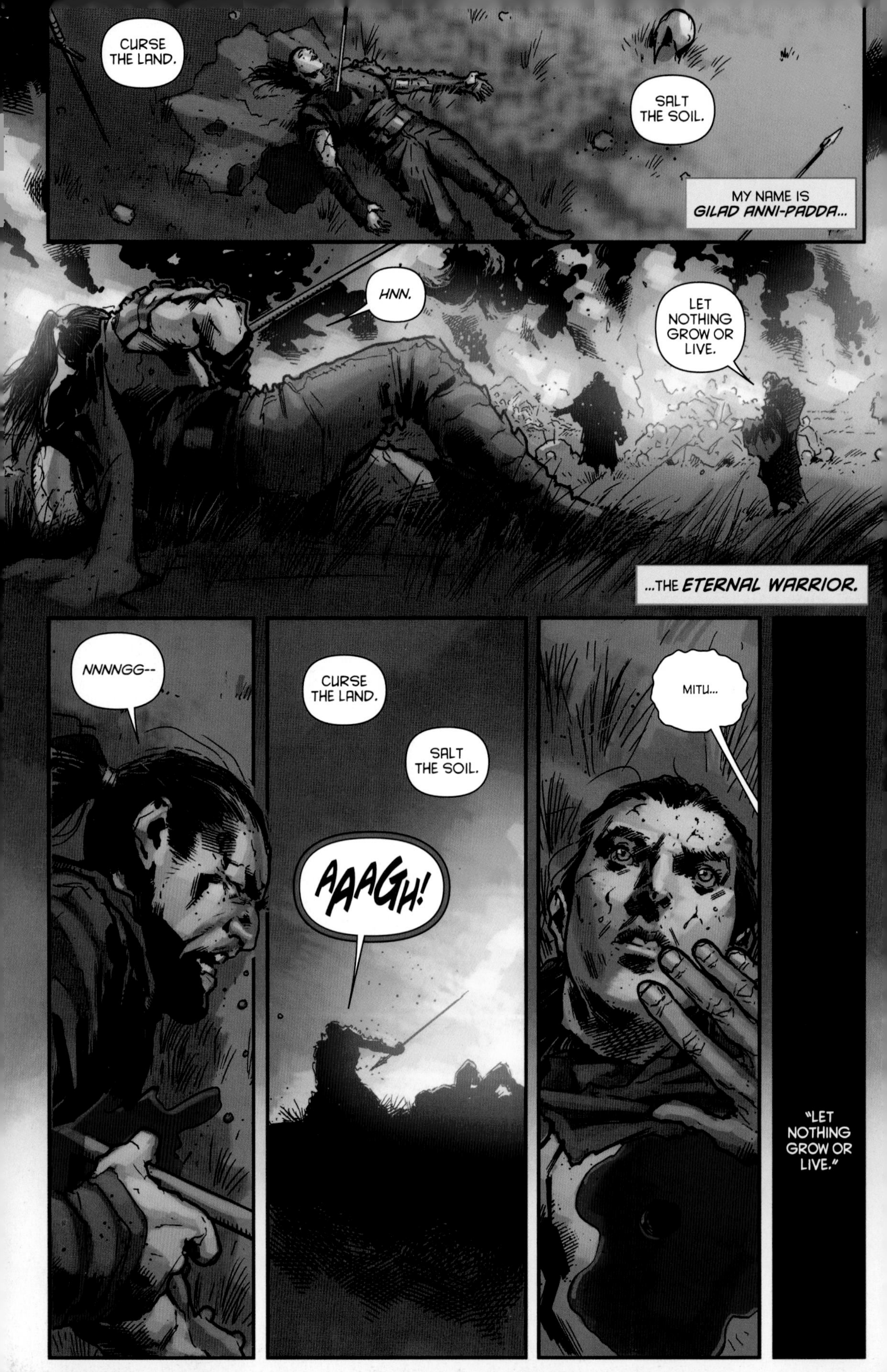
CURSE THE LAND.
SALT THE SOIL.
MY NAME IS GILAD ANNI-PADDA...
HNN.
LET NOTHING GROW OR LIVE.
...THE ETERNAL WARRIOR.
NNNNGG--
CURSE THE LAND.
SALT THE SOIL.
AAAGH!
MITU...
"LET NOTHING GROW OR LIVE."

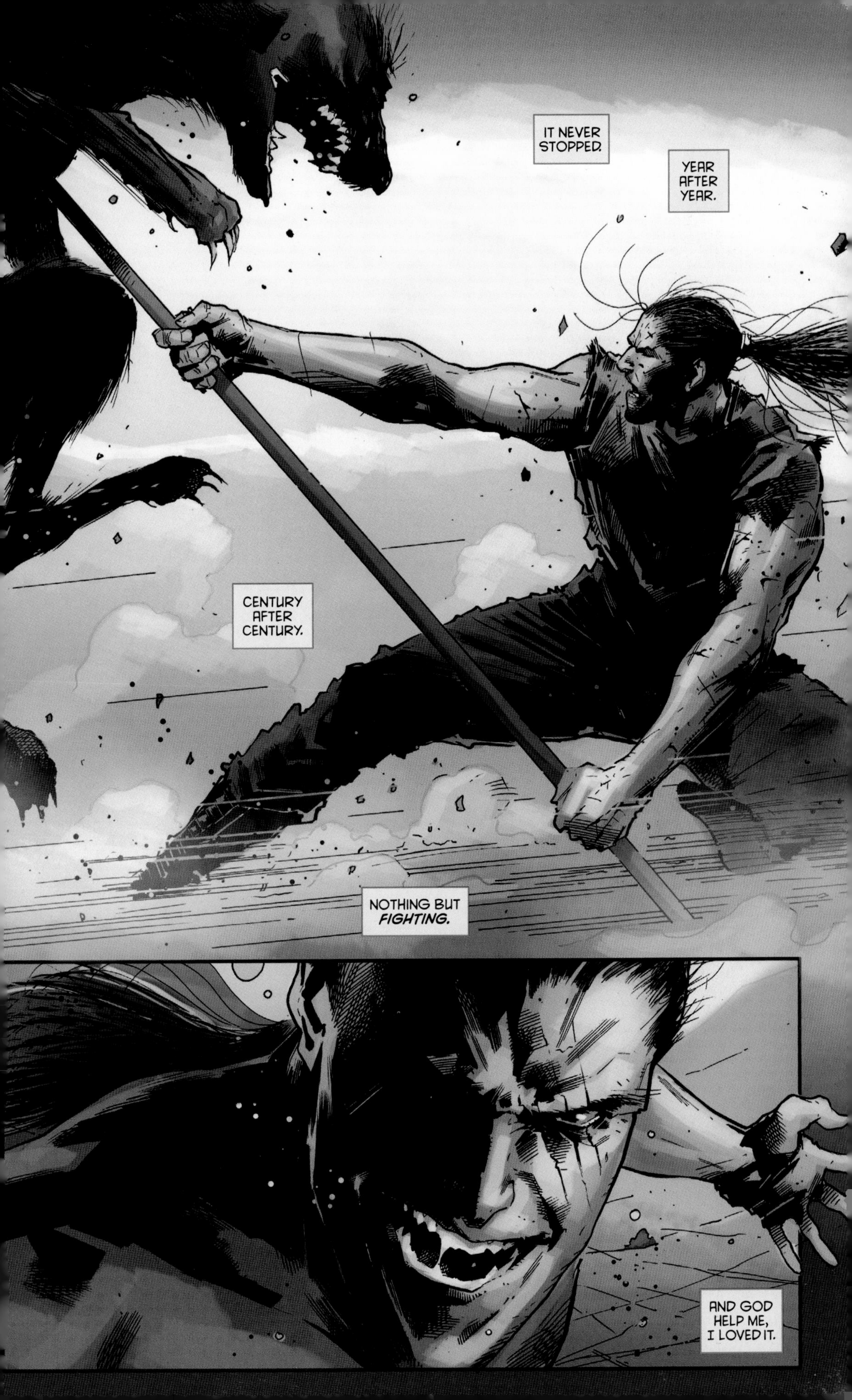
IT NEVER STOPPED.
YEAR AFTER YEAR.
CENTURY AFTER CENTURY.
NOTHING BUT *FIGHTING.*
AND GOD HELP ME, I LOVED IT.

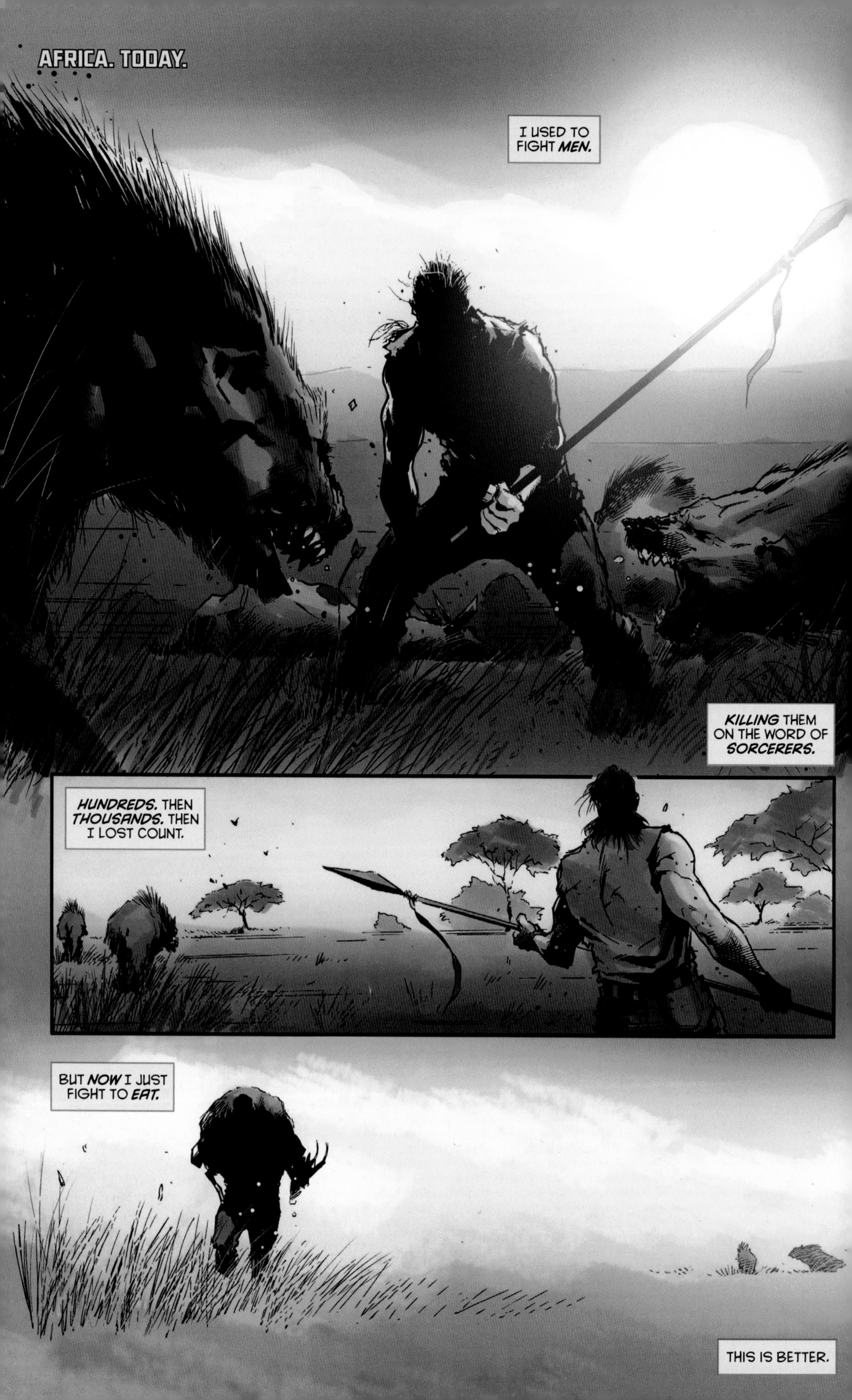
AFRICA. TODAY.
I USED TO FIGHT MEN.
KILLING THEM ON THE WORD OF SORCERERS.
HUNDREDS. THEN THOUSANDS. THEN I LOST COUNT.
BUT NOW I JUST FIGHT TO EAT.
THIS IS BETTER.

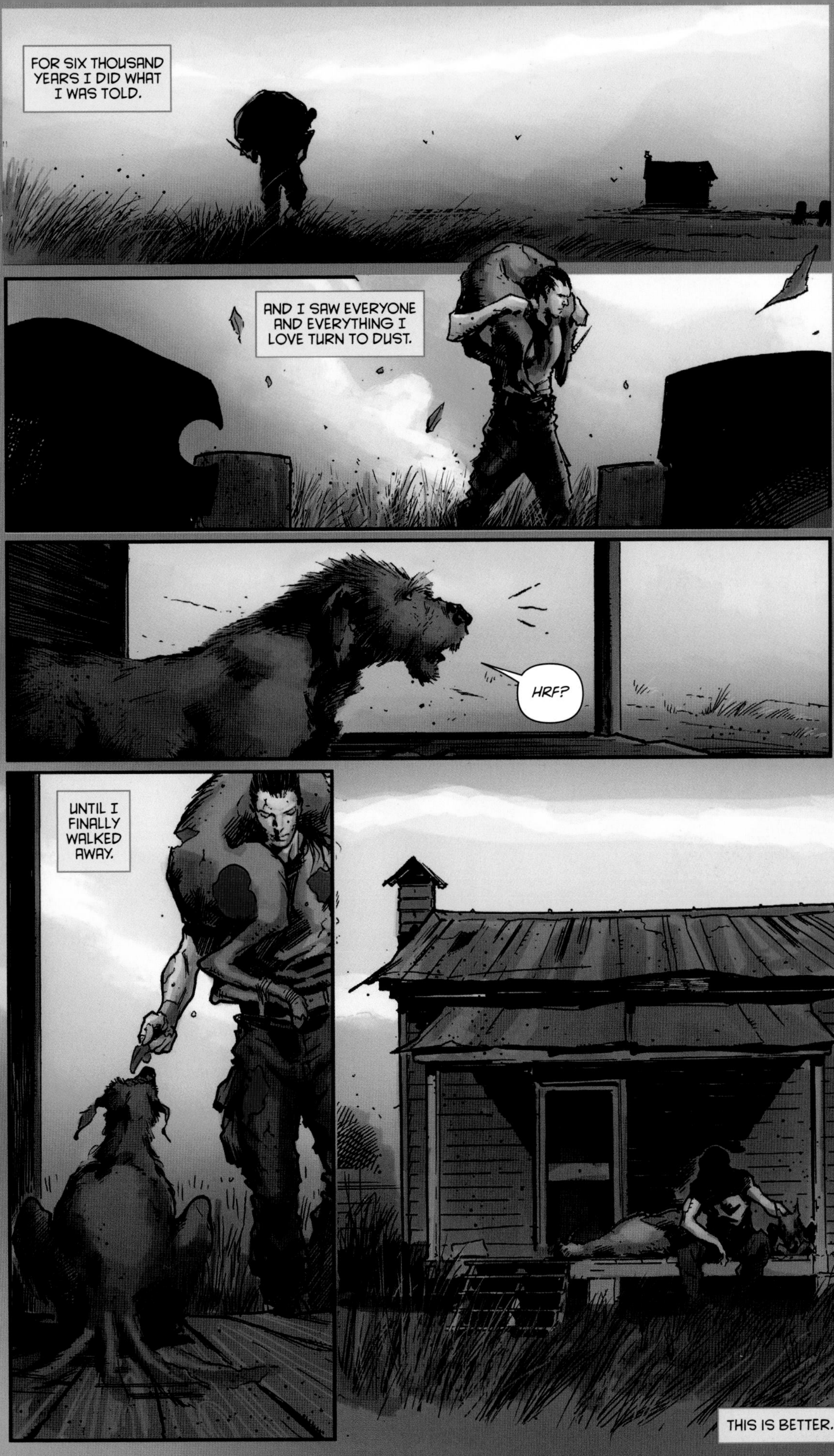
FOR SIX THOUSAND YEARS I DID WHAT I WAS TOLD.
AND I SAW EVERYONE AND EVERYTHING I LOVE TURN TO DUST.
HRF?
UNTIL I FINALLY WALKED AWAY.
THIS IS BETTER.

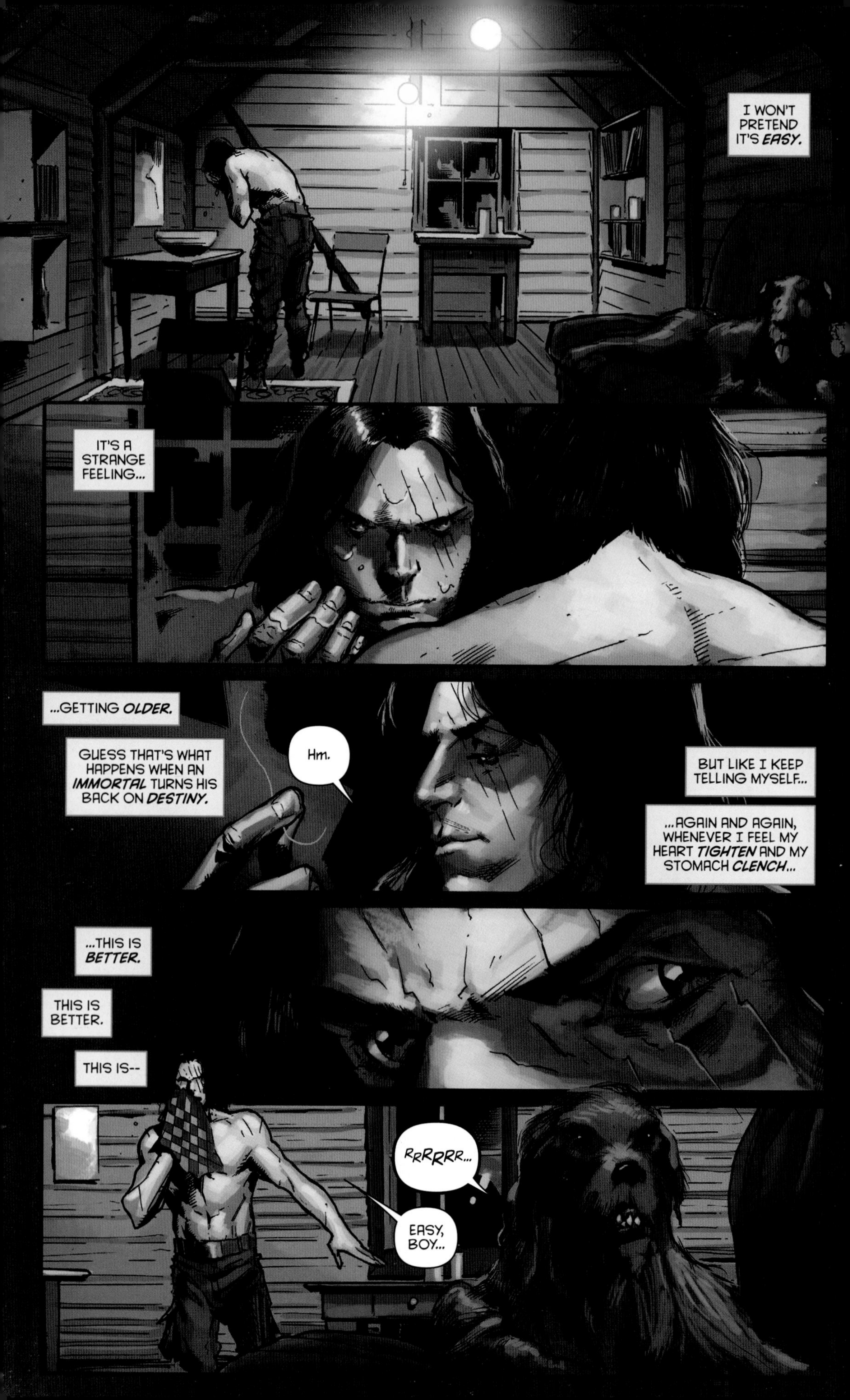
I WON'T PRETEND IT'S EASY.
IT'S A STRANGE FEELING...
...GETTING OLDER.
GUESS THAT'S WHAT HAPPENS WHEN AN IMMORTAL TURNS HIS BACK ON DESTINY.
Hm.
BUT LIKE I KEEP TELLING MYSELF...
...AGAIN AND AGAIN, WHENEVER I FEEL MY HEART TIGHTEN AND MY STOMACH CLENCH...
...THIS IS BETTER.
THIS IS BETTER.
THIS IS--
RRRRRR...
EASY, BOY...

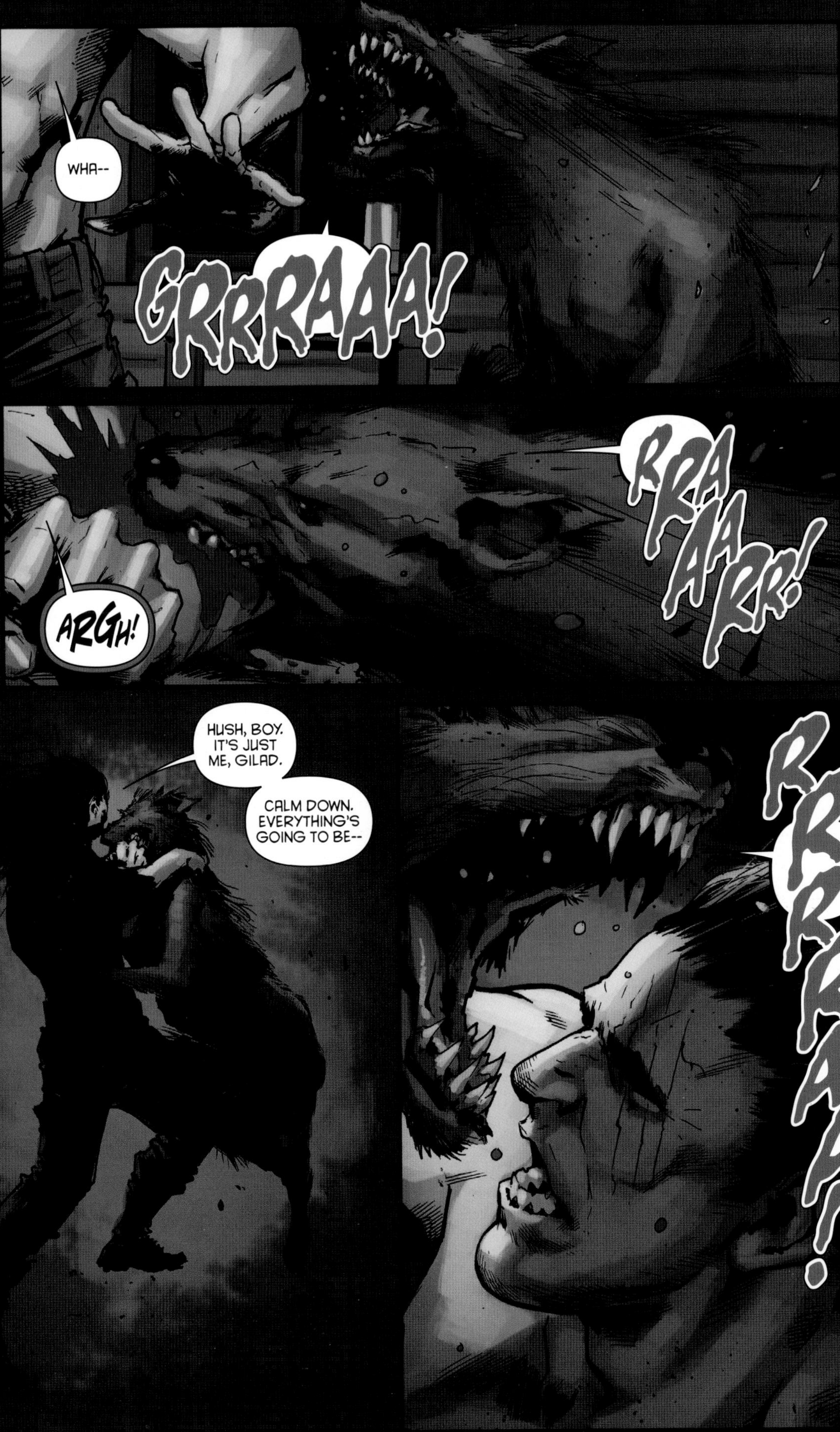
WHA--
GRRRAAA!
RRRAAARRR!
ARGH!
HUSH, BOY. IT'S JUST ME, GILAD.
CALM DOWN. EVERYTHING'S GOING TO BE--
RRRRRAAA!

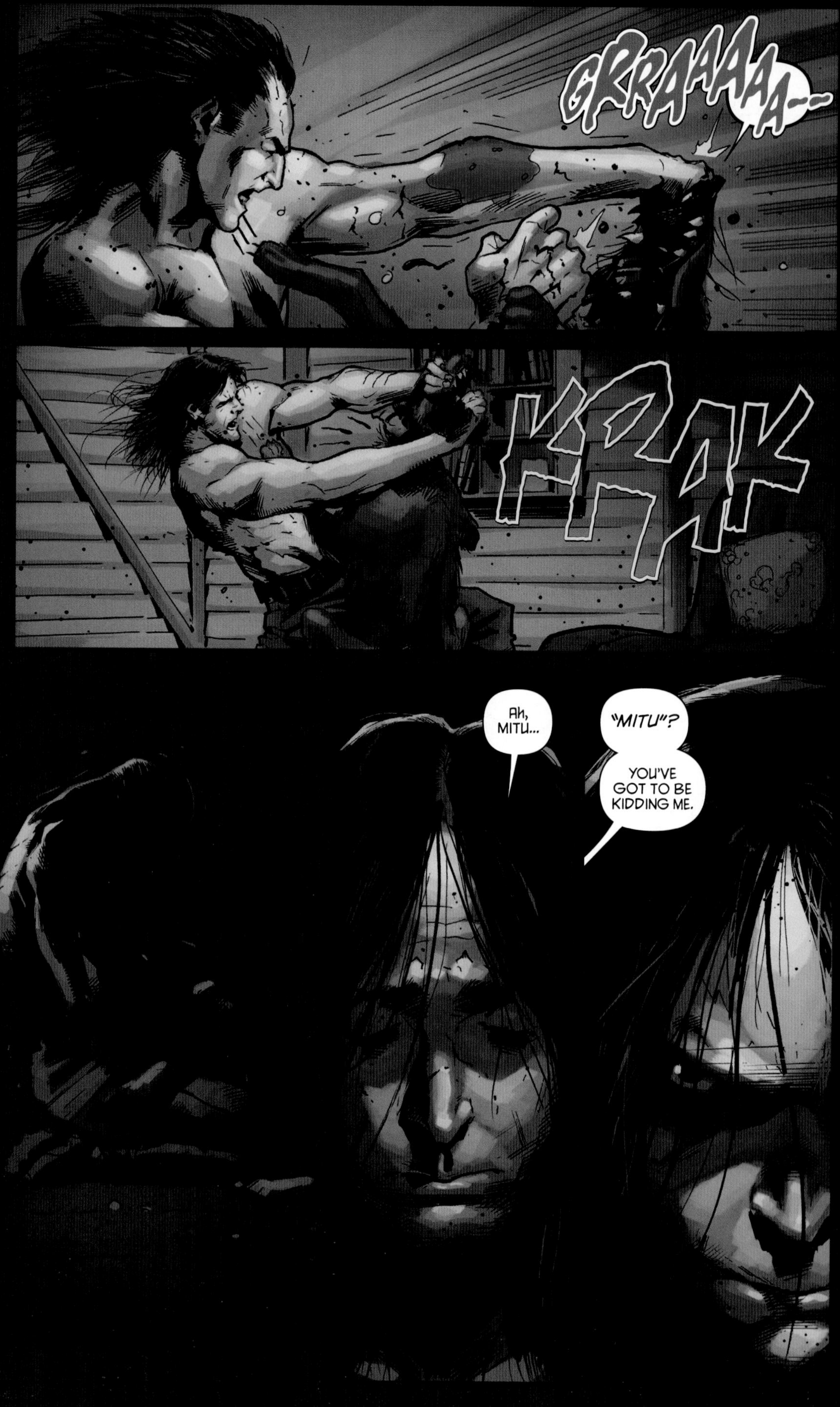
GRRAAAAAA--
KRAK
Ah, MITU...
"MITU"?
YOU'VE GOT TO BE KIDDING ME.

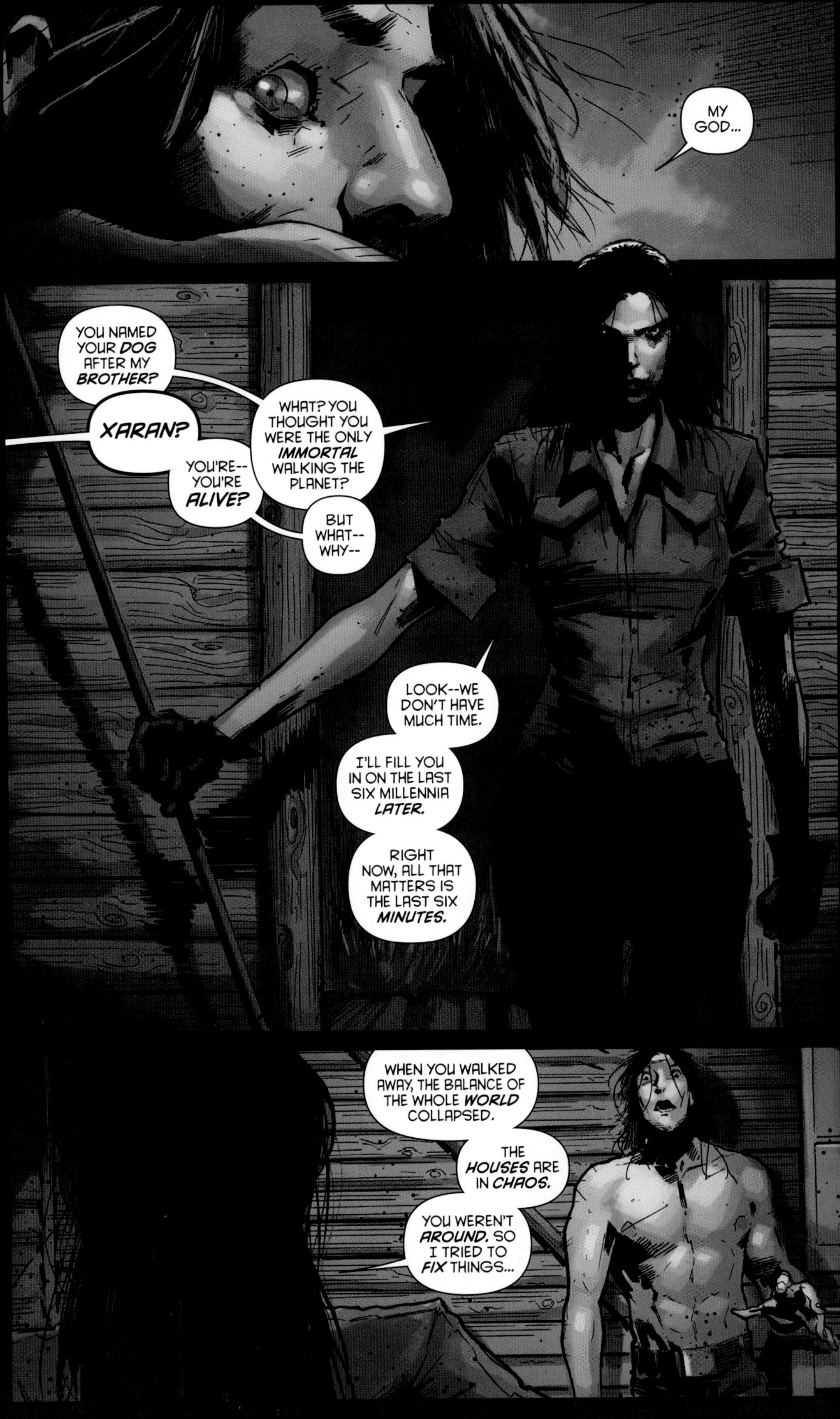
MY GOD...
YOU NAMED YOUR DOG AFTER MY BROTHER?
XARAN?
YOU'RE-- YOU'RE ALIVE?
WHAT? YOU THOUGHT YOU WERE THE ONLY IMMORTAL WALKING THE PLANET?
BUT WHAT-- WHY--
LOOK--WE DON'T HAVE MUCH TIME.
I'LL FILL YOU IN ON THE LAST SIX MILLENNIA LATER.
RIGHT NOW, ALL THAT MATTERS IS THE LAST SIX MINUTES.
WHEN YOU WALKED AWAY, THE BALANCE OF THE WHOLE WORLD COLLAPSED.
THE HOUSES ARE IN CHAOS.
YOU WEREN'T AROUND. SO I TRIED TO FIX THINGS...

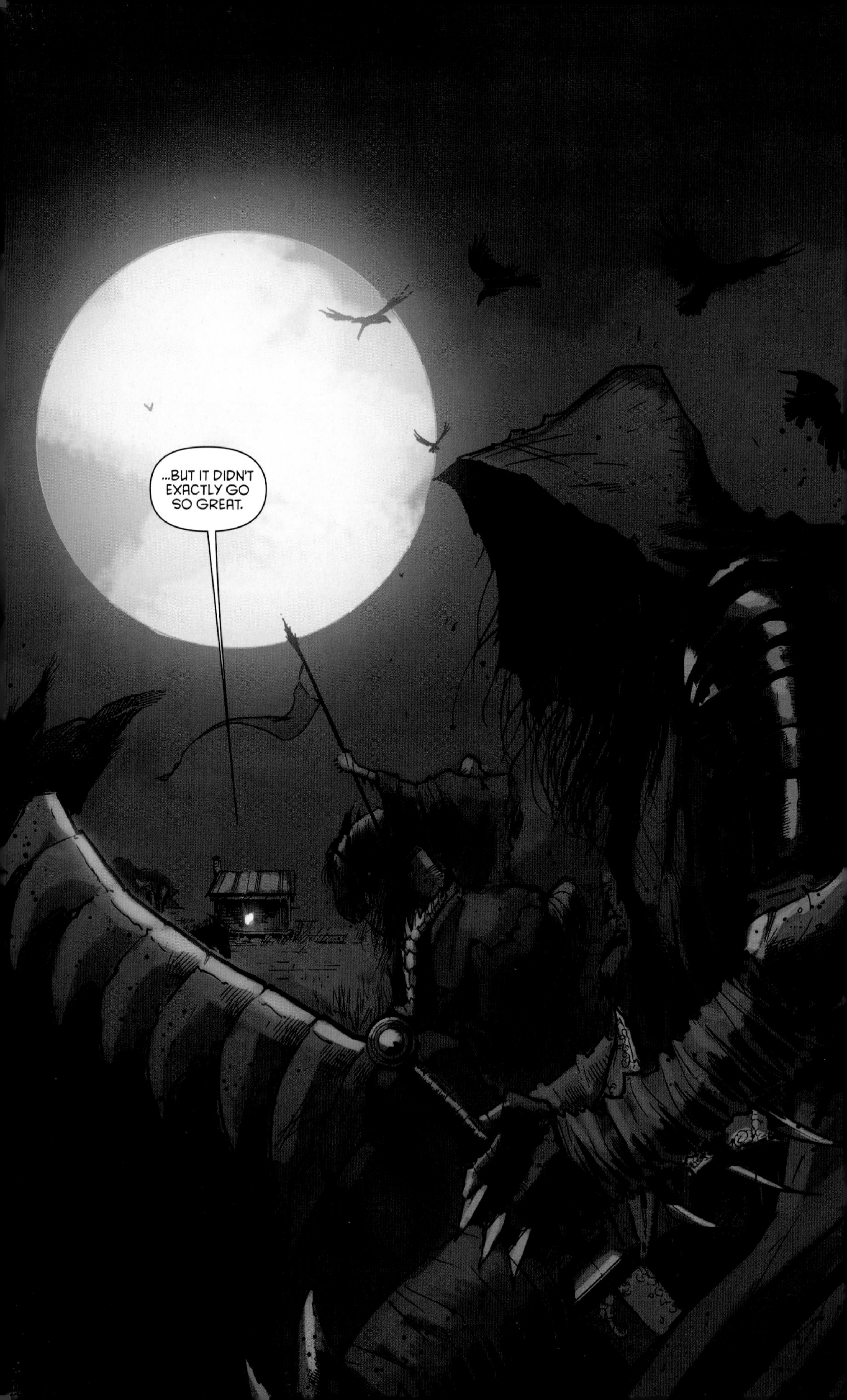
...BUT IT DIDN'T EXACTLY GO SO GREAT.

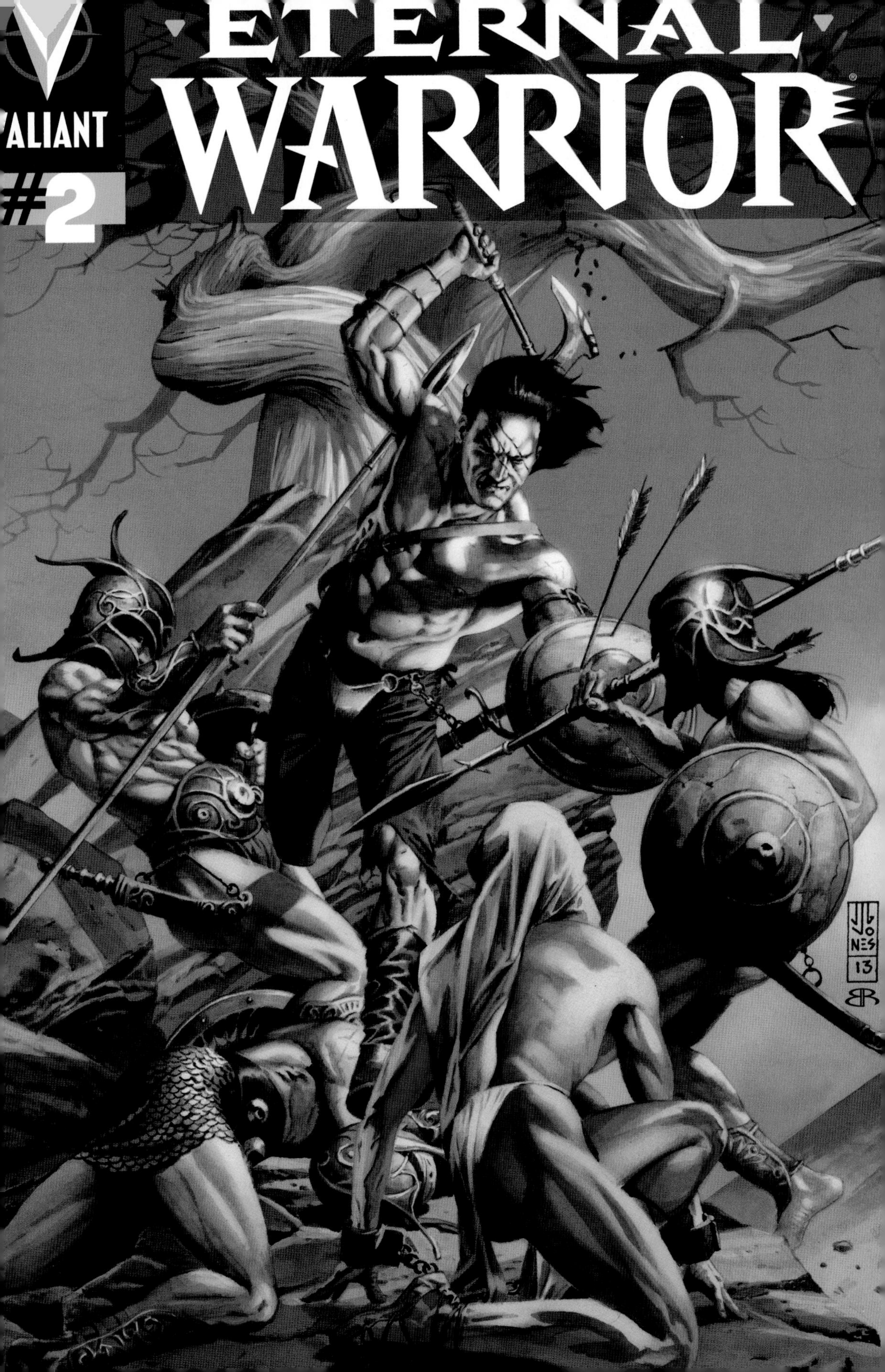

VALIANT
#2
ETERNAL WARRIOR

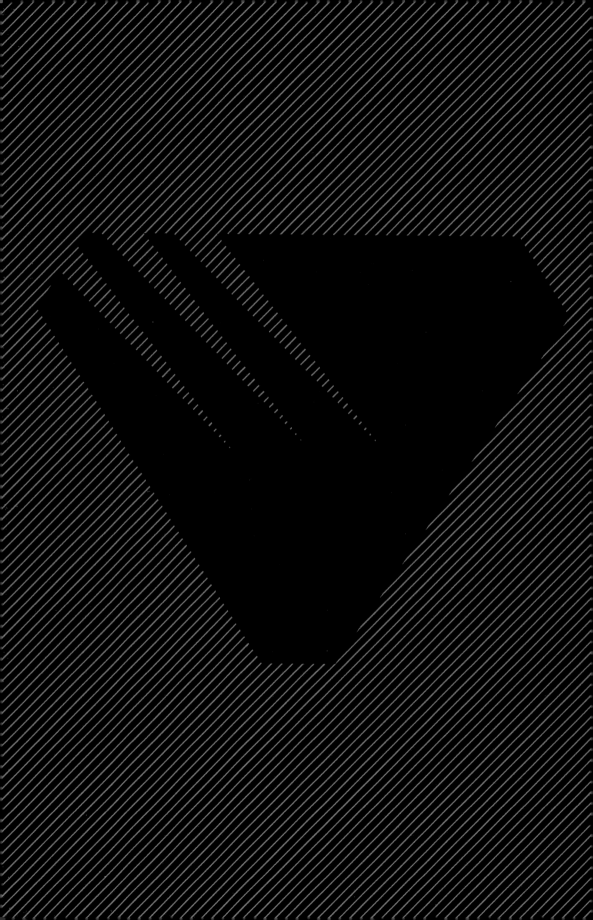

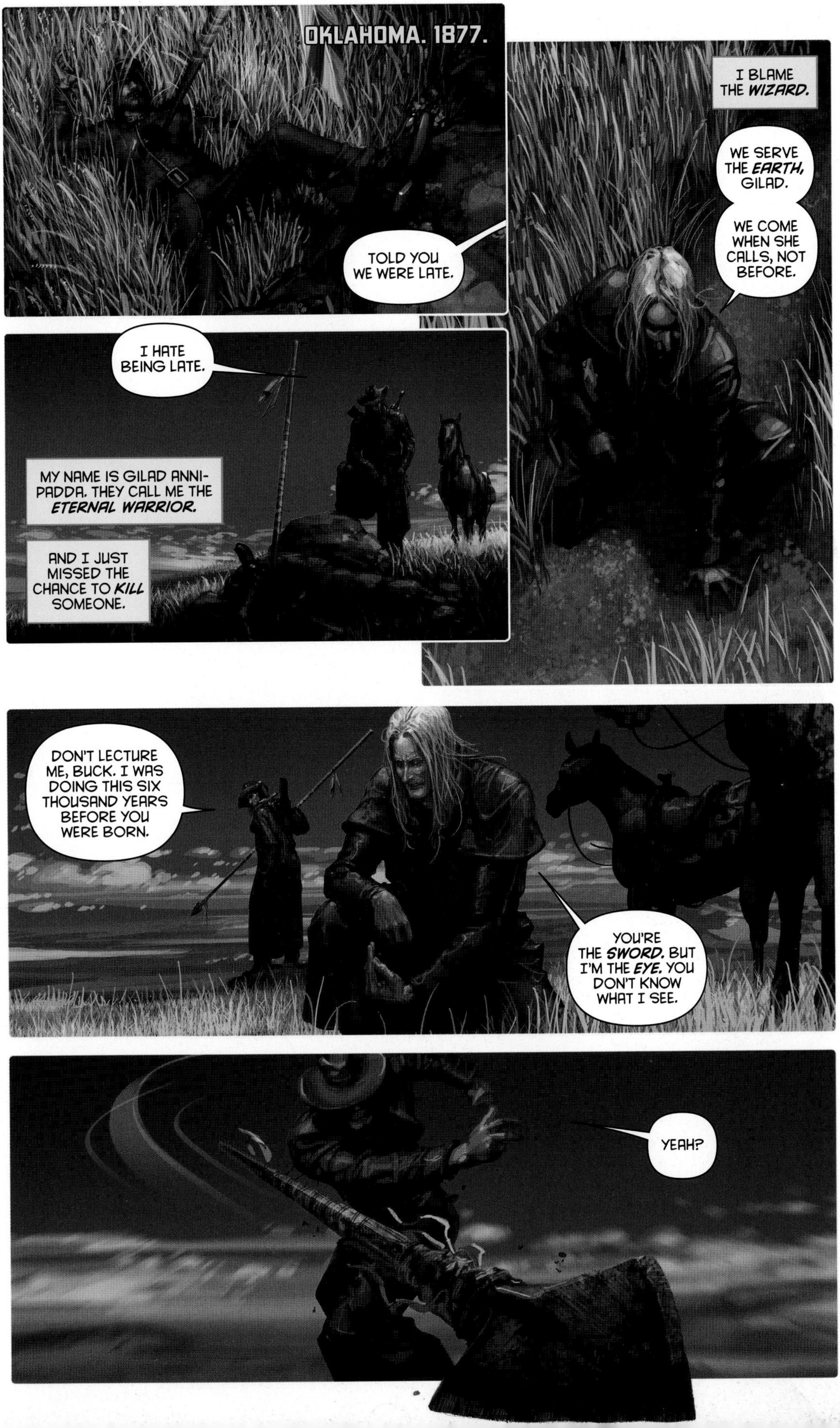
OKLAHOMA. 1877.
TOLD YOU WE WERE LATE.
I BLAME THE WIZARD.
WE SERVE THE EARTH, GILAD.
WE COME WHEN SHE CALLS, NOT BEFORE.
I HATE BEING LATE.
MY NAME IS GILAD ANNI-PADDA. THEY CALL ME THE ETERNAL WARRIOR.
AND I JUST MISSED THE CHANCE TO KILL SOMEONE.
DON'T LECTURE ME, BUCK. I WAS DOING THIS SIX THOUSAND YEARS BEFORE YOU WERE BORN.
YOU'RE THE SWORD. BUT I'M THE EYE. YOU DON'T KNOW WHAT I SEE.
YEAH?

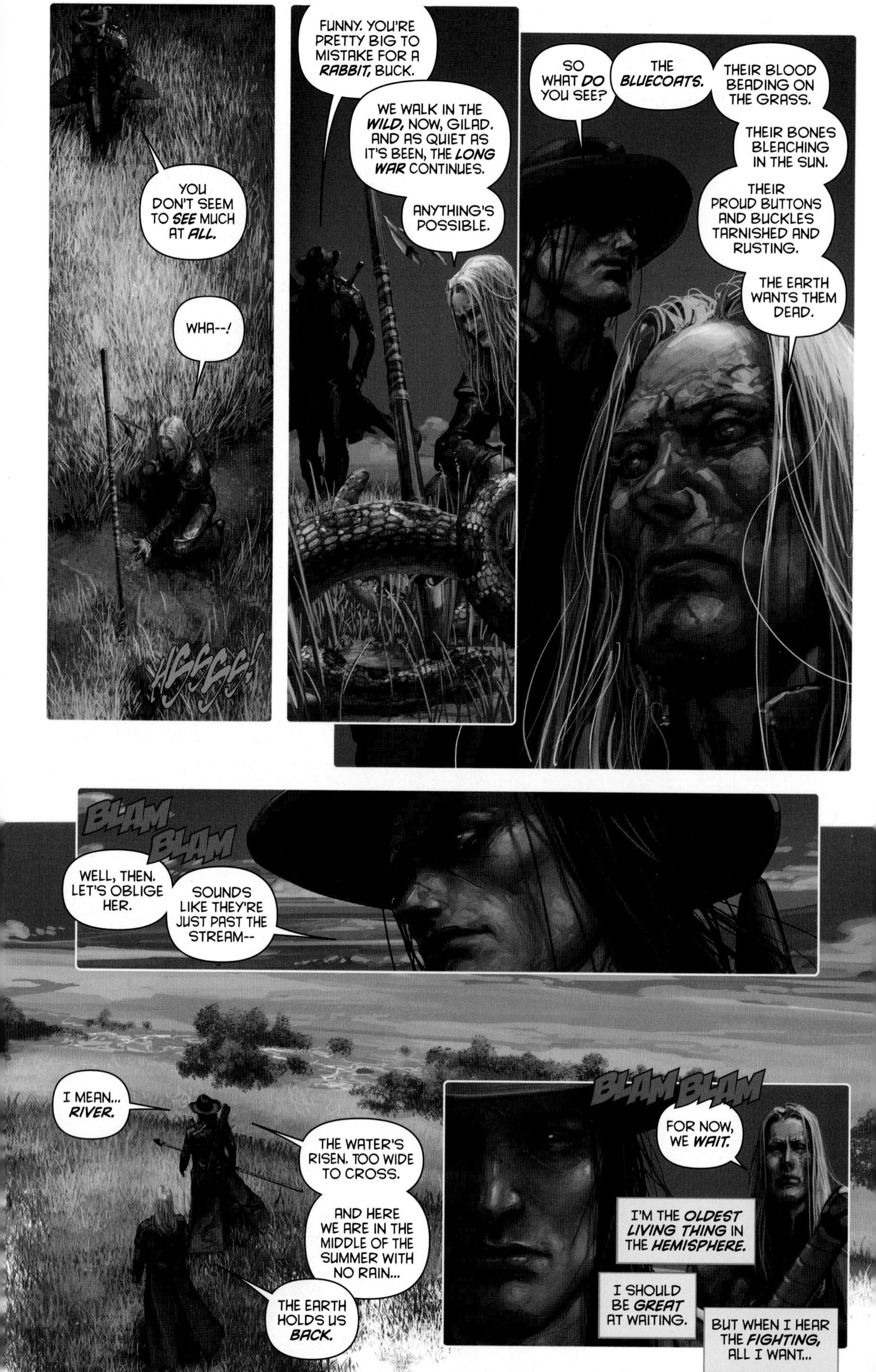
YOU DON'T SEEM TO SEE MUCH AT ALL.
WHA--!
HSSSS!
FUNNY. YOU'RE PRETTY BIG TO MISTAKE FOR A RABBIT, BUCK.
WE WALK IN THE WILD, NOW, GILAD. AND AS QUIET AS IT'S BEEN, THE LONG WAR CONTINUES.
ANYTHING'S POSSIBLE.
SO WHAT DO YOU SEE?
THE BLUECOATS.
THEIR BLOOD BEADING ON THE GRASS.
THEIR BONES BLEACHING IN THE SUN.
THEIR PROUD BUTTONS AND BUCKLES TARNISHED AND RUSTING.
THE EARTH WANTS THEM DEAD.
BLAM BLAM
WELL, THEN. LET'S OBLIGE HER.
SOUNDS LIKE THEY'RE JUST PAST THE STREAM--
I MEAN... RIVER.
THE WATER'S RISEN. TOO WIDE TO CROSS.
AND HERE WE ARE IN THE MIDDLE OF THE SUMMER WITH NO RAIN...
THE EARTH HOLDS US BACK.
BLAM BLAM
FOR NOW, WE WAIT.
I'M THE OLDEST LIVING THING IN THE HEMISPHERE.
I SHOULD BE GREAT AT WAITING.
BUT WHEN I HEAR THE FIGHTING, ALL I WANT...

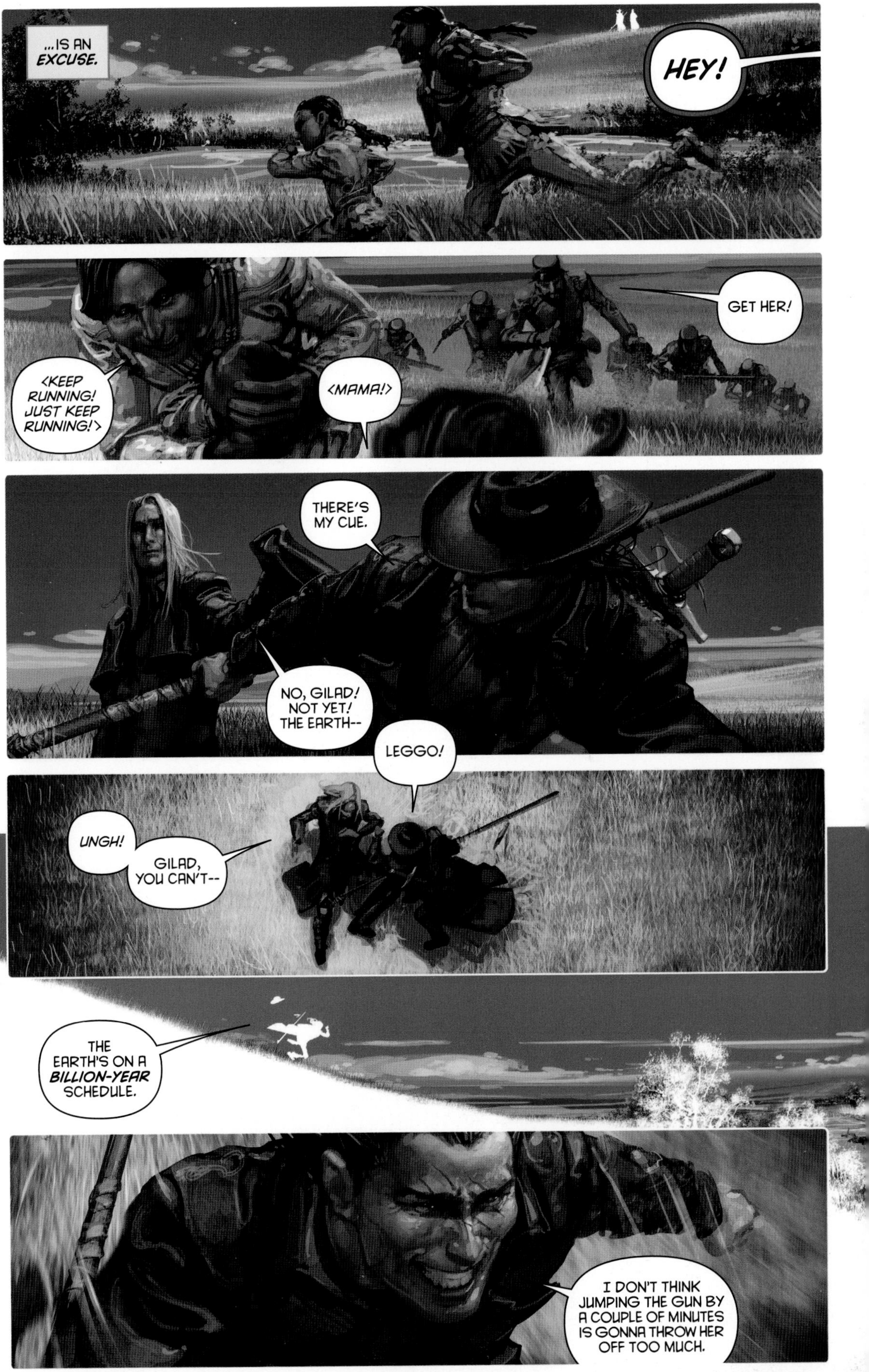
...IS AN EXCUSE.
HEY!
GET HER!
<KEEP RUNNING! JUST KEEP RUNNING!>
<MAMA!>
THERE'S MY CUE.
NO, GILAD! NOT YET! THE EARTH--
LEGGO!
UNGH!
GILAD, YOU CAN'T--
THE EARTH'S ON A BILLION-YEAR SCHEDULE.
I DON'T THINK JUMPING THE GUN BY A COUPLE OF MINUTES IS GONNA THROW HER OFF TOO MUCH.

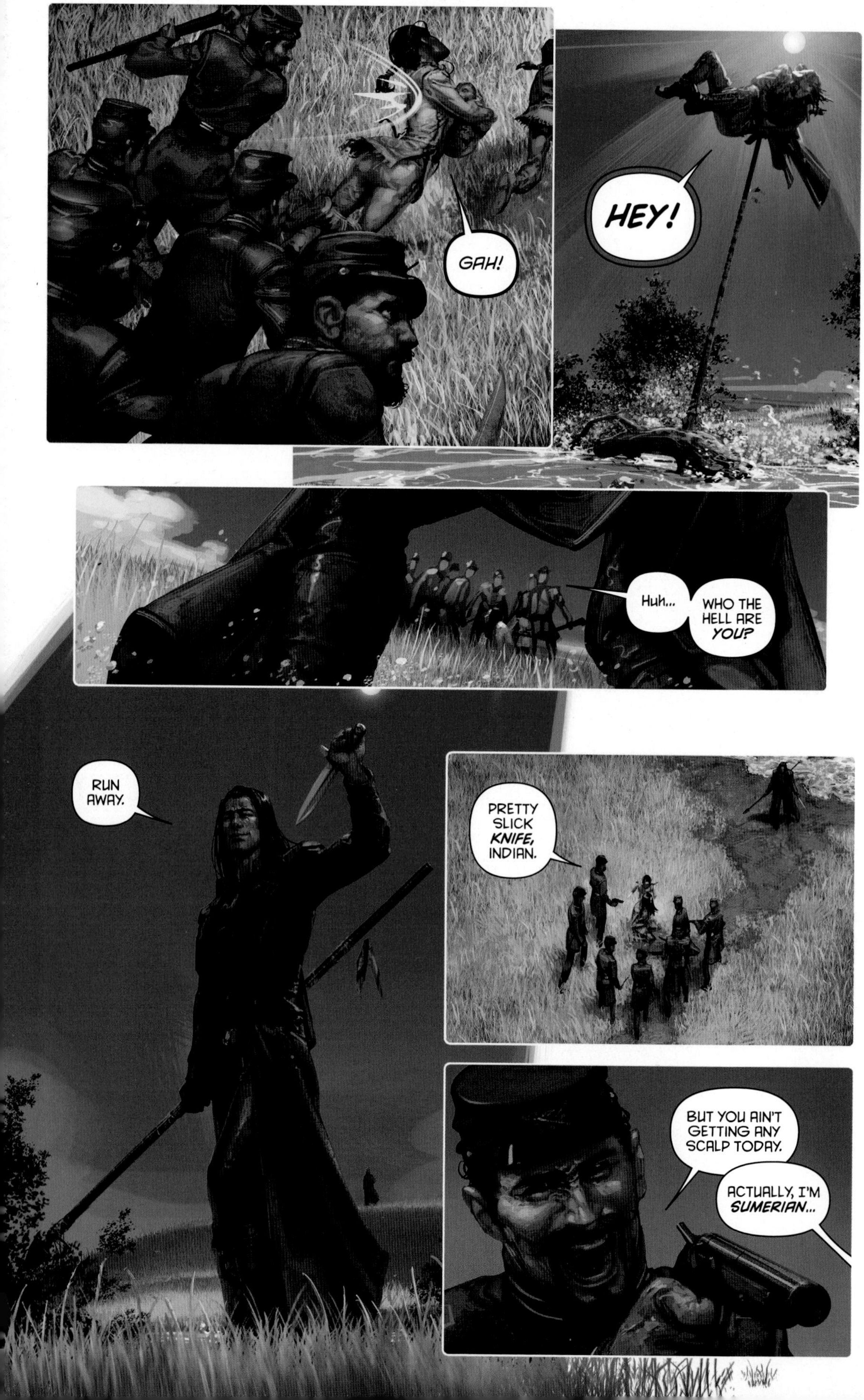
GAH!
HEY!
Huh...
WHO THE HELL ARE YOU?
RUN AWAY.
PRETTY SLICK KNIFE, INDIAN.
BUT YOU AIN'T GETTING ANY SCALP TODAY.
ACTUALLY, I'M SUMERIAN...

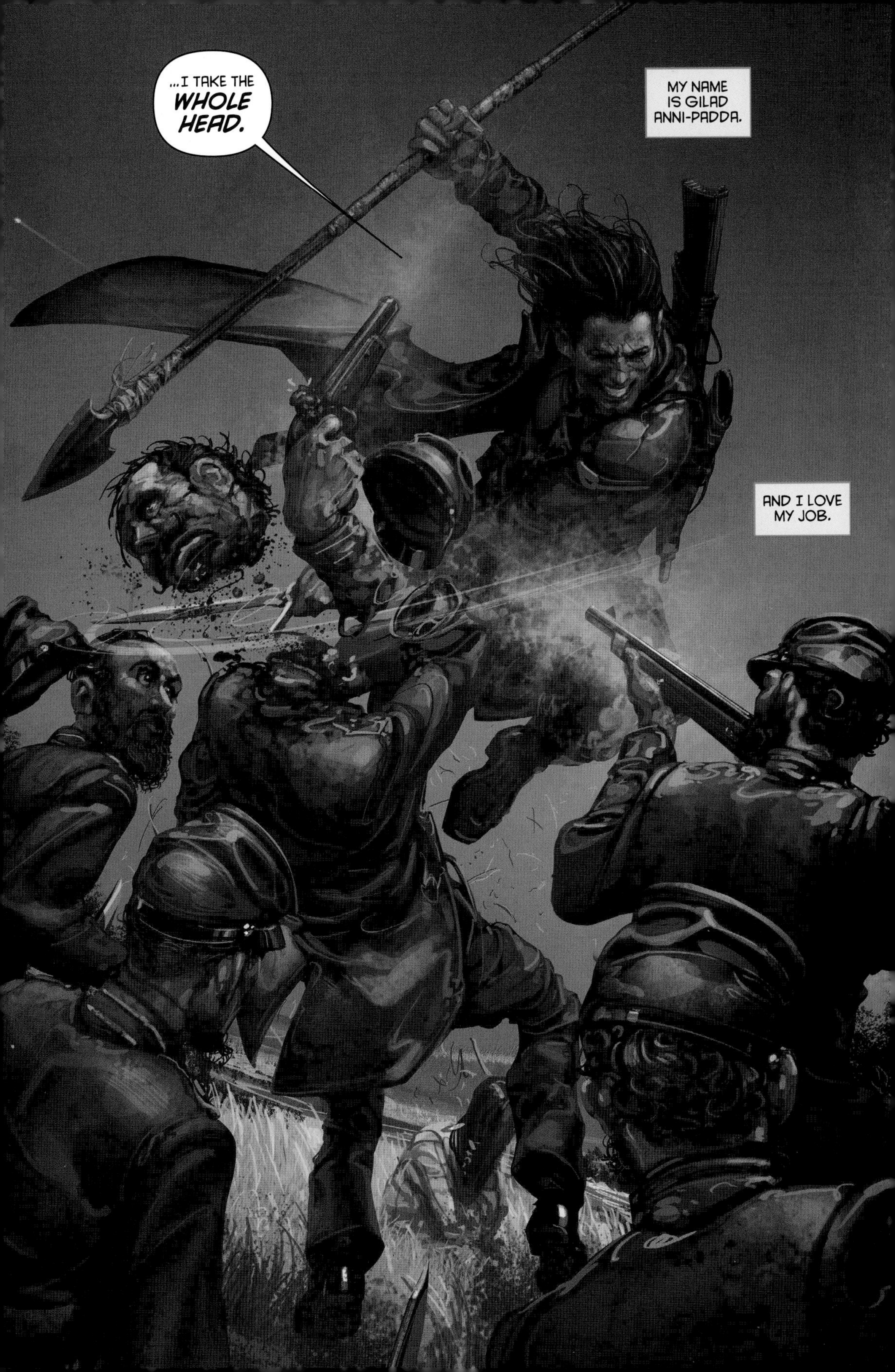
...I TAKE THE WHOLE HEAD.
MY NAME IS GILAD ANNI-PADDA.
AND I LOVE MY JOB.

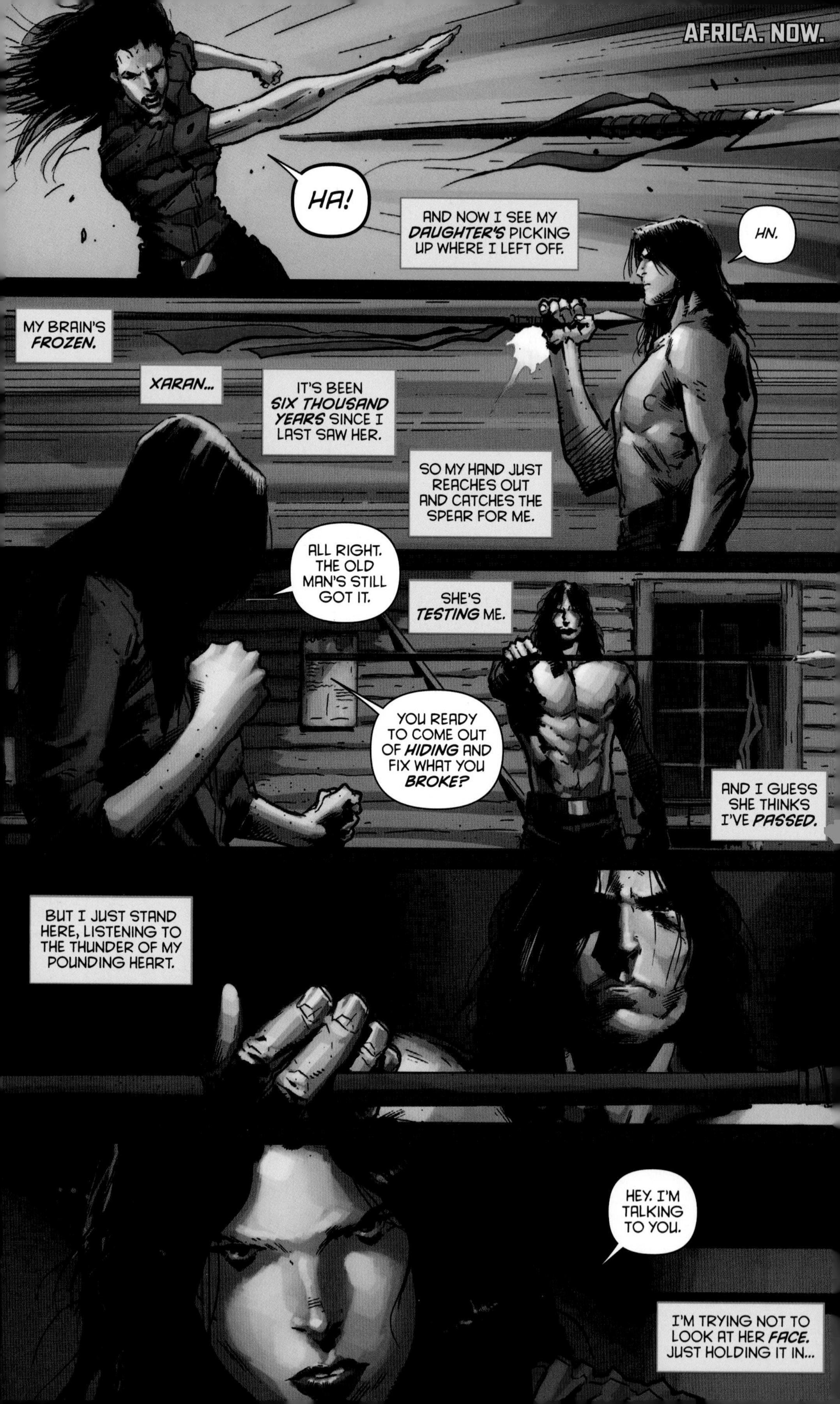
AFRICA. NOW.
HA!
AND NOW I SEE MY DAUGHTER'S PICKING UP WHERE I LEFT OFF.
HN.
MY BRAIN'S FROZEN.
XARAN...
IT'S BEEN SIX THOUSAND YEARS SINCE I LAST SAW HER.
SO MY HAND JUST REACHES OUT AND CATCHES THE SPEAR FOR ME.
ALL RIGHT. THE OLD MAN'S STILL GOT IT.
SHE'S TESTING ME.
YOU READY TO COME OUT OF HIDING AND FIX WHAT YOU BROKE?
AND I GUESS SHE THINKS I'VE PASSED.
BUT I JUST STAND HERE, LISTENING TO THE THUNDER OF MY POUNDING HEART.
HEY. I'M TALKING TO YOU.
I'M TRYING NOT TO LOOK AT HER FACE. JUST HOLDING IT IN...

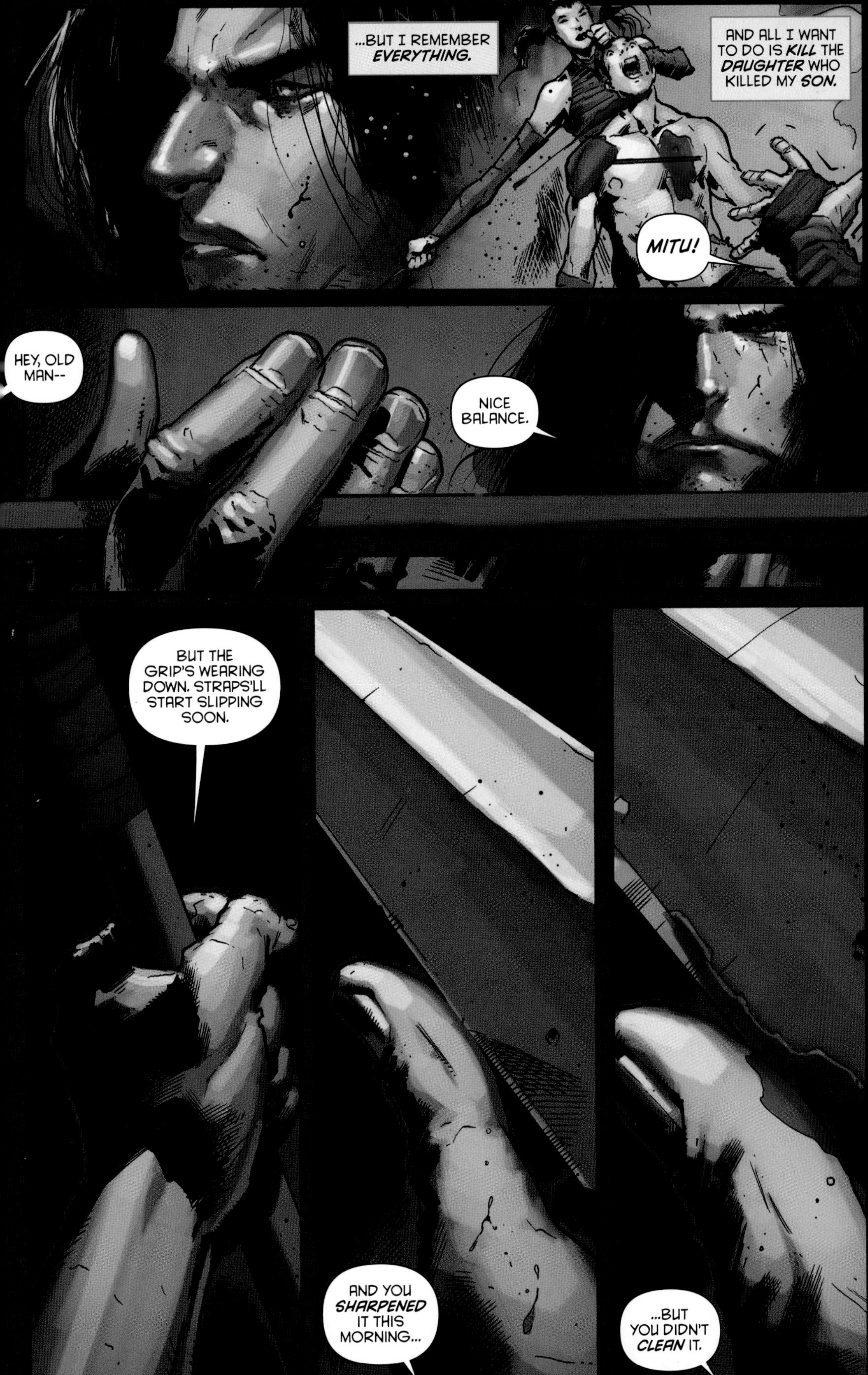
...BUT I REMEMBER EVERYTHING.
AND ALL I WANT TO DO IS KILL THE DAUGHTER WHO KILLED MY SON.
MITU!
HEY, OLD MAN--
NICE BALANCE.
BUT THE GRIP'S WEARING DOWN. STRAPS'LL START SLIPPING SOON.
AND YOU SHARPENED IT THIS MORNING...
...BUT YOU DIDN'T CLEAN IT.

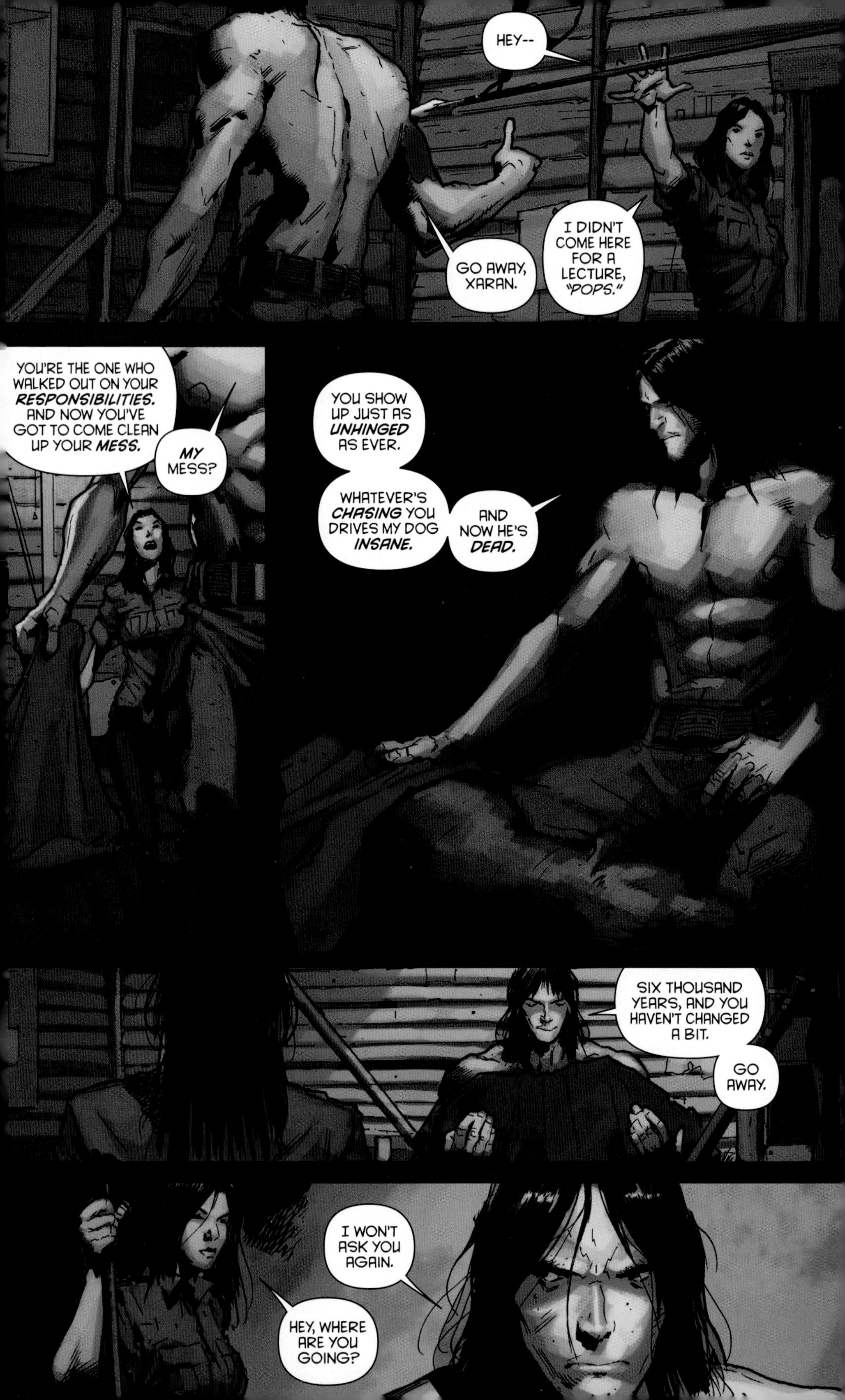
HEY--
GO AWAY, XARAN.
I DIDN'T COME HERE FOR A LECTURE, "POPS."
YOU'RE THE ONE WHO WALKED OUT ON YOUR RESPONSIBILITIES. AND NOW YOU'VE GOT TO COME CLEAN UP YOUR MESS.
MY MESS?
YOU SHOW UP JUST AS UNHINGED AS EVER.
WHATEVER'S CHASING YOU DRIVES MY DOG INSANE.
AND NOW HE'S DEAD.
SIX THOUSAND YEARS, AND YOU HAVEN'T CHANGED A BIT.
GO AWAY.
I WON'T ASK YOU AGAIN.
HEY, WHERE ARE YOU GOING?

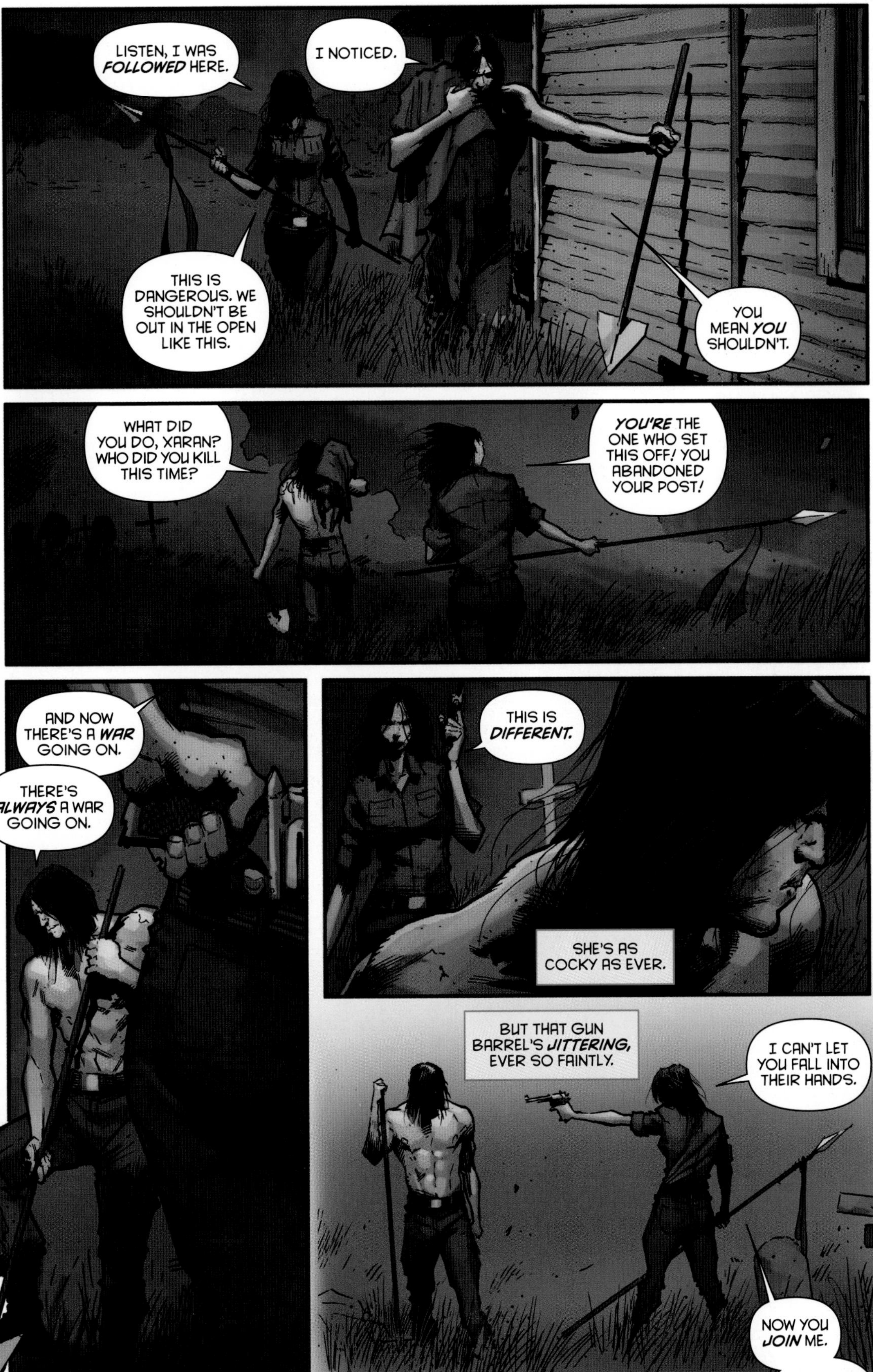
LISTEN, I WAS FOLLOWED HERE.
I NOTICED.
THIS IS DANGEROUS. WE SHOULDN'T BE OUT IN THE OPEN LIKE THIS.
YOU MEAN YOU SHOULDN'T.
WHAT DID YOU DO, XARAN? WHO DID YOU KILL THIS TIME?
YOU'RE THE ONE WHO SET THIS OFF! YOU ABANDONED YOUR POST!
AND NOW THERE'S A WAR GOING ON.
THERE'S ALWAYS A WAR GOING ON.
THIS IS DIFFERENT.
SHE'S AS COCKY AS EVER.
BUT THAT GUN BARREL'S JITTERING, EVER SO FAINTLY.
I CAN'T LET YOU FALL INTO THEIR HANDS.
NOW YOU JOIN ME.
OR I BLOW YOUR HEAD OFF.

I CAN HEAR HER BREATH. STEADY, BUT RAGGED.

SHE'S RUNNING ON ADRENALINE.

PROBABLY HASN'T SLEPT IN THREE DAYS.

SHE'S ACTUALLY...*SCARED.*

BUT NOT OF *ME.*

"THIS IS DIFFERENT"?

YES. YOU HAVE NO IDEA. THIS WORLD... IT *NEEDS* US, GILAD.

BUT I KNOW WHERE THIS KIND OF TALK LEADS.

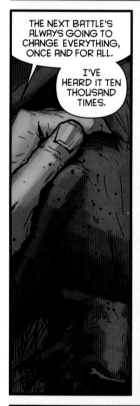

THE NEXT BATTLE'S ALWAYS GOING TO CHANGE EVERYTHING, ONCE AND FOR ALL.

I'VE HEARD IT TEN THOUSAND TIMES.

AND IT'S ALWAYS A LIE.

LOOK. I'LL MAKE THIS *SIMPLE.*

YOU HELP ME *FIX* WHAT YOU *BROKE* OR--

KAAAA!!

I DON'T KNOW WHAT'S GOING ON IN HER HEAD ANY LONGER.

WHETHER SHE THINKS SHE'S FIGHTING FOR SOMETHING BIGGER...OR SHE'S JUST TRYING TO SAVE HER SKIN.

BUT IN THE END, IT DOESN'T REALLY MATTER.

GET READY, XARAN...

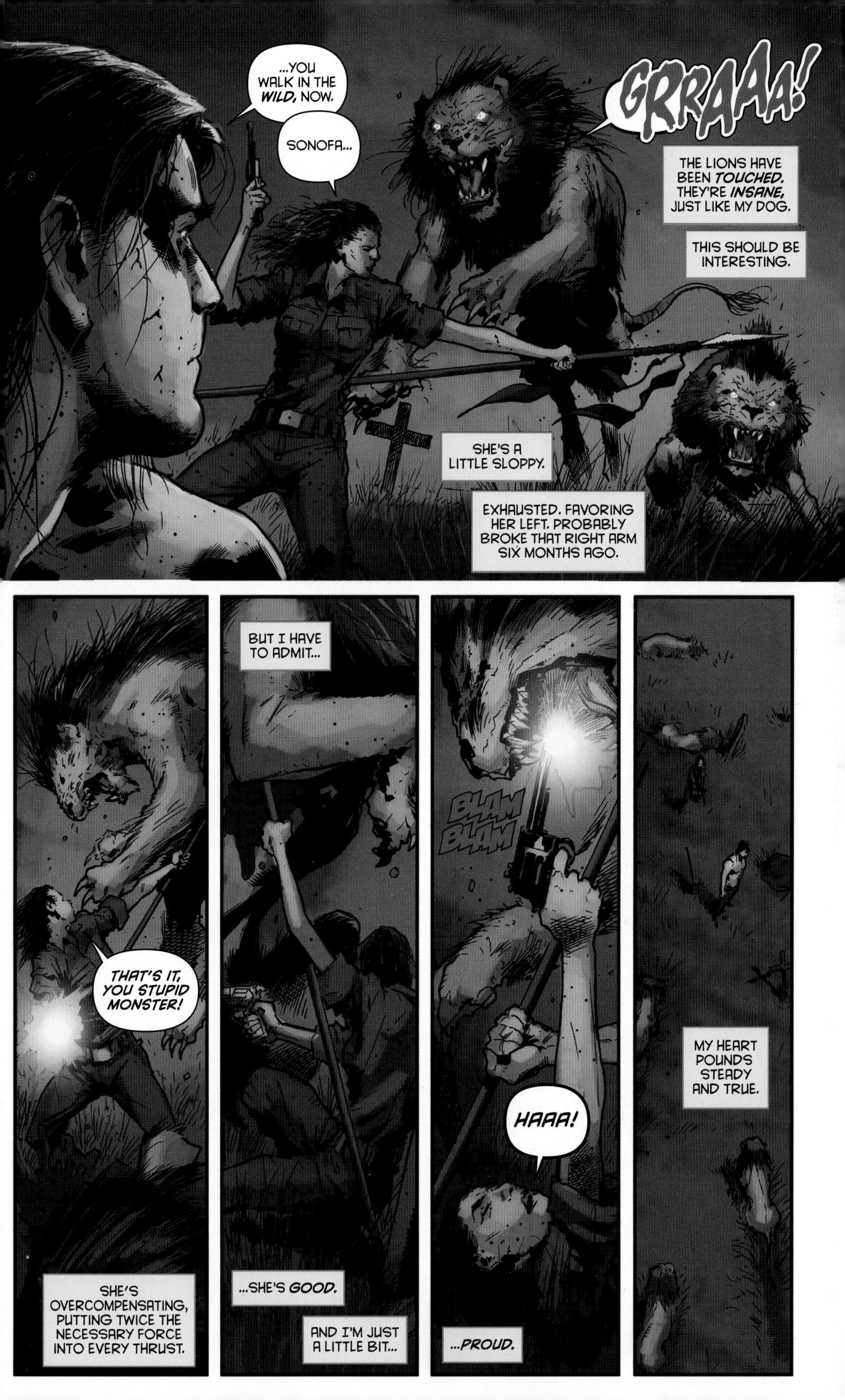
...YOU WALK IN THE WILD, NOW.
SONOFA...
GRRAAA!
THE LIONS HAVE BEEN TOUCHED. THEY'RE INSANE, JUST LIKE MY DOG.
THIS SHOULD BE INTERESTING.
SHE'S A LITTLE SLOPPY.
EXHAUSTED. FAVORING HER LEFT. PROBABLY BROKE THAT RIGHT ARM SIX MONTHS AGO.
THAT'S IT, YOU STUPID MONSTER!
SHE'S OVERCOMPENSATING, PUTTING TWICE THE NECESSARY FORCE INTO EVERY THRUST.
BUT I HAVE TO ADMIT...
...SHE'S GOOD.
AND I'M JUST A LITTLE BIT...
BLAM BLAM
HAAA!
...PROUD.
MY HEART POUNDS STEADY AND TRUE.

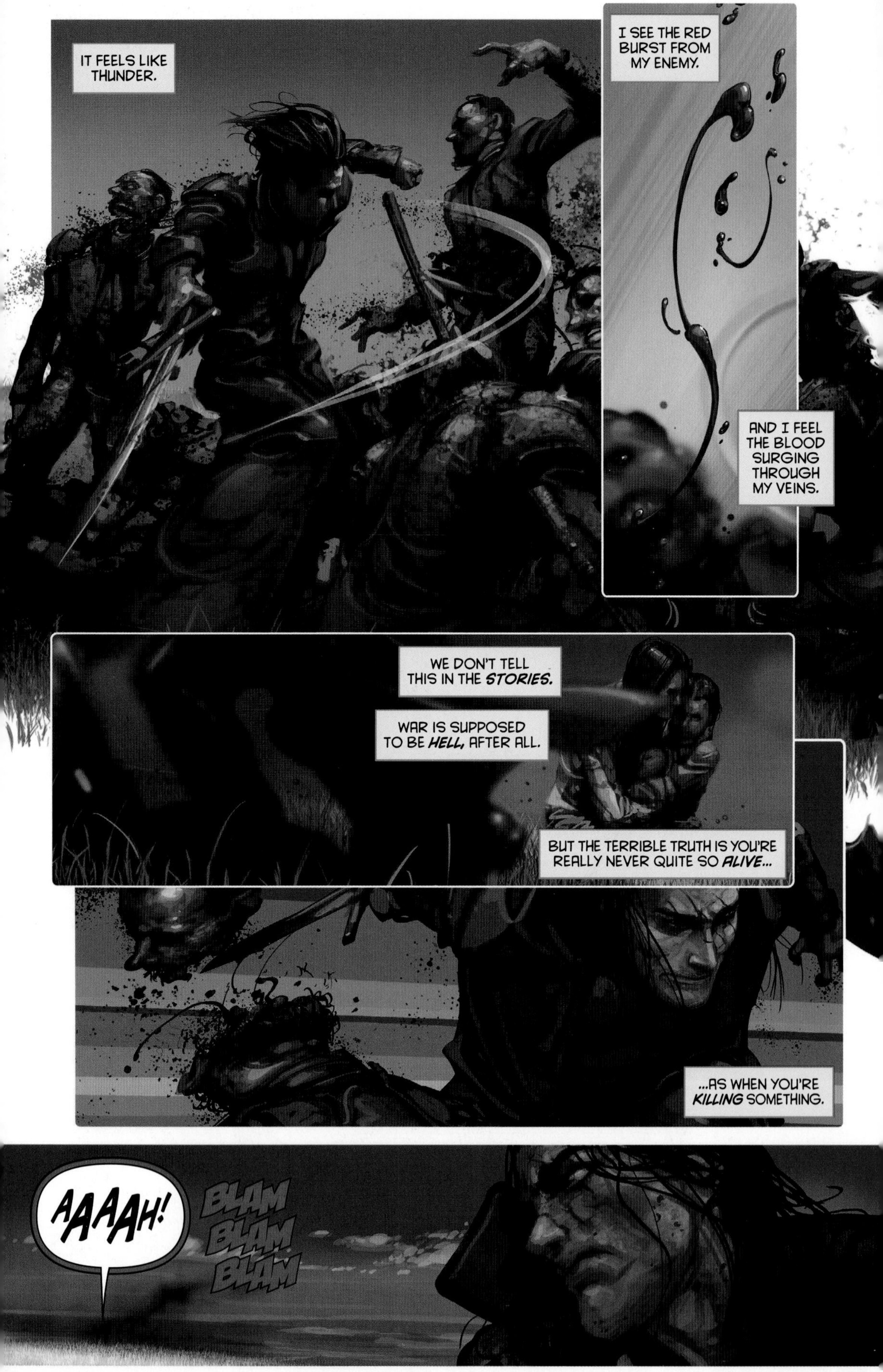

IT FEELS LIKE THUNDER.
I SEE THE RED BURST FROM MY ENEMY.
AND I FEEL THE BLOOD SURGING THROUGH MY VEINS.
WE DON'T TELL THIS IN THE *STORIES.*
WAR IS SUPPOSED TO BE *HELL,* AFTER ALL.
BUT THE TERRIBLE TRUTH IS YOU'RE REALLY NEVER QUITE SO *ALIVE*...
...AS WHEN YOU'RE *KILLING* SOMETHING.
AAAAH!
BLAM
BLAM
BLAM

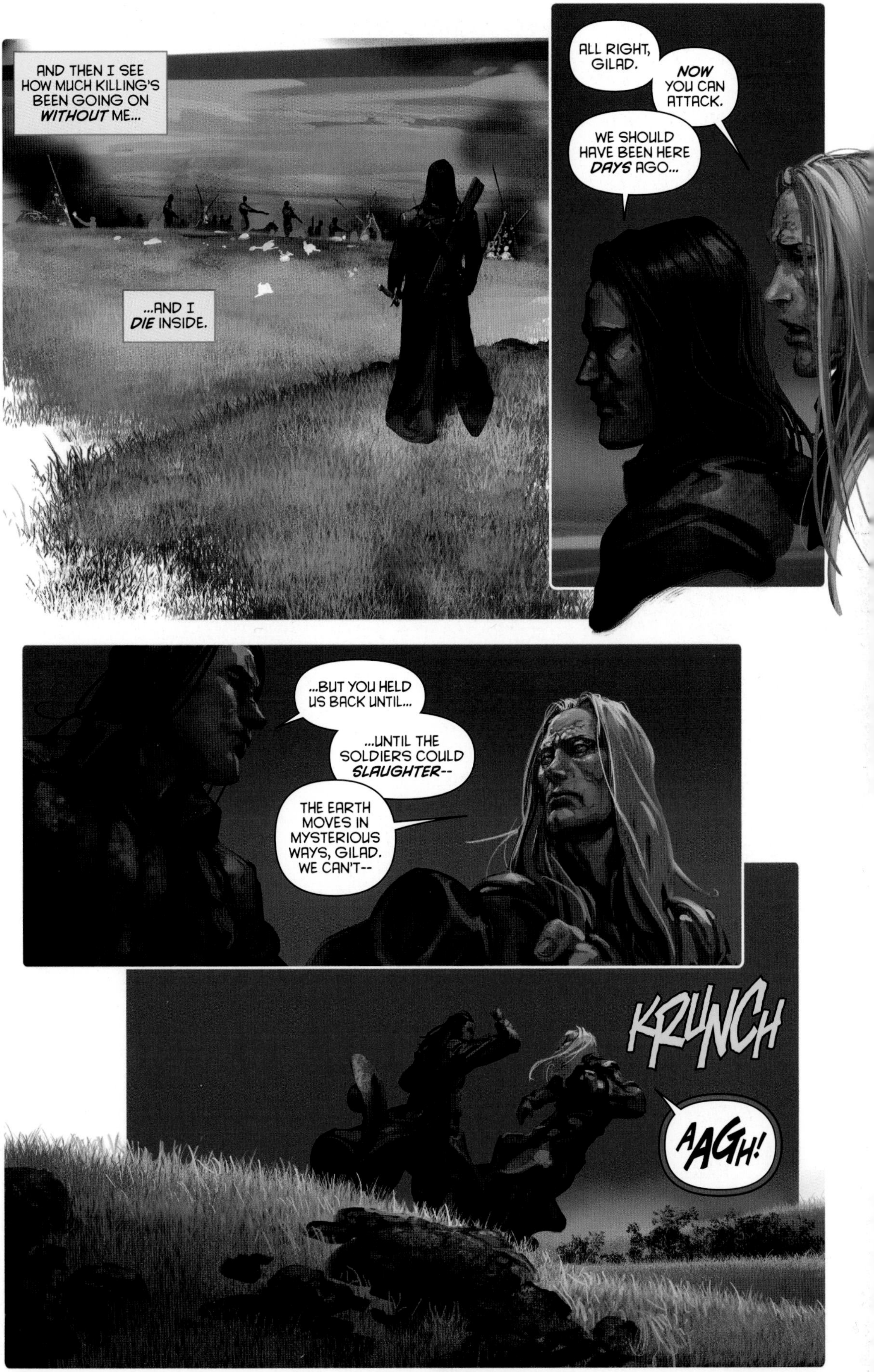

AND THEN I SEE HOW MUCH KILLING'S BEEN GOING ON WITHOUT ME...
...AND I DIE INSIDE.
ALL RIGHT, GILAD.
NOW YOU CAN ATTACK.
WE SHOULD HAVE BEEN HERE DAYS AGO...
...BUT YOU HELD US BACK UNTIL...
...UNTIL THE SOLDIERS COULD SLAUGHTER--
THE EARTH MOVES IN MYSTERIOUS WAYS, GILAD. WE CAN'T--
KRUNCH
AAGH!

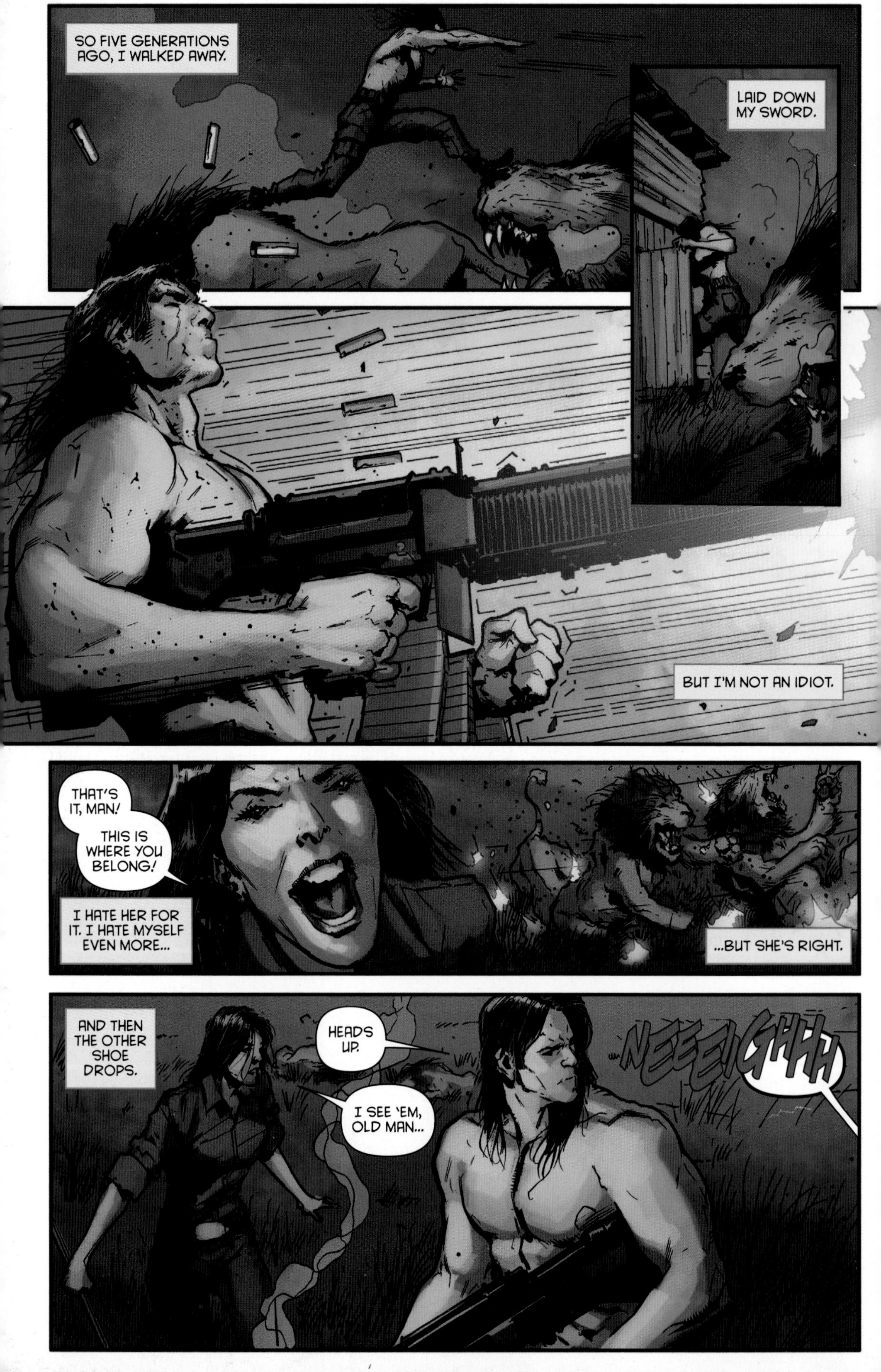
SO FIVE GENERATIONS AGO, I WALKED AWAY.
LAID DOWN MY SWORD.
BUT I'M NOT AN IDIOT.
THAT'S IT, MAN!
THIS IS WHERE YOU BELONG!
I HATE HER FOR IT. I HATE MYSELF EVEN MORE...
...BUT SHE'S RIGHT.
AND THEN THE OTHER SHOE DROPS.
HEADS UP.
I SEE 'EM, OLD MAN...
NEEEIGHHH

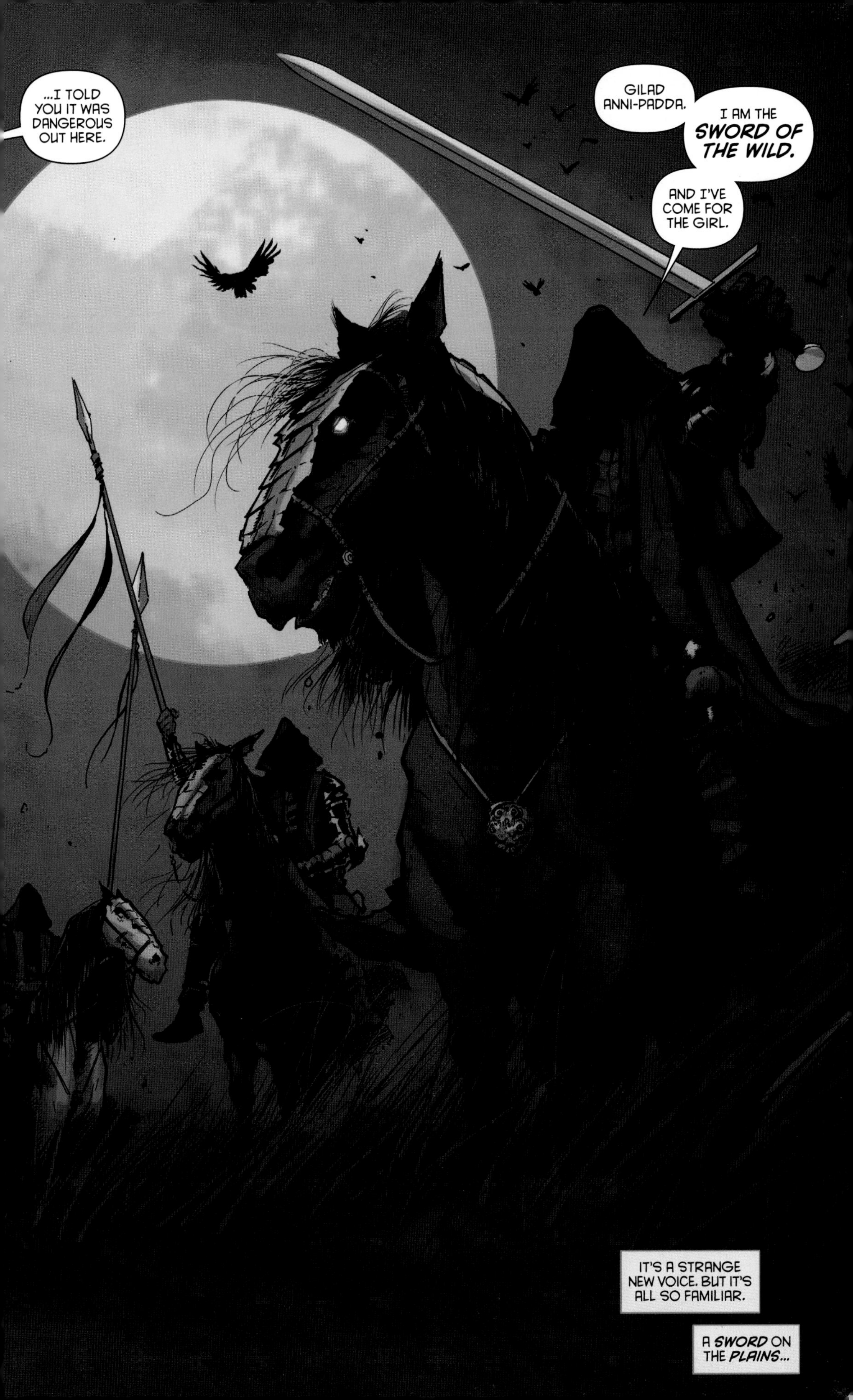
...I TOLD YOU IT WAS DANGEROUS OUT HERE.
GILAD ANNI-PADDA.
I AM THE SWORD OF THE WILD.
AND I'VE COME FOR THE GIRL.
IT'S A STRANGE NEW VOICE. BUT IT'S ALL SO FAMILIAR.
A SWORD ON THE PLAINS...

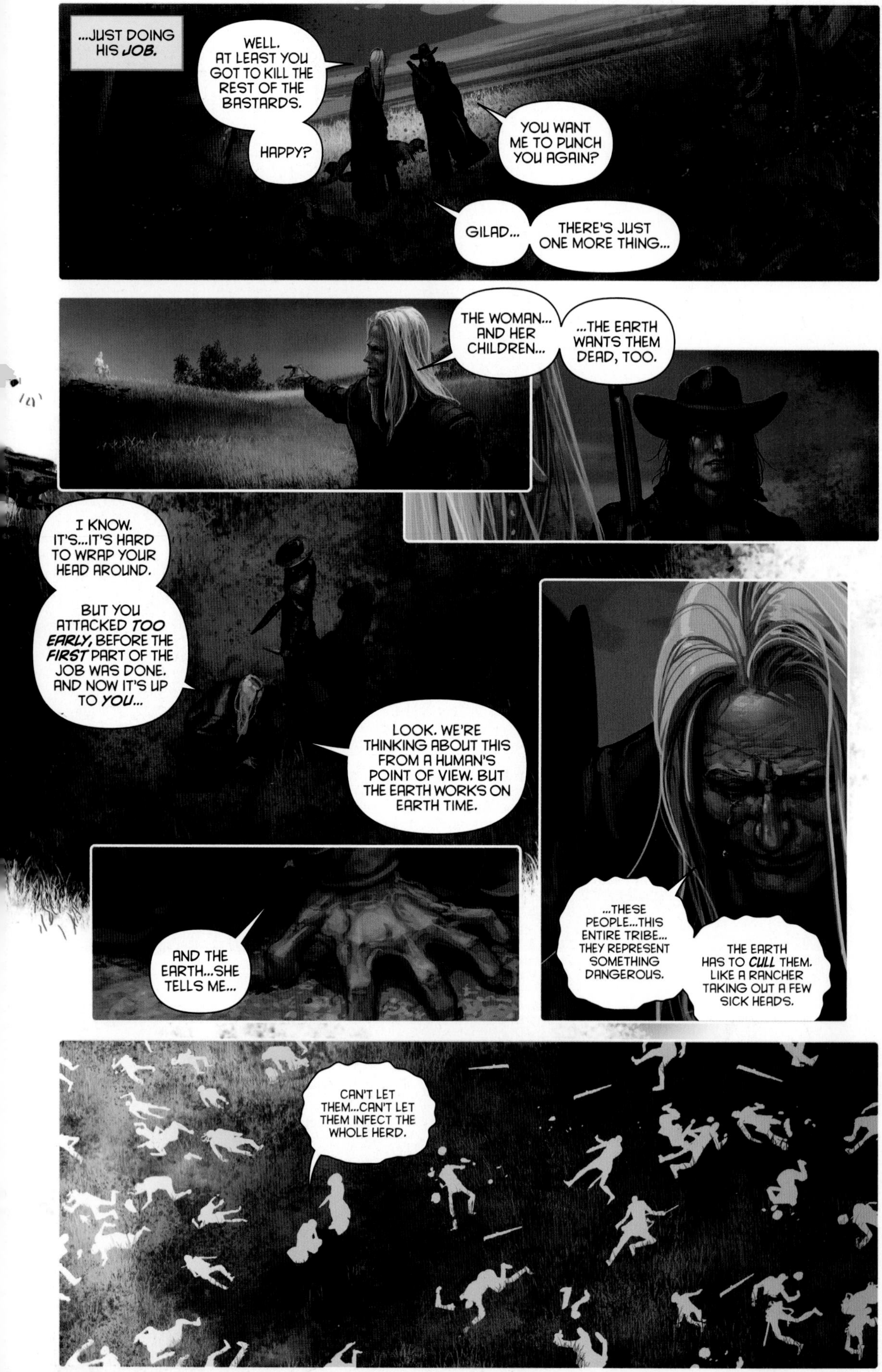
...JUST DOING HIS *JOB.*
WELL. AT LEAST YOU GOT TO KILL THE REST OF THE BASTARDS.
HAPPY?
YOU WANT ME TO PUNCH YOU AGAIN?
GILAD...
THERE'S JUST ONE MORE THING...
THE WOMAN... AND HER CHILDREN...
...THE EARTH WANTS THEM DEAD, TOO.
I KNOW. IT'S...IT'S HARD TO WRAP YOUR HEAD AROUND.
BUT YOU ATTACKED *TOO EARLY,* BEFORE THE *FIRST* PART OF THE JOB WAS DONE. AND NOW IT'S UP TO *YOU...*
LOOK. WE'RE THINKING ABOUT THIS FROM A HUMAN'S POINT OF VIEW. BUT THE EARTH WORKS ON EARTH TIME.
AND THE EARTH...SHE TELLS ME...
...THESE PEOPLE...THIS ENTIRE TRIBE... THEY REPRESENT SOMETHING DANGEROUS.
THE EARTH HAS TO *CULL* THEM. LIKE A RANCHER TAKING OUT A FEW SICK HEADS.
CAN'T LET THEM...CAN'T LET THEM INFECT THE WHOLE HERD.

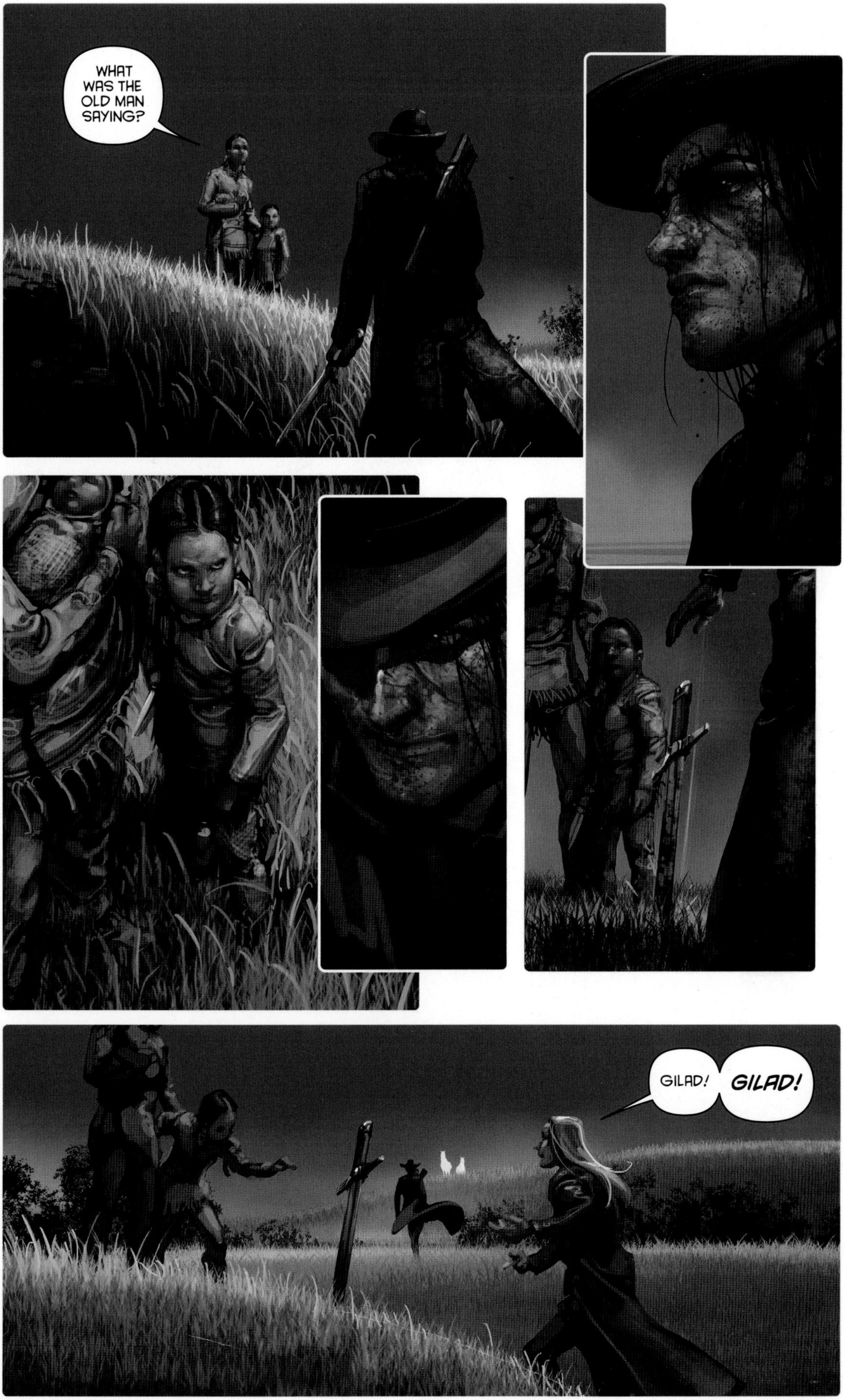
WHAT WAS THE OLD MAN SAYING?
GILAD!
GILAD!

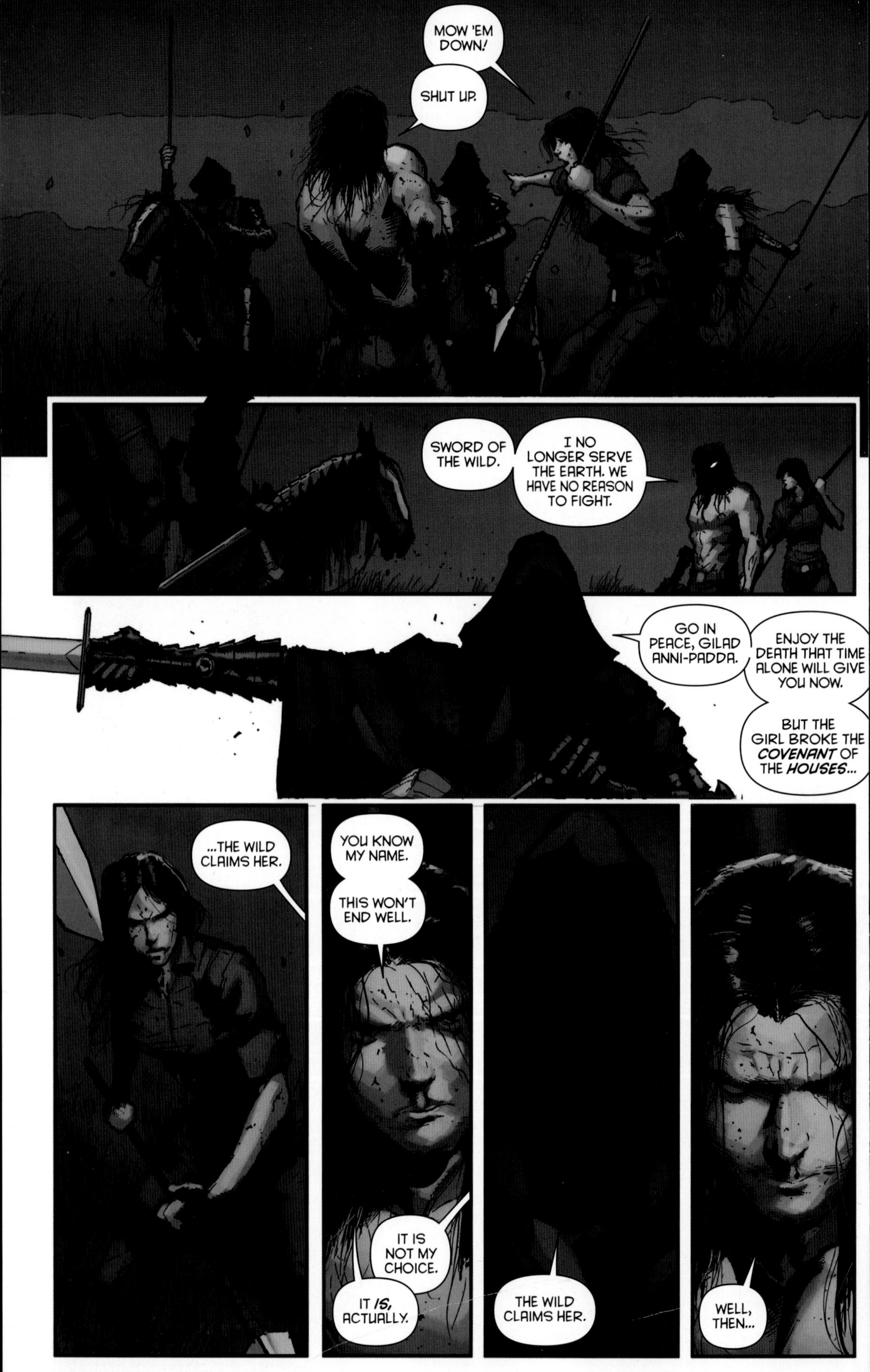
MOW 'EM DOWN!
SHUT UP.
SWORD OF THE WILD.
I NO LONGER SERVE THE EARTH. WE HAVE NO REASON TO FIGHT.
GO IN PEACE, GILAD ANNI-PADDA.
ENJOY THE DEATH THAT TIME ALONE WILL GIVE YOU NOW.
BUT THE GIRL BROKE THE COVENANT OF THE HOUSES...
...THE WILD CLAIMS HER.
YOU KNOW MY NAME.
THIS WON'T END WELL.
IT IS NOT MY CHOICE.
IT IS, ACTUALLY.
THE WILD CLAIMS HER.
WELL, THEN...

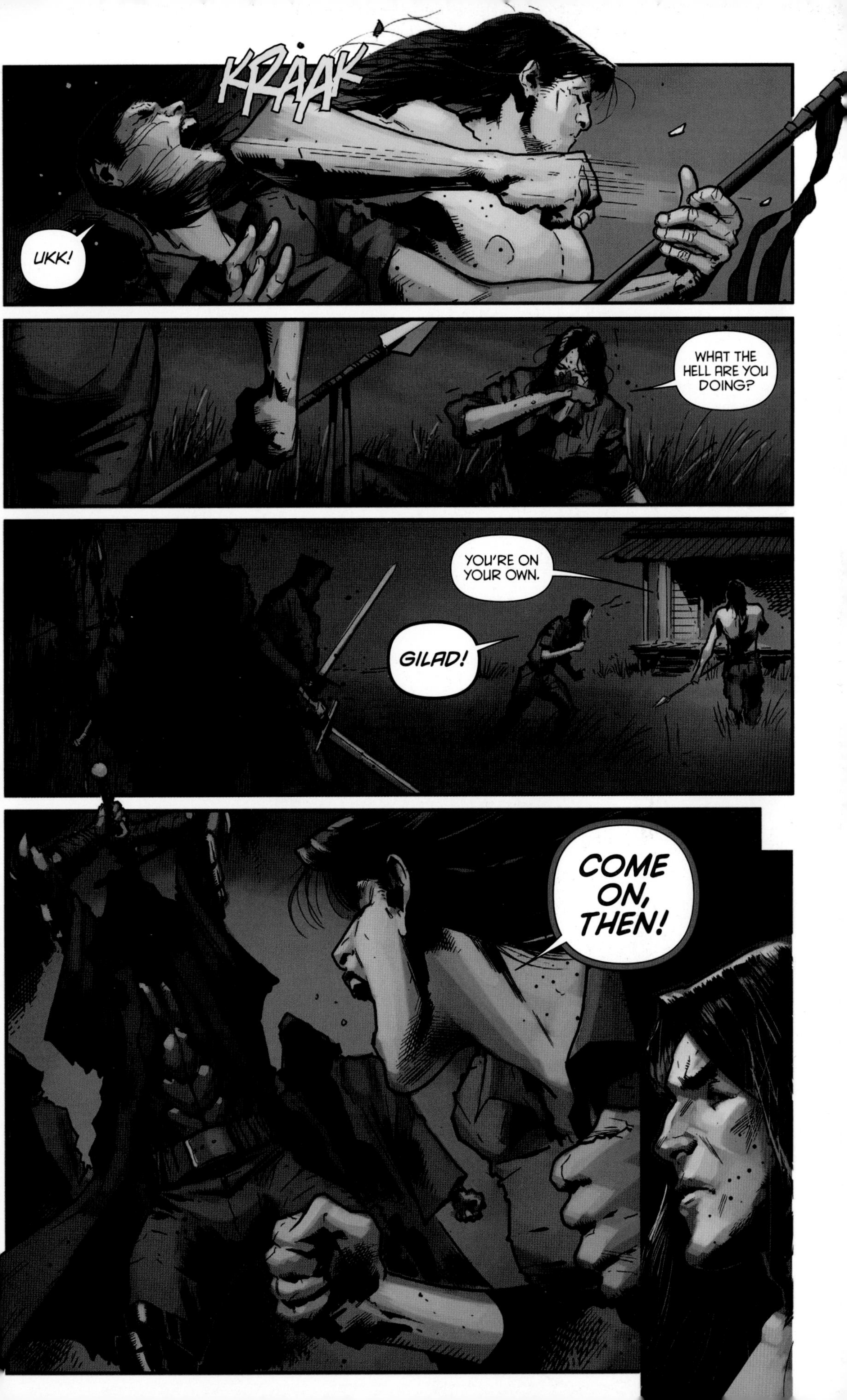
KRAAK
UKK!
WHAT THE HELL ARE YOU DOING?
YOU'RE ON YOUR OWN.
GILAD!
COME ON, THEN!

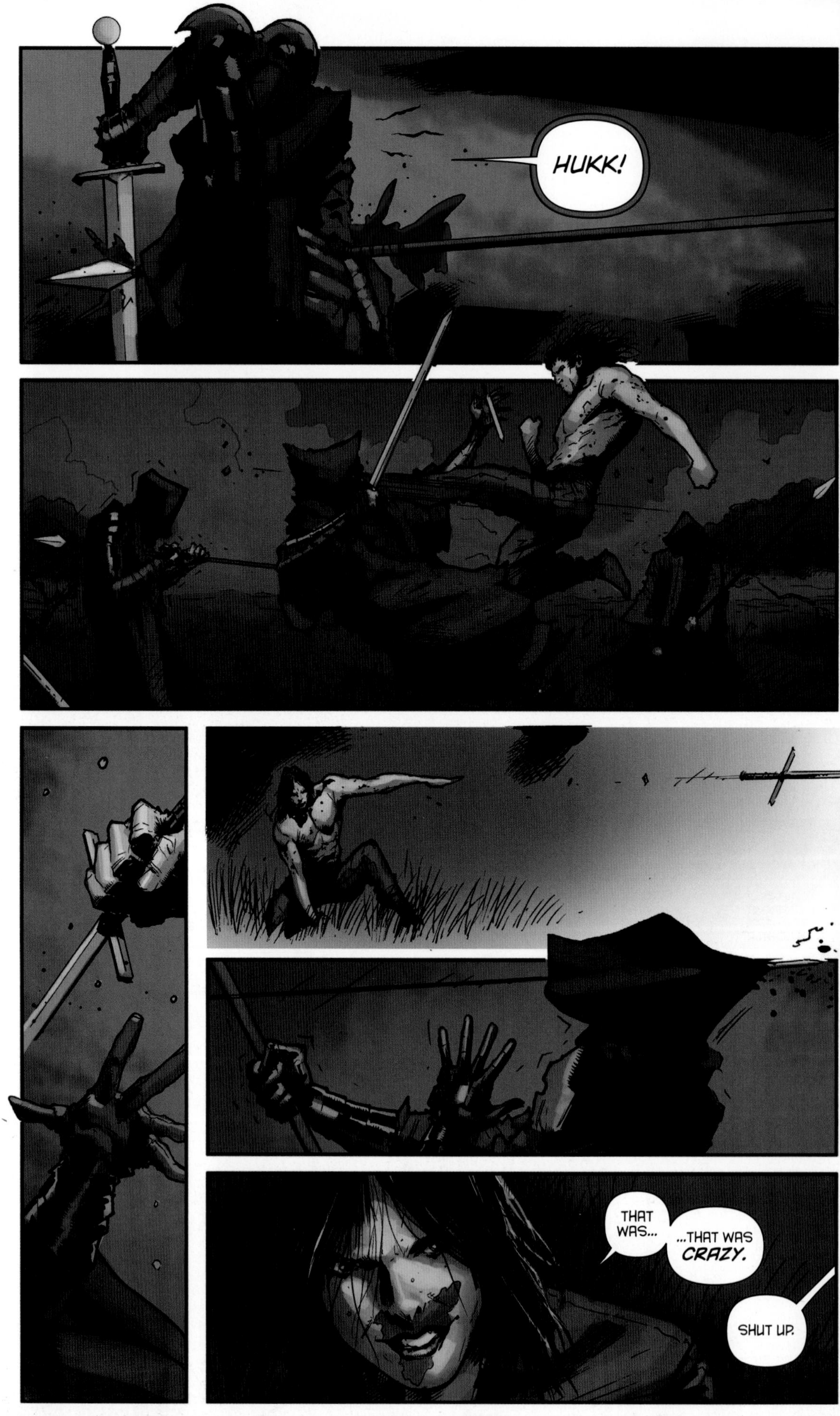
HUKK!
THAT WAS...
...THAT WAS CRAZY.
SHUT UP.

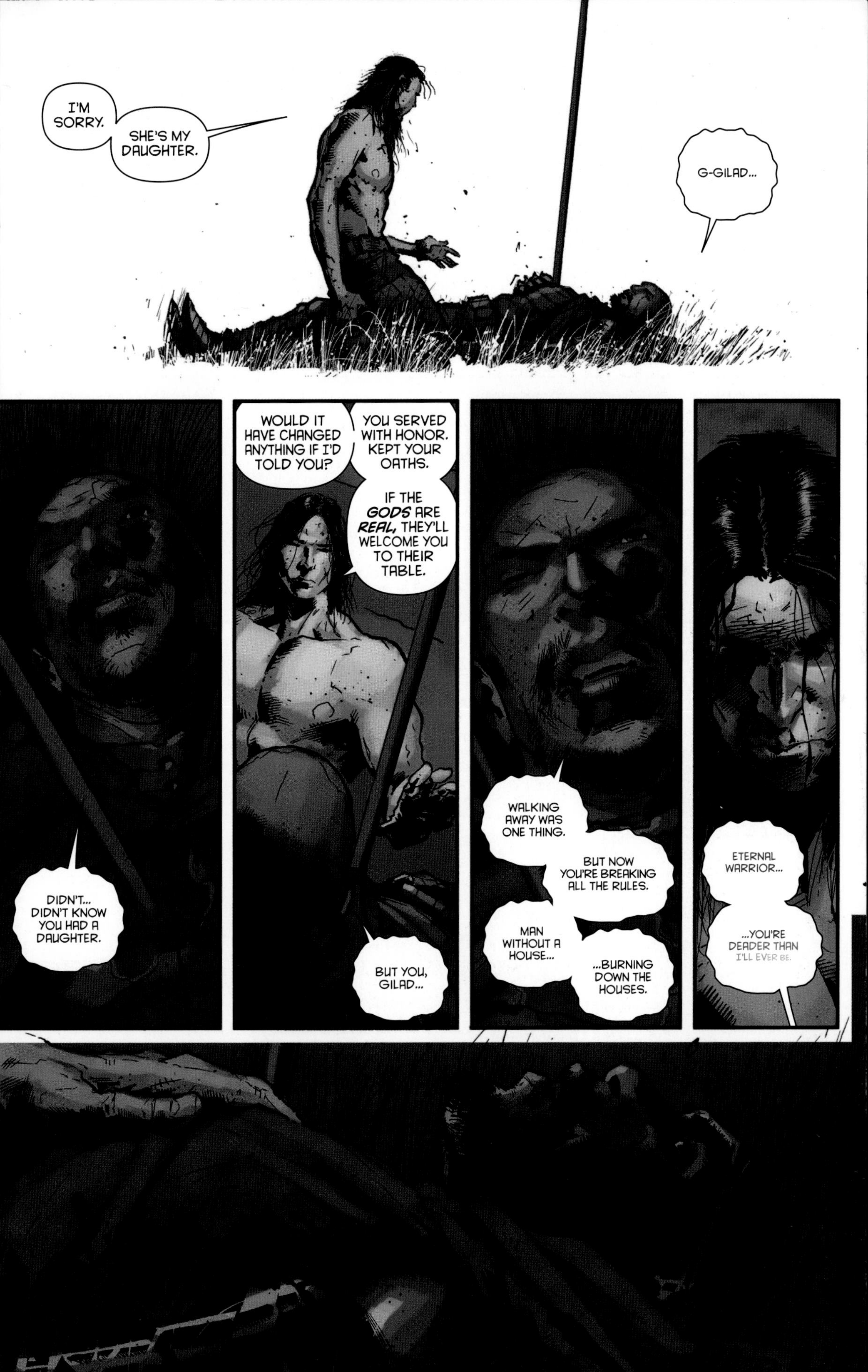
I'M SORRY.
SHE'S MY DAUGHTER.
G-GILAD...
DIDN'T... DIDN'T KNOW YOU HAD A DAUGHTER.
WOULD IT HAVE CHANGED ANYTHING IF I'D TOLD YOU?
YOU SERVED WITH HONOR. KEPT YOUR OATHS.
IF THE GODS ARE REAL, THEY'LL WELCOME YOU TO THEIR TABLE.
BUT YOU, GILAD...
WALKING AWAY WAS ONE THING.
BUT NOW YOU'RE BREAKING ALL THE RULES.
MAN WITHOUT A HOUSE...
...BURNING DOWN THE HOUSES.
ETERNAL WARRIOR...
...YOU'RE DEADER THAN I'LL EVER BE.

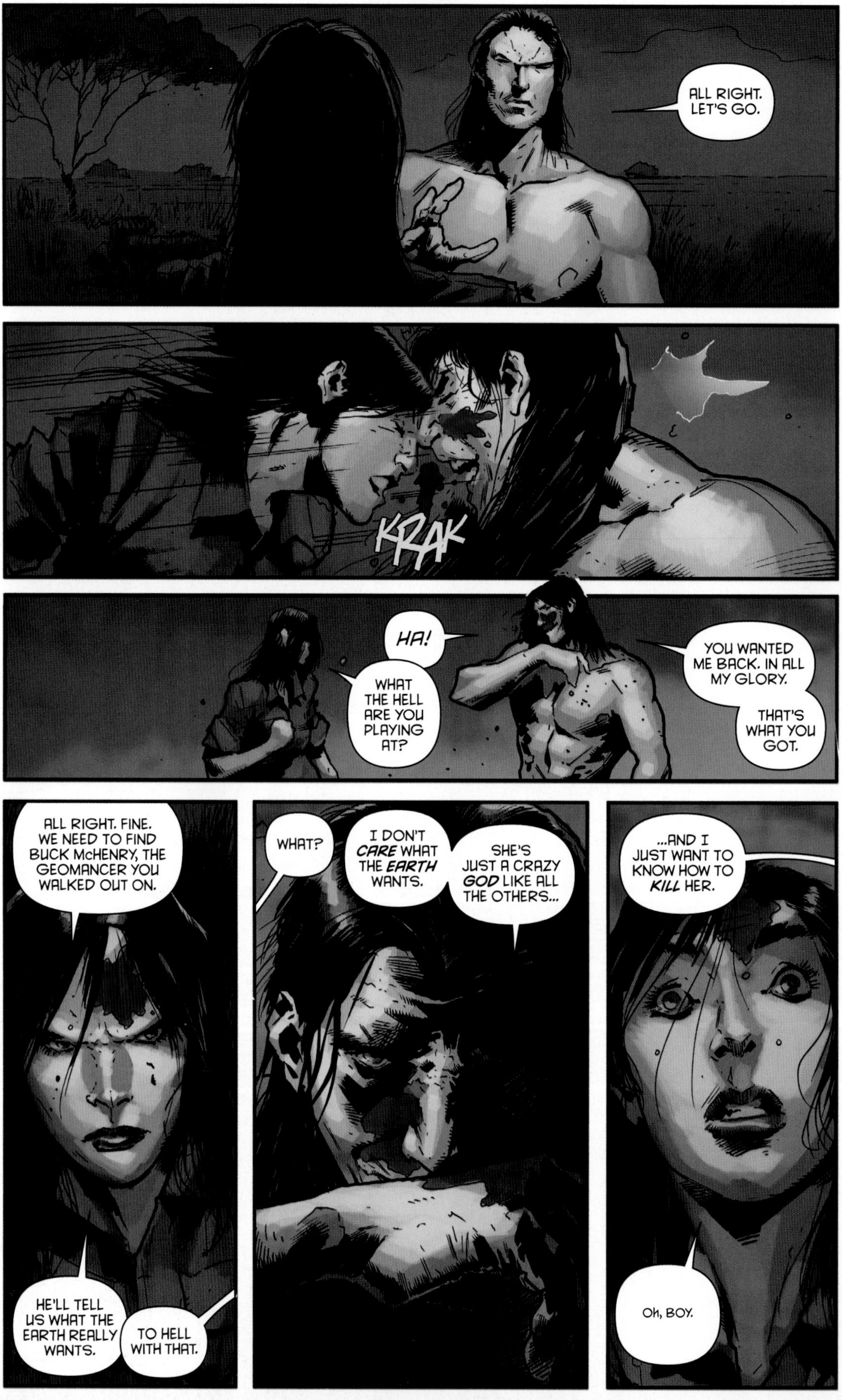
ALL RIGHT. LET'S GO.
KRAK
HA!
WHAT THE HELL ARE YOU PLAYING AT?
YOU WANTED ME BACK. IN ALL MY GLORY.
THAT'S WHAT YOU GOT.
ALL RIGHT. FINE. WE NEED TO FIND BUCK McHENRY, THE GEOMANCER YOU WALKED OUT ON.
HE'LL TELL US WHAT THE EARTH REALLY WANTS.
TO HELL WITH THAT.
WHAT?
I DON'T CARE WHAT THE EARTH WANTS.
SHE'S JUST A CRAZY GOD LIKE ALL THE OTHERS...
...AND I JUST WANT TO KNOW HOW TO KILL HER.
Oh, BOY.

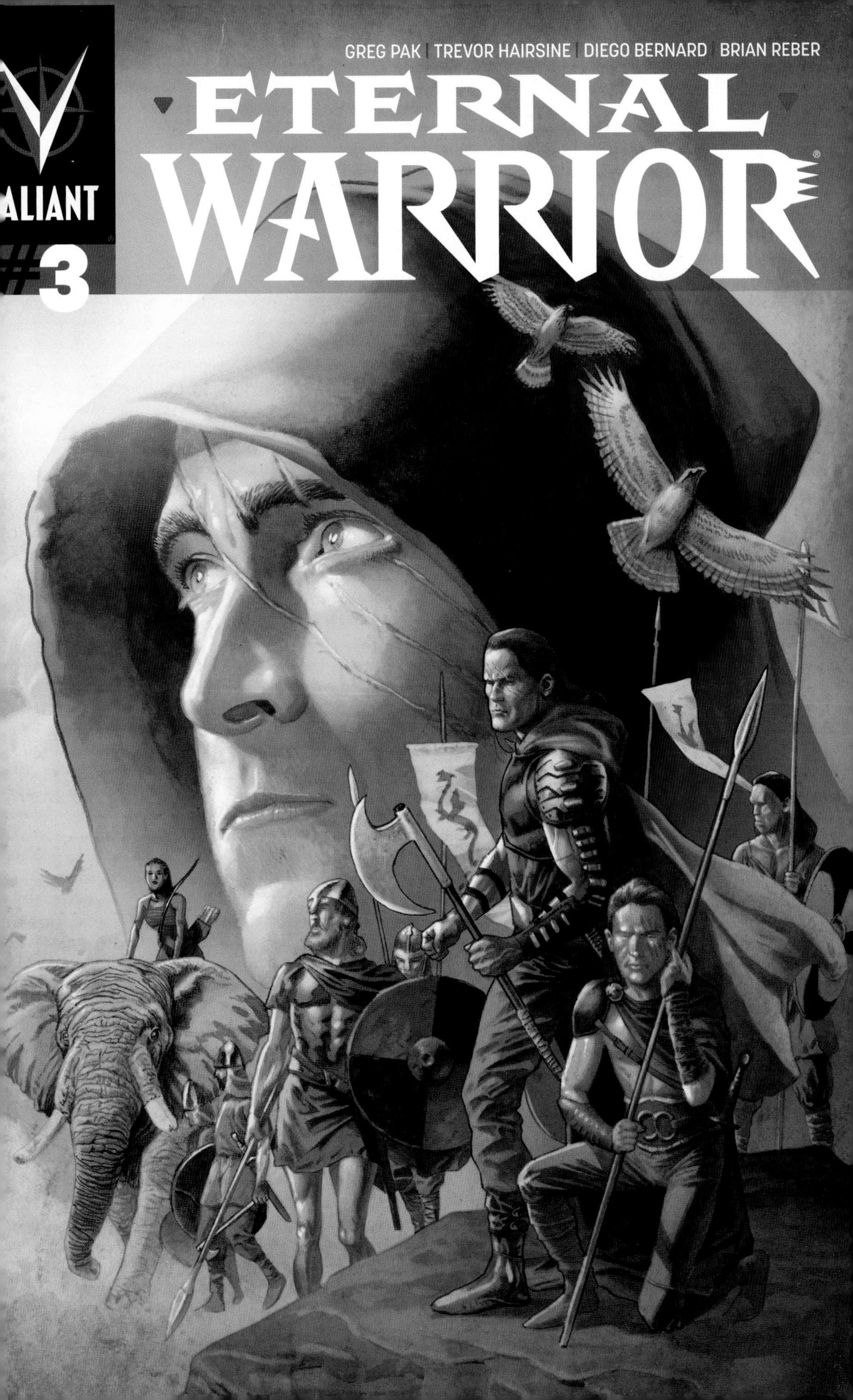
GREG PAK | TREVOR HAIRSINE | DIEGO BERNARD | BRIAN REBER
ETERNAL
WARRIOR
VALIANT
#3

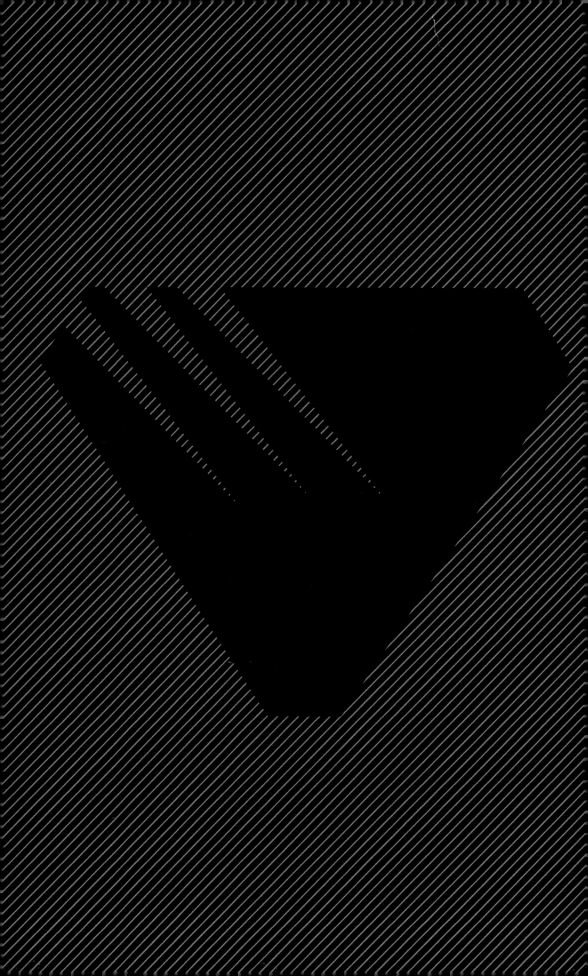

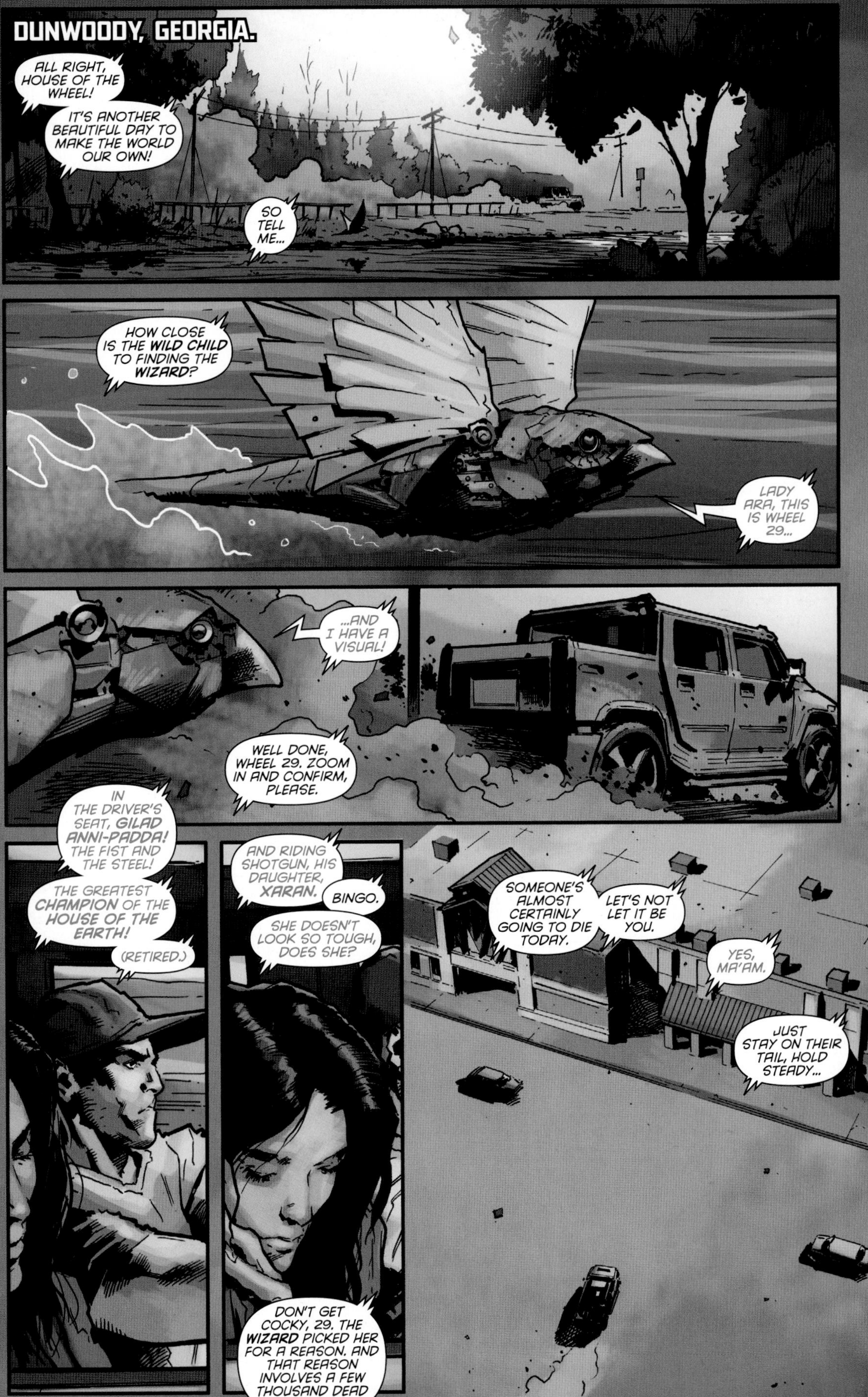
DUNWOODY, GEORGIA.
ALL RIGHT, HOUSE OF THE WHEEL!
IT'S ANOTHER BEAUTIFUL DAY TO MAKE THE WORLD OUR OWN!
SO TELL ME...
HOW CLOSE IS THE WILD CHILD TO FINDING THE WIZARD?
LADY ARA, THIS IS WHEEL 29...
...AND I HAVE A VISUAL!
WELL DONE, WHEEL 29. ZOOM IN AND CONFIRM, PLEASE.
IN THE DRIVER'S SEAT, GILAD ANNI-PADDA! THE FIST AND THE STEEL!
THE GREATEST CHAMPION OF THE HOUSE OF THE EARTH!
(RETIRED.)
AND RIDING SHOTGUN, HIS DAUGHTER, XARAN.
BINGO.
SHE DOESN'T LOOK SO TOUGH, DOES SHE?
DON'T GET COCKY, 29. THE WIZARD PICKED HER FOR A REASON. AND THAT REASON INVOLVES A FEW THOUSAND DEAD BODIES.
SOMEONE'S ALMOST CERTAINLY GOING TO DIE TODAY.
LET'S NOT LET IT BE YOU.
YES, MA'AM.
JUST STAY ON THEIR TAIL, HOLD STEADY...

"...AND WAIT FOR THE BIG GUNS."
ALE
THEY JUST LET YOU BUY THIS STUFF OFF THE SHELF?
WELCOME TO AMERICA.
I LIKE IT.
DISCOUN
IMO
BARGAIN ** OF ** THE WEEK!!

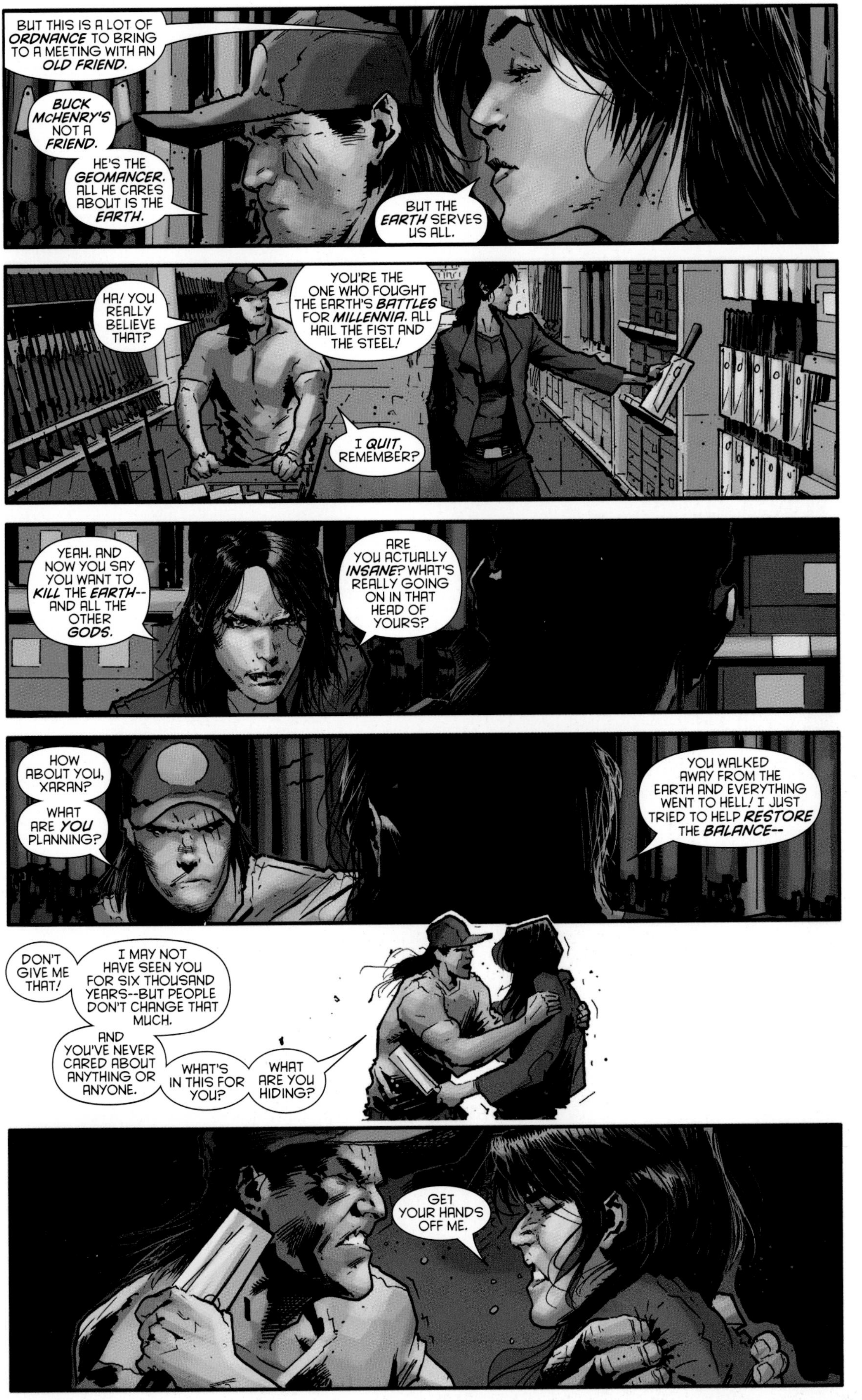
BUT THIS IS A LOT OF ORDNANCE TO BRING TO A MEETING WITH AN OLD FRIEND.
BUCK MCHENRY'S NOT A FRIEND.
HE'S THE GEOMANCER. ALL HE CARES ABOUT IS THE EARTH.
BUT THE EARTH SERVES US ALL.
HA! YOU REALLY BELIEVE THAT?
YOU'RE THE ONE WHO FOUGHT THE EARTH'S BATTLES FOR MILLENNIA. ALL HAIL THE FIST AND THE STEEL!
I QUIT, REMEMBER?
YEAH. AND NOW YOU SAY YOU WANT TO KILL THE EARTH-- AND ALL THE OTHER GODS.
ARE YOU ACTUALLY INSANE? WHAT'S REALLY GOING ON IN THAT HEAD OF YOURS?
HOW ABOUT YOU, XARAN?
WHAT ARE YOU PLANNING?
YOU WALKED AWAY FROM THE EARTH AND EVERYTHING WENT TO HELL! I JUST TRIED TO HELP RESTORE THE BALANCE--
DON'T GIVE ME THAT!
I MAY NOT HAVE SEEN YOU FOR SIX THOUSAND YEARS--BUT PEOPLE DON'T CHANGE THAT MUCH.
AND YOU'VE NEVER CARED ABOUT ANYTHING OR ANYONE.
WHAT'S IN THIS FOR YOU?
WHAT ARE YOU HIDING?
GET YOUR HANDS OFF ME.

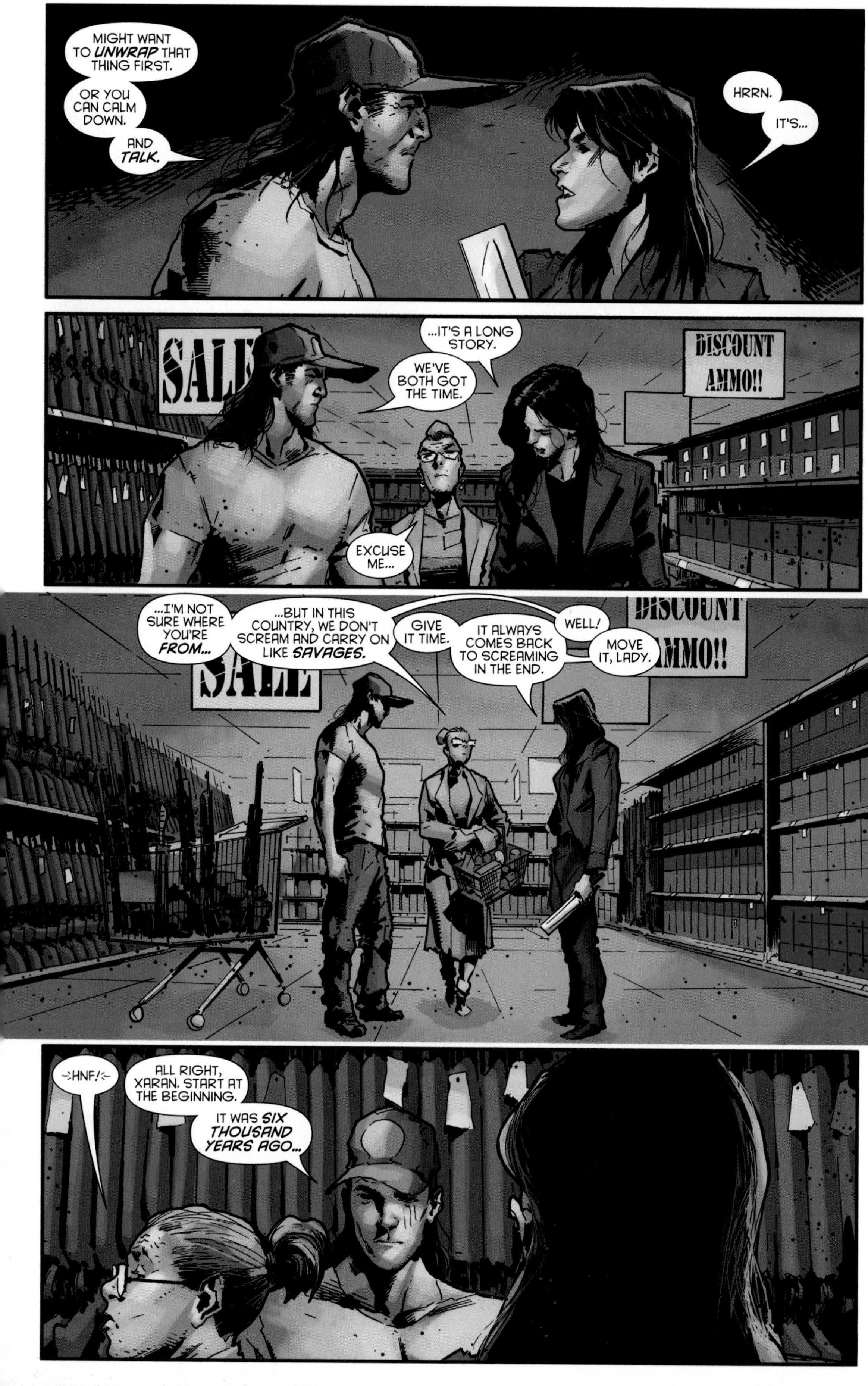

MIGHT WANT TO UNWRAP THAT THING FIRST.
OR YOU CAN CALM DOWN.
AND TALK.
HRRN.
IT'S...
...IT'S A LONG STORY.
WE'VE BOTH GOT THE TIME.
SALE
DISCOUNT AMMO!!
EXCUSE ME...
...I'M NOT SURE WHERE YOU'RE FROM...
...BUT IN THIS COUNTRY, WE DON'T SCREAM AND CARRY ON LIKE SAVAGES.
GIVE IT TIME.
IT ALWAYS COMES BACK TO SCREAMING IN THE END.
WELL!
MOVE IT, LADY.
SALE
DISCOUNT AMMO!!
HNF!
ALL RIGHT, XARAN. START AT THE BEGINNING.
IT WAS SIX THOUSAND YEARS AGO...

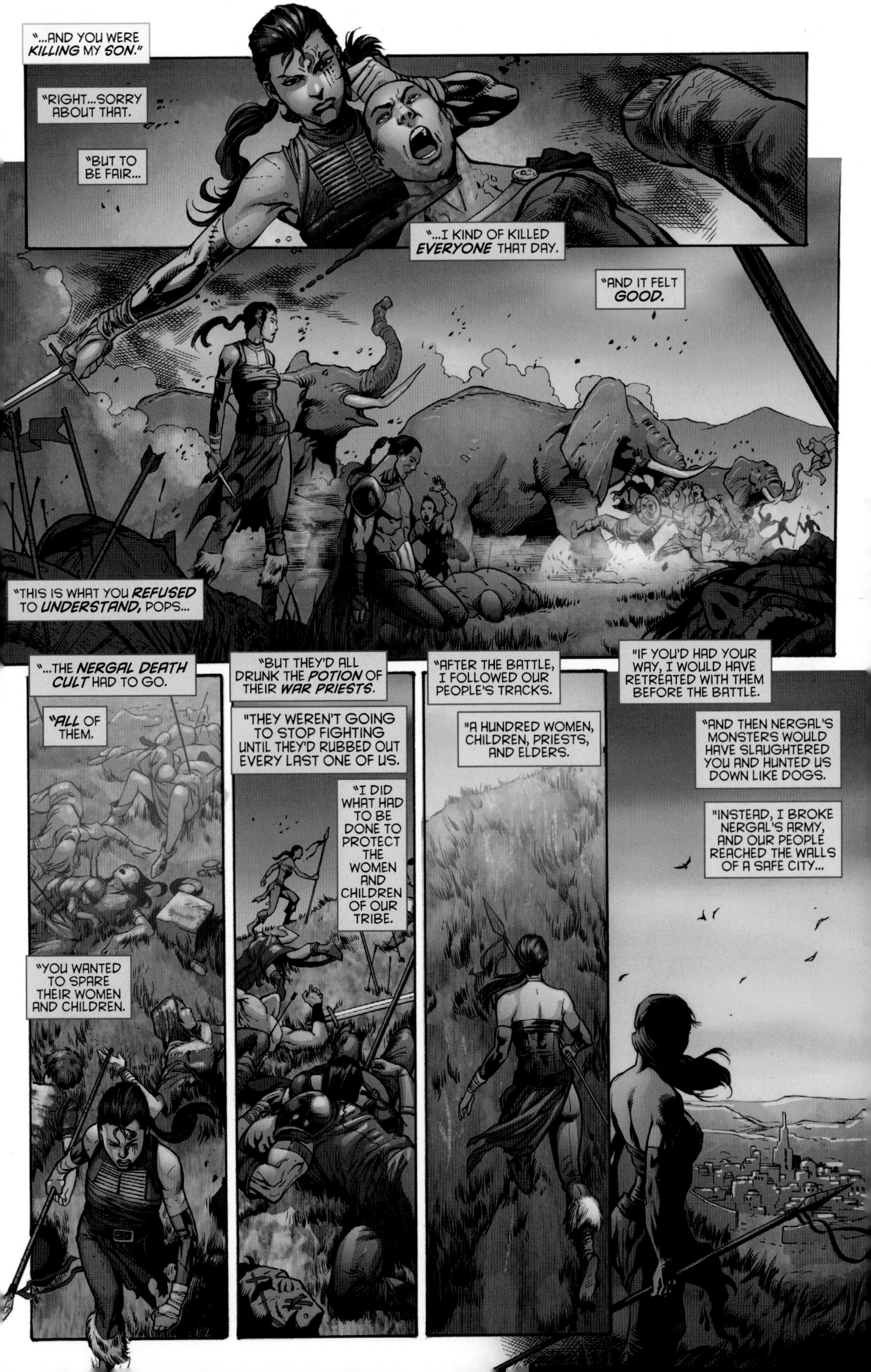
"...AND YOU WERE KILLING MY SON."
"RIGHT...SORRY ABOUT THAT.
"BUT TO BE FAIR...
"...I KIND OF KILLED EVERYONE THAT DAY.
"AND IT FELT GOOD.
"THIS IS WHAT YOU REFUSED TO UNDERSTAND, POPS...
"...THE NERGAL DEATH CULT HAD TO GO.
"ALL OF THEM.
"YOU WANTED TO SPARE THEIR WOMEN AND CHILDREN.
"BUT THEY'D ALL DRUNK THE POTION OF THEIR WAR PRIESTS.
"THEY WEREN'T GOING TO STOP FIGHTING UNTIL THEY'D RUBBED OUT EVERY LAST ONE OF US.
"I DID WHAT HAD TO BE DONE TO PROTECT THE WOMEN AND CHILDREN OF OUR TRIBE.
"AFTER THE BATTLE, I FOLLOWED OUR PEOPLE'S TRACKS.
"A HUNDRED WOMEN, CHILDREN, PRIESTS, AND ELDERS.
"IF YOU'D HAD YOUR WAY, I WOULD HAVE RETREATED WITH THEM BEFORE THE BATTLE.
"AND THEN NERGAL'S MONSTERS WOULD HAVE SLAUGHTERED YOU AND HUNTED US DOWN LIKE DOGS.
"INSTEAD, I BROKE NERGAL'S ARMY, AND OUR PEOPLE REACHED THE WALLS OF A SAFE CITY...

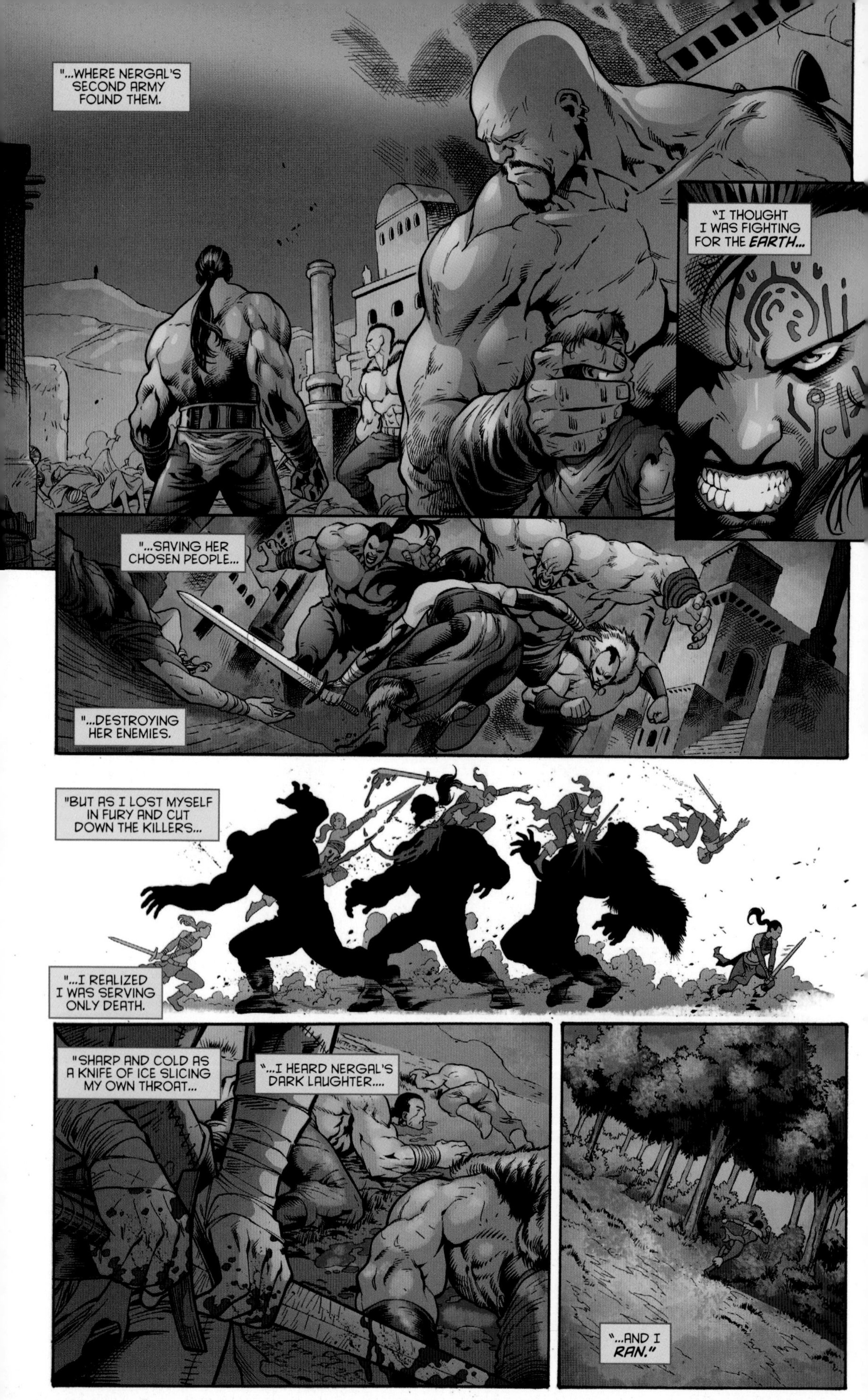
"...WHERE NERGAL'S SECOND ARMY FOUND THEM.
"I THOUGHT I WAS FIGHTING FOR THE EARTH...
"...SAVING HER CHOSEN PEOPLE...
"...DESTROYING HER ENEMIES.
"BUT AS I LOST MYSELF IN FURY AND CUT DOWN THE KILLERS...
"...I REALIZED I WAS SERVING ONLY DEATH.
"SHARP AND COLD AS A KNIFE OF ICE SLICING MY OWN THROAT...
"...I HEARD NERGAL'S DARK LAUGHTER....
"...AND I RAN."

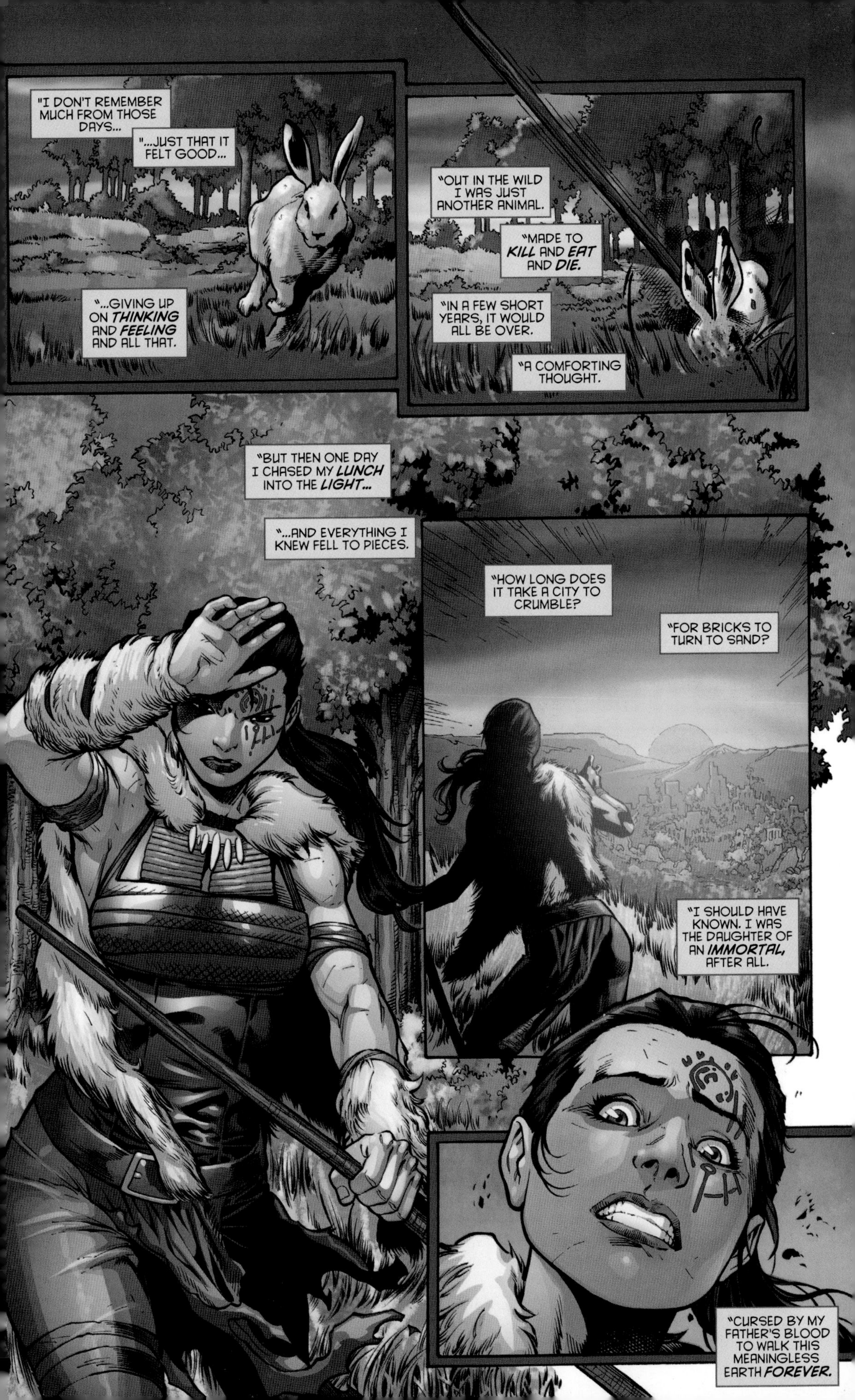
"I DON'T REMEMBER MUCH FROM THOSE DAYS...
"...JUST THAT IT FELT GOOD...
"...GIVING UP ON *THINKING* AND *FEELING* AND ALL THAT.
"OUT IN THE WILD I WAS JUST ANOTHER ANIMAL.
"MADE TO *KILL* AND *EAT* AND *DIE.*
"IN A FEW SHORT YEARS, IT WOULD ALL BE OVER.
"A COMFORTING THOUGHT.
"BUT THEN ONE DAY I CHASED MY *LUNCH* INTO THE *LIGHT...*
"...AND EVERYTHING I KNEW FELL TO PIECES.
"HOW LONG DOES IT TAKE A CITY TO CRUMBLE?
"FOR BRICKS TO TURN TO SAND?
"I SHOULD HAVE KNOWN. I WAS THE DAUGHTER OF AN *IMMORTAL,* AFTER ALL.
"CURSED BY MY FATHER'S BLOOD TO WALK THIS MEANINGLESS EARTH *FOREVER.*

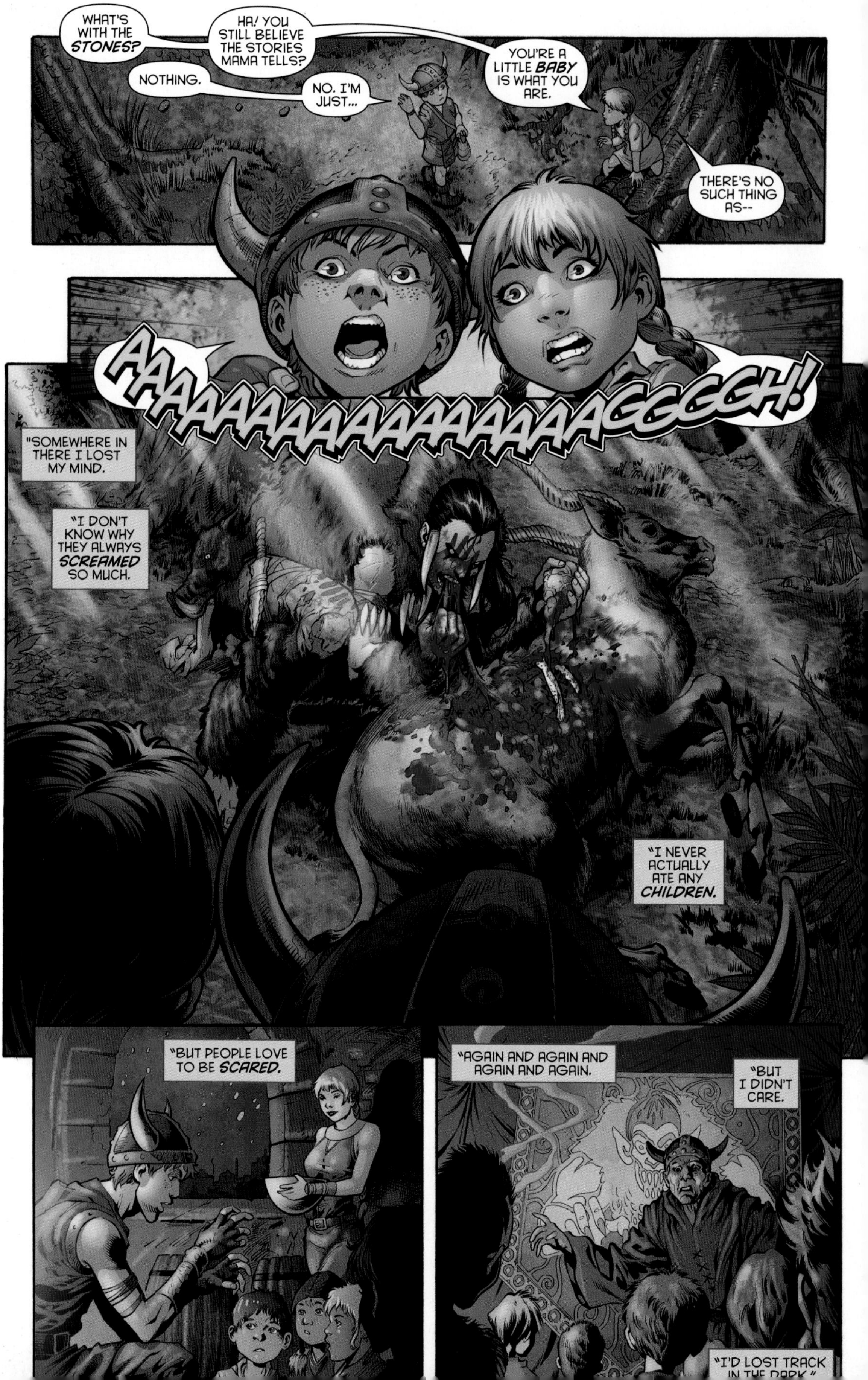
WHAT'S WITH THE STONES?
NOTHING.
HA! YOU STILL BELIEVE THE STORIES MAMA TELLS?
NO. I'M JUST...
YOU'RE A LITTLE BABY IS WHAT YOU ARE.
THERE'S NO SUCH THING AS--
AAAAAAAAAAAAAAAAAGGGGH!
"SOMEWHERE IN THERE I LOST MY MIND.
"I DON'T KNOW WHY THEY ALWAYS SCREAMED SO MUCH.
"I NEVER ACTUALLY ATE ANY CHILDREN.
"BUT PEOPLE LOVE TO BE SCARED.
"AGAIN AND AGAIN AND AGAIN AND AGAIN.
"BUT I DIDN'T CARE.
"I'D LOST TRACK

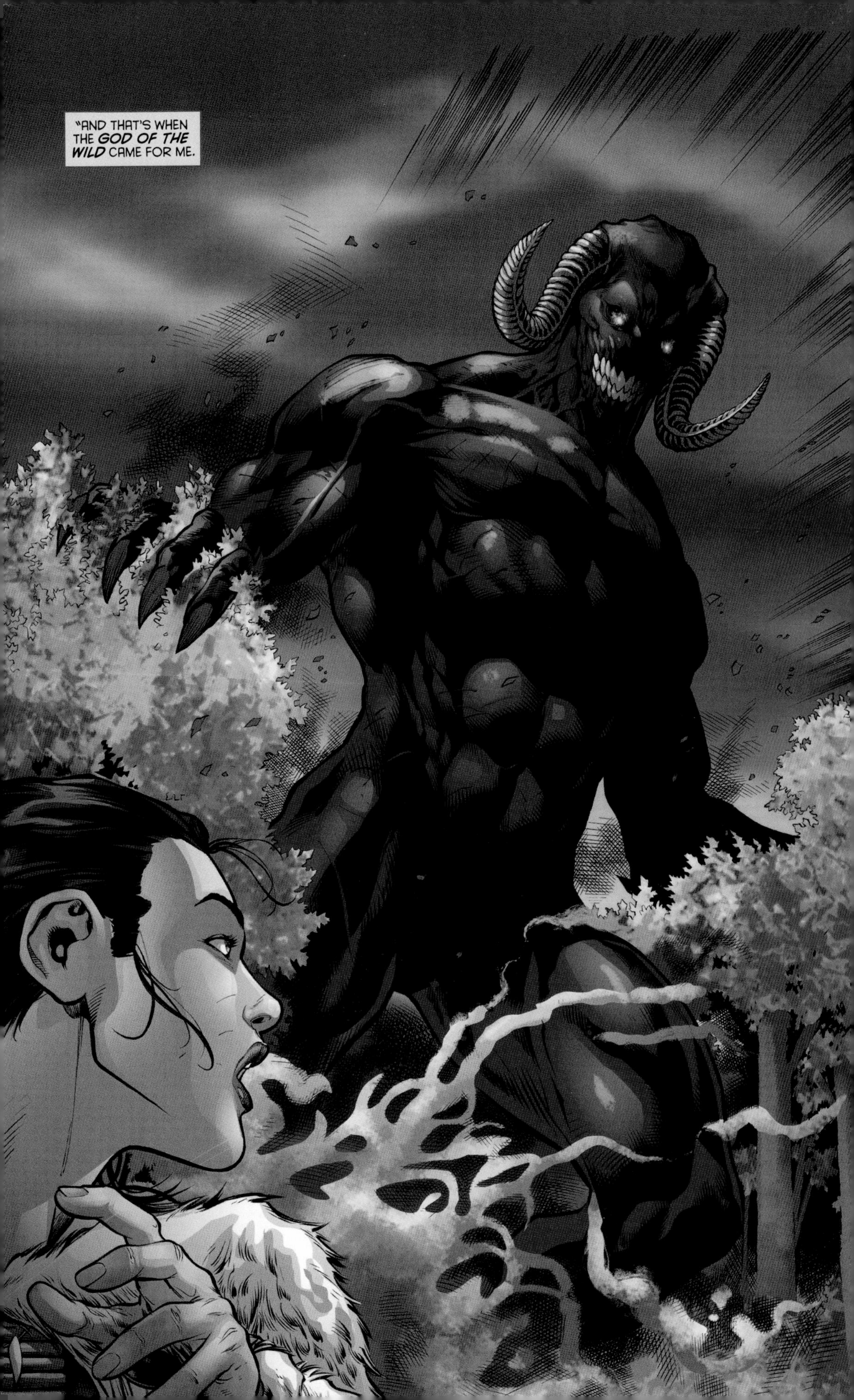
"AND THAT'S WHEN THE ***GOD OF THE WILD*** CAME FOR ME.

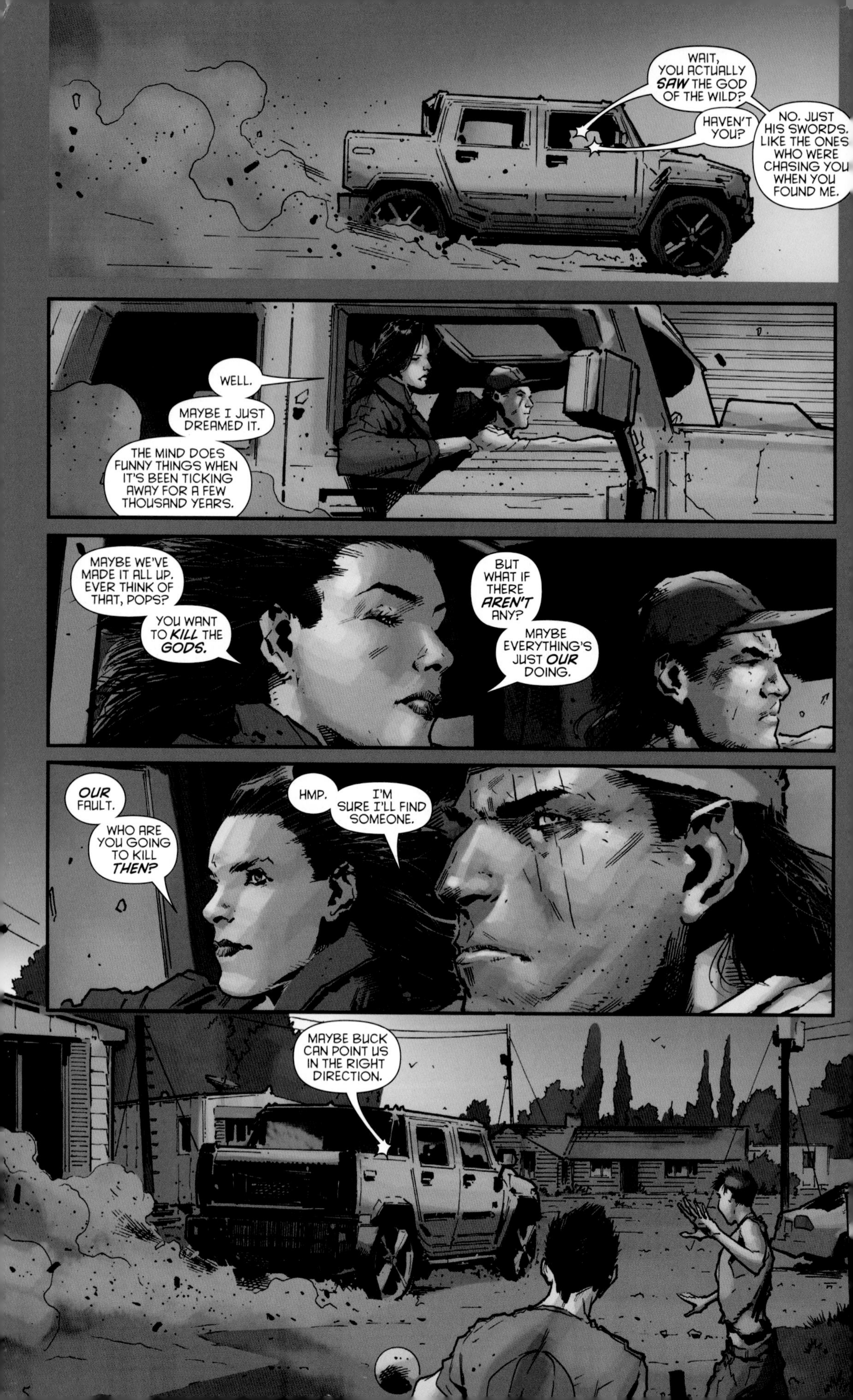
WAIT, YOU ACTUALLY SAW THE GOD OF THE WILD?
HAVEN'T YOU?
NO. JUST HIS SWORDS. LIKE THE ONES WHO WERE CHASING YOU WHEN YOU FOUND ME.
WELL.
MAYBE I JUST DREAMED IT.
THE MIND DOES FUNNY THINGS WHEN IT'S BEEN TICKING AWAY FOR A FEW THOUSAND YEARS.
MAYBE WE'VE MADE IT ALL UP. EVER THINK OF THAT, POPS?
YOU WANT TO KILL THE GODS.
BUT WHAT IF THERE AREN'T ANY?
MAYBE EVERYTHING'S JUST OUR DOING.
OUR FAULT.
WHO ARE YOU GOING TO KILL THEN?
HMP.
I'M SURE I'LL FIND SOMEONE.
MAYBE BUCK CAN POINT US IN THE RIGHT DIRECTION.

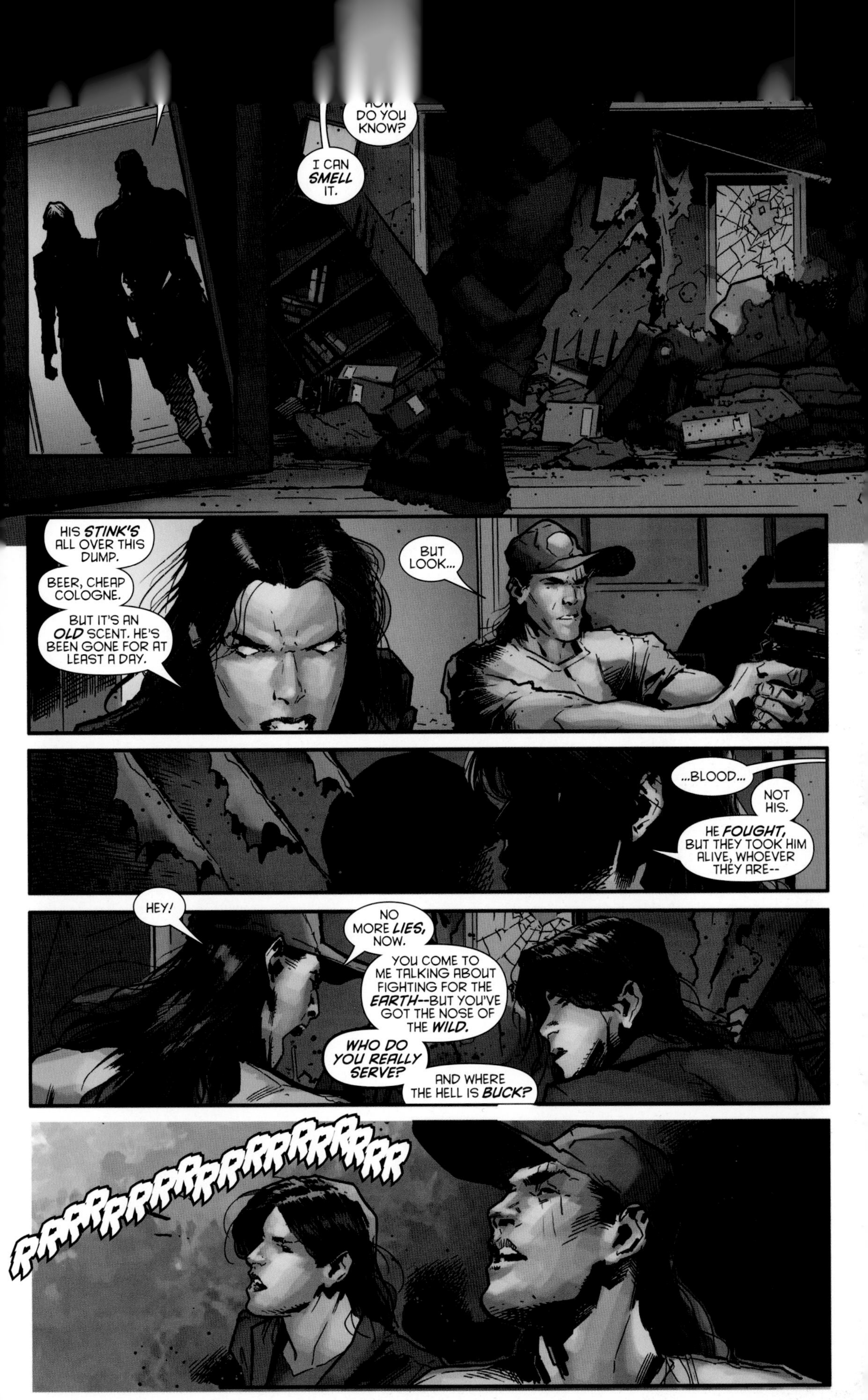

DO YOU KNOW?
I CAN SMELL IT.
HIS STINK'S ALL OVER THIS DUMP.
BEER, CHEAP COLOGNE.
BUT IT'S AN OLD SCENT. HE'S BEEN GONE FOR AT LEAST A DAY.
BUT LOOK...
...BLOOD...
NOT HIS.
HE FOUGHT, BUT THEY TOOK HIM ALIVE, WHOEVER THEY ARE--
HEY!
NO MORE LIES, NOW.
YOU COME TO ME TALKING ABOUT FIGHTING FOR THE EARTH--BUT YOU'VE GOT THE NOSE OF THE WILD.
WHO DO YOU REALLY SERVE?
AND WHERE THE HELL IS BUCK?
RRRRRRRRRRRRRRRRRRRR

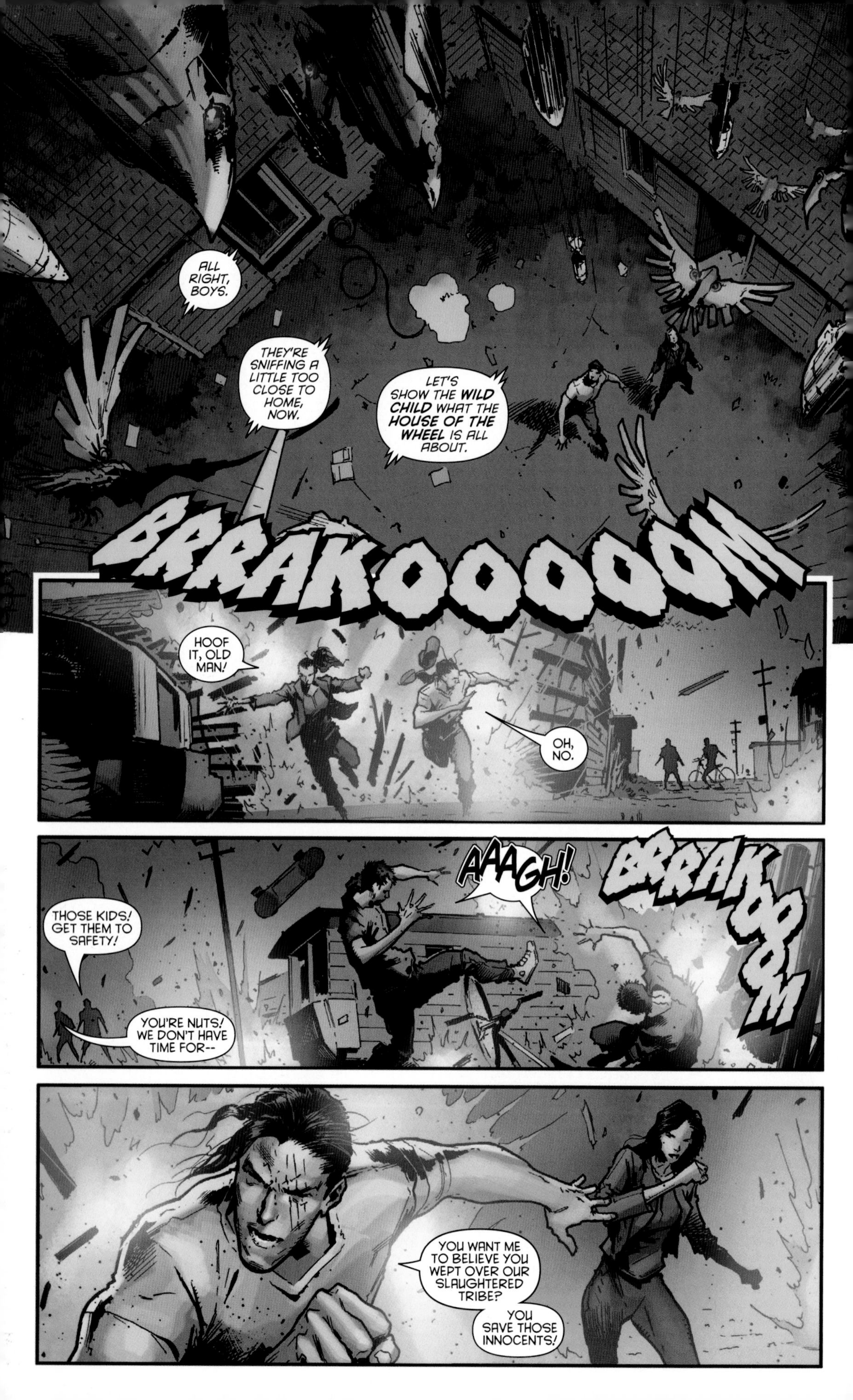
ALL RIGHT, BOYS.
THEY'RE SNIFFING A LITTLE TOO CLOSE TO HOME, NOW.
LET'S SHOW THE WILD CHILD WHAT THE HOUSE OF THE WHEEL IS ALL ABOUT.
BRRAKOOOOOOM
HOOF IT, OLD MAN!
OH, NO.
THOSE KIDS! GET THEM TO SAFETY!
YOU'RE NUTS! WE DON'T HAVE TIME FOR--
AAAGH!
BRRAKOOOM
YOU WANT ME TO BELIEVE YOU WEPT OVER OUR SLAUGHTERED TRIBE?
YOU SAVE THOSE INNOCENTS!

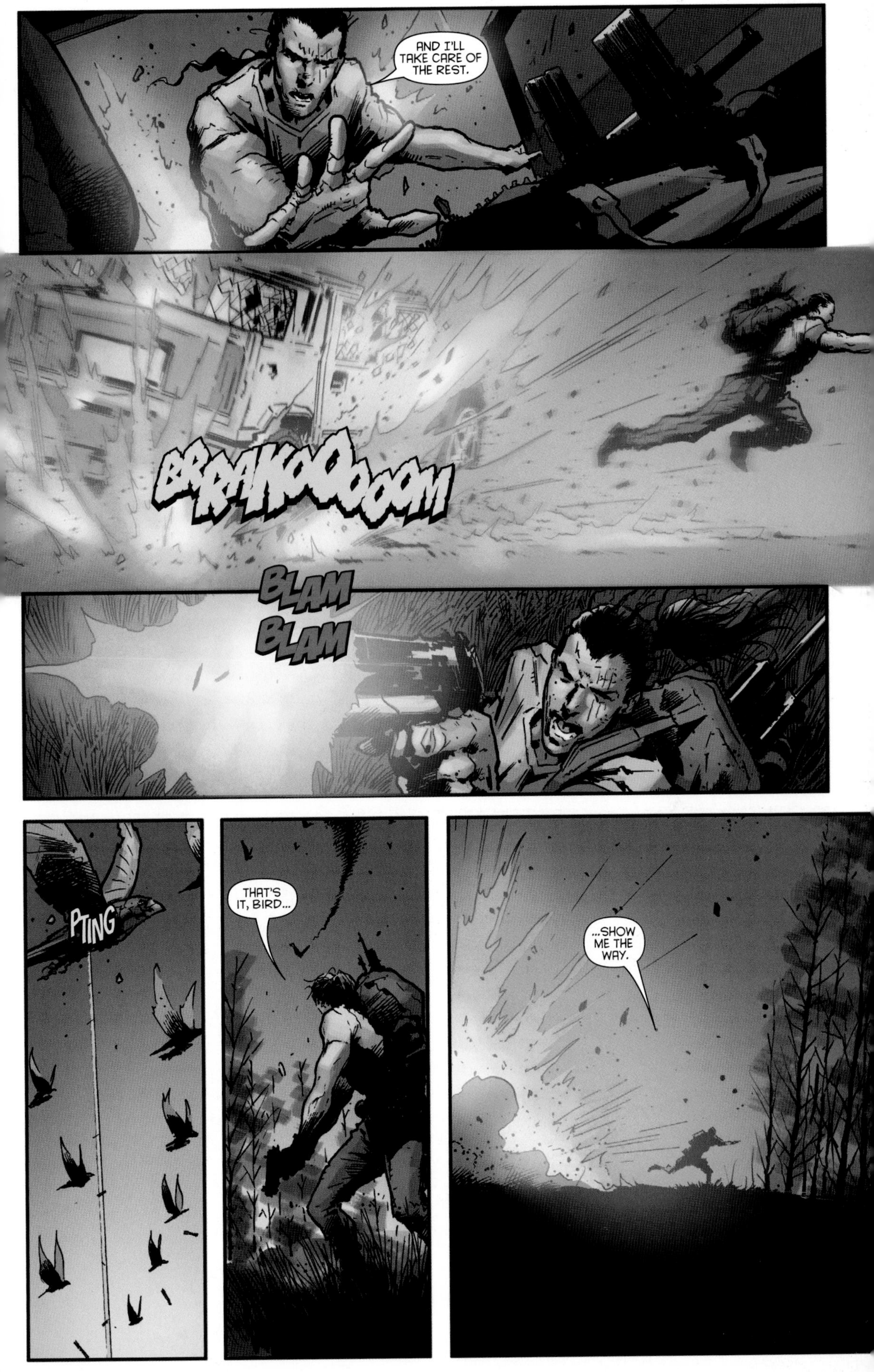
AND I'LL TAKE CARE OF THE REST.
BRRAKOOOOOOM
BLAM
BLAM
PTING
THAT'S IT, BIRD...
...SHOW ME THE WAY.

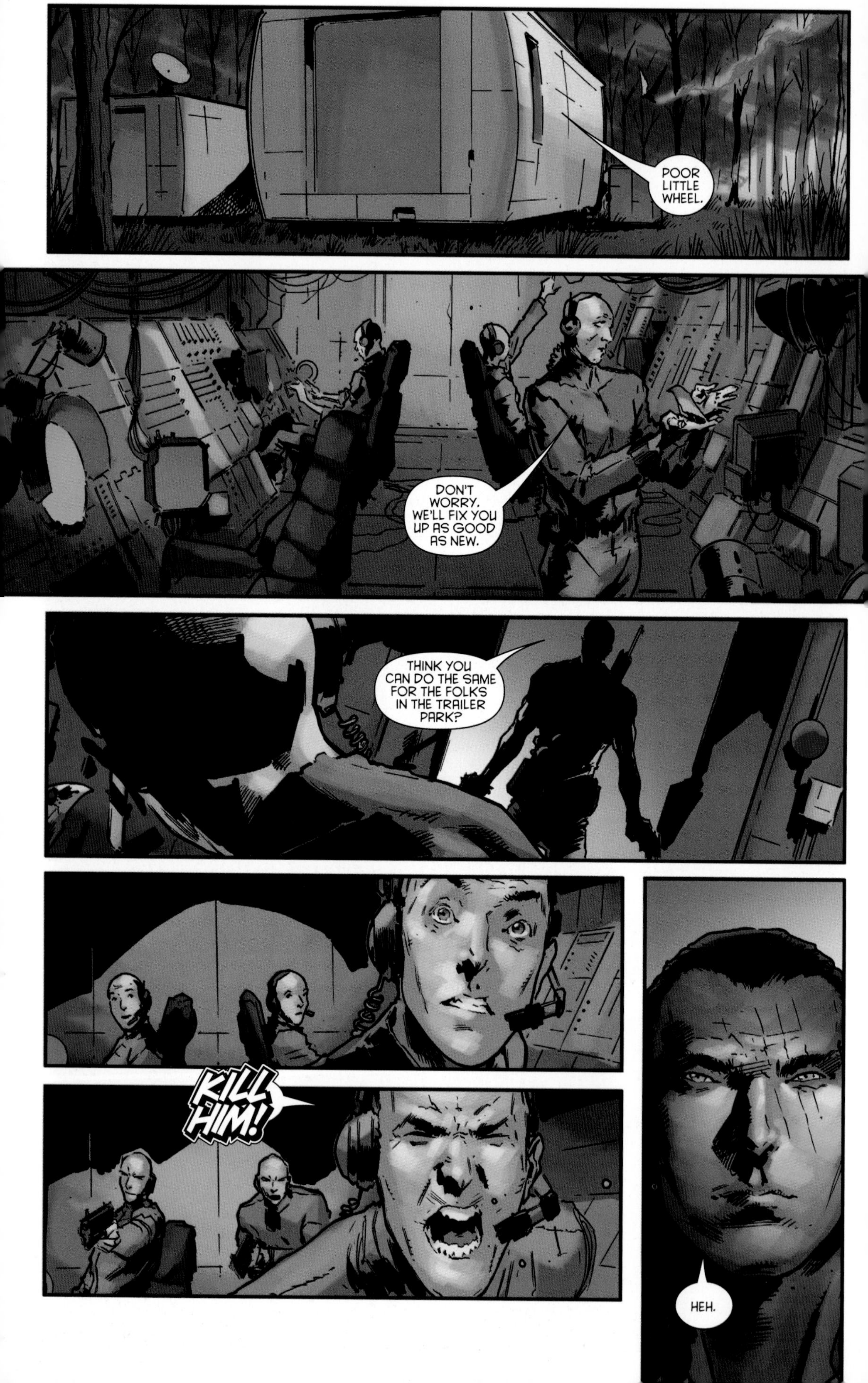
POOR LITTLE WHEEL.
DON'T WORRY. WE'LL FIX YOU UP AS GOOD AS NEW.
THINK YOU CAN DO THE SAME FOR THE FOLKS IN THE TRAILER PARK?
KILL HIM!
HEH.

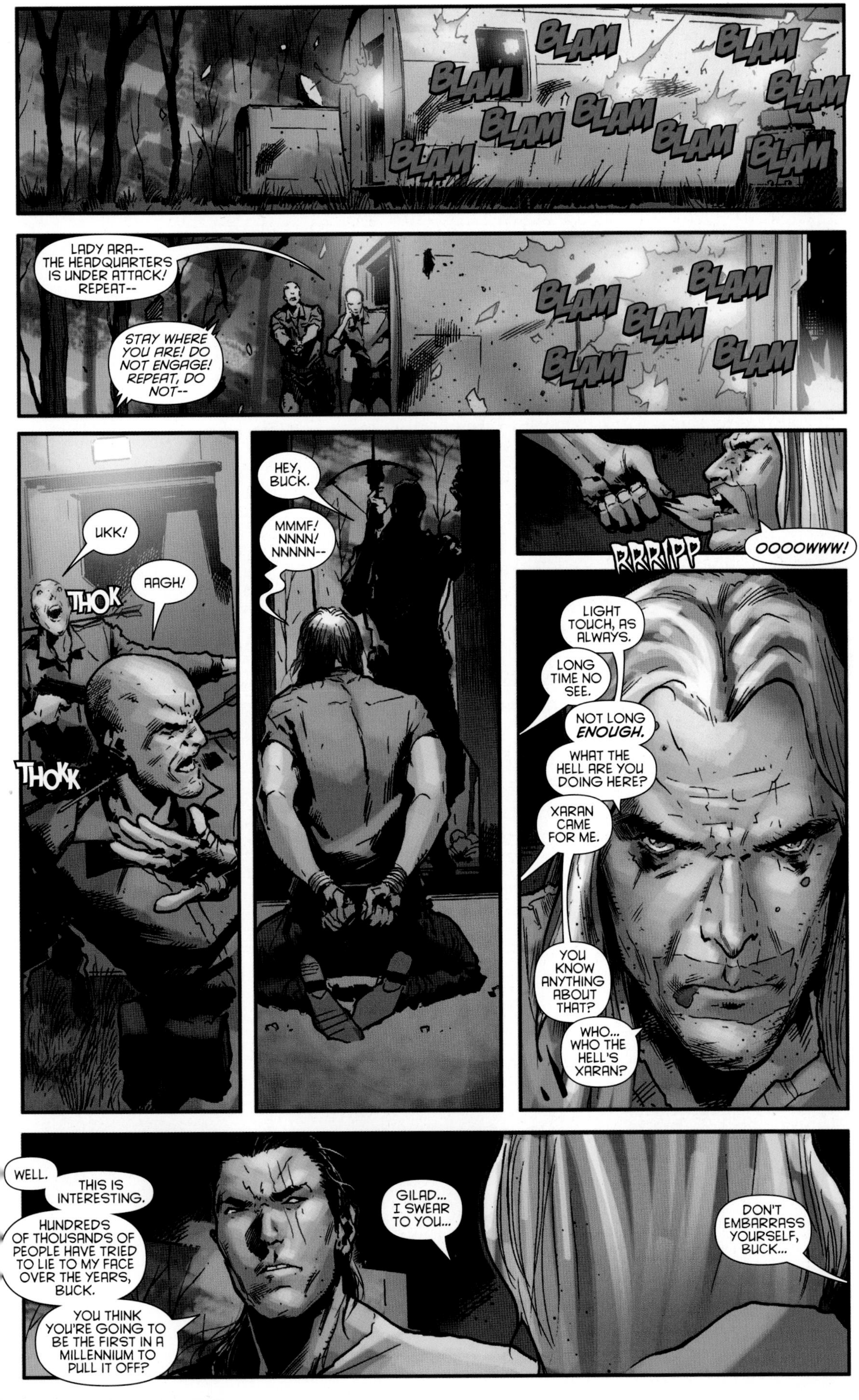
BLAM
BLAM
BLAM
BLAM
BLAM
BLAM
BLAM
BLAM
BLAM
LADY ARA-- THE HEADQUARTERS IS UNDER ATTACK! REPEAT--
STAY WHERE YOU ARE! DO NOT ENGAGE! REPEAT, DO NOT--
BLAM
BLAM
BLAM
BLAM
BLAM
UKK!
THOK
AAGH!
THOKK
HEY, BUCK.
MMMF! NNNN! NNNNN--
RRRIPP
OOOOWWW!
LIGHT TOUCH, AS ALWAYS.
LONG TIME NO SEE.
NOT LONG ENOUGH.
WHAT THE HELL ARE YOU DOING HERE?
XARAN CAME FOR ME.
YOU KNOW ANYTHING ABOUT THAT?
WHO... WHO THE HELL'S XARAN?
WELL.
THIS IS INTERESTING.
HUNDREDS OF THOUSANDS OF PEOPLE HAVE TRIED TO LIE TO MY FACE OVER THE YEARS, BUCK.
YOU THINK YOU'RE GOING TO BE THE FIRST IN A MILLENNIUM TO PULL IT OFF?
GILAD... I SWEAR TO YOU...
DON'T EMBARRASS YOURSELF, BUCK...

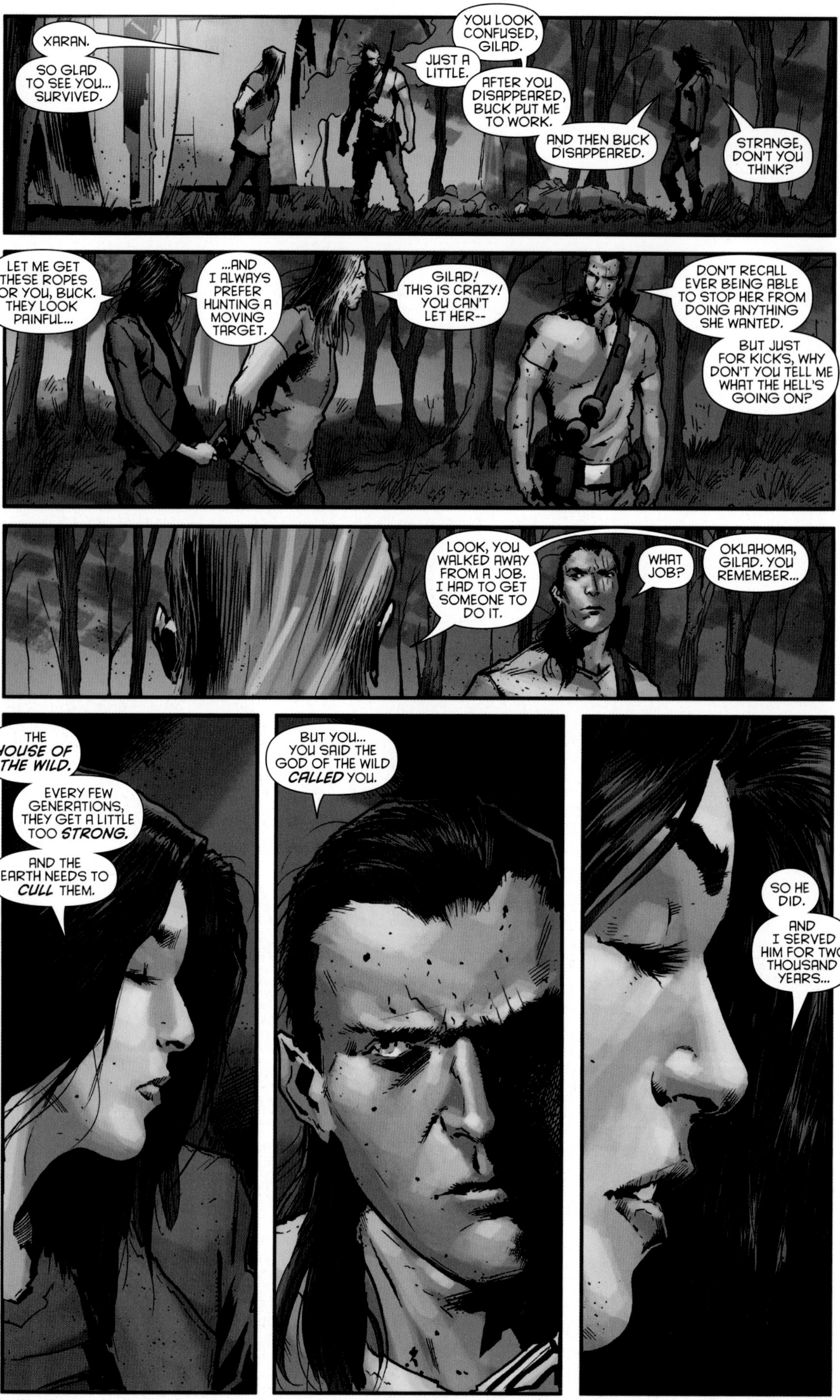
XARAN.
SO GLAD TO SEE YOU... SURVIVED.
YOU LOOK CONFUSED, GILAD.
JUST A LITTLE.
AFTER YOU DISAPPEARED, BUCK PUT ME TO WORK.
AND THEN BUCK DISAPPEARED.
STRANGE, DON'T YOU THINK?
LET ME GET THESE ROPES FOR YOU, BUCK. THEY LOOK PAINFUL...
...AND I ALWAYS PREFER HUNTING A MOVING TARGET.
GILAD! THIS IS CRAZY! YOU CAN'T LET HER--
DON'T RECALL EVER BEING ABLE TO STOP HER FROM DOING ANYTHING SHE WANTED.
BUT JUST FOR KICKS, WHY DON'T YOU TELL ME WHAT THE HELL'S GOING ON?
LOOK, YOU WALKED AWAY FROM A JOB. I HAD TO GET SOMEONE TO DO IT.
WHAT JOB?
OKLAHOMA, GILAD. YOU REMEMBER...
THE ***HOUSE OF THE WILD.***
EVERY FEW GENERATIONS, THEY GET A LITTLE TOO ***STRONG.***
AND THE EARTH NEEDS TO ***CULL*** THEM.
BUT YOU... YOU SAID THE GOD OF THE WILD ***CALLED*** YOU.
SO HE DID.
AND I SERVED HIM FOR TWO THOUSAND YEARS...

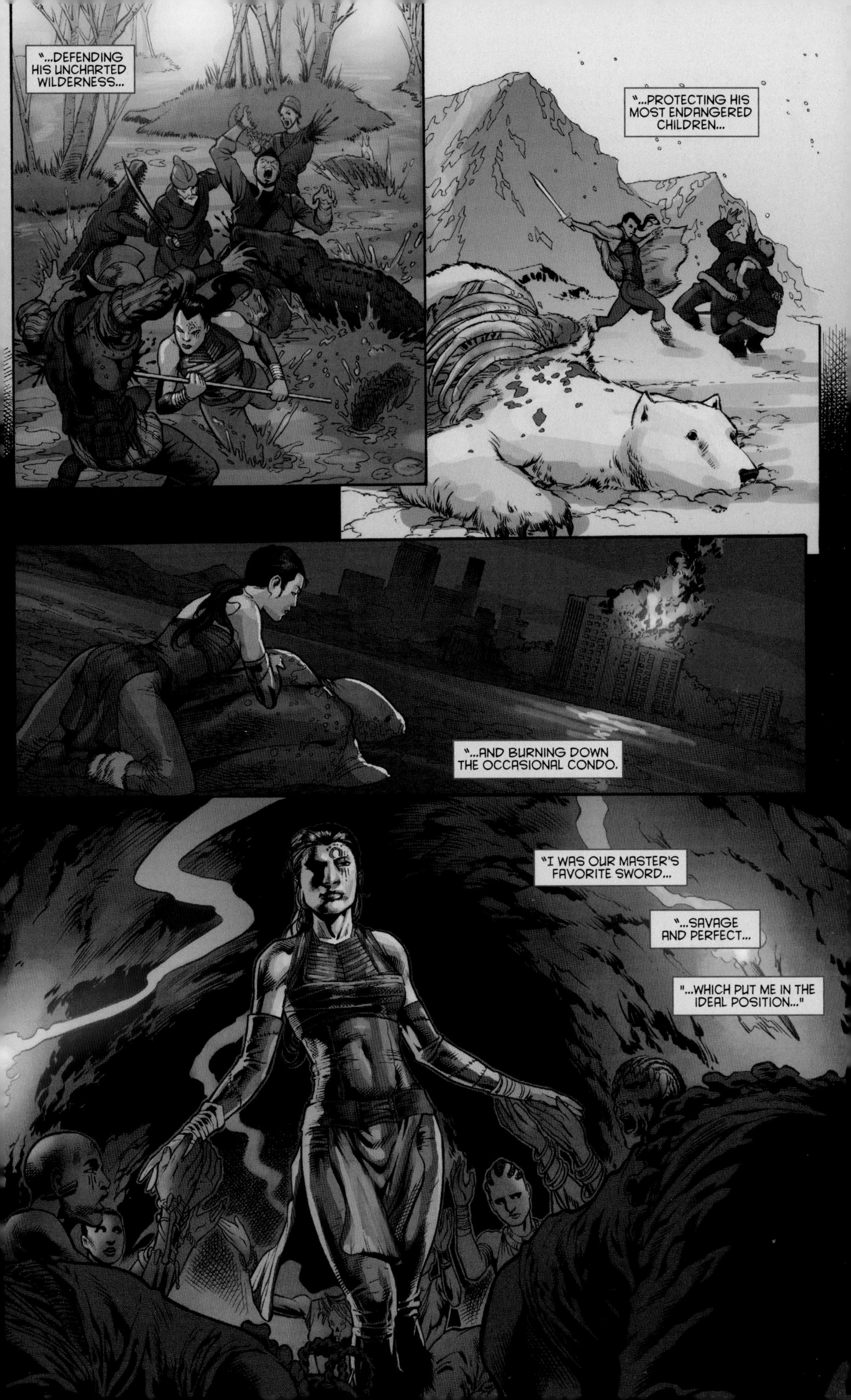
"...DEFENDING HIS UNCHARTED WILDERNESS...
"...PROTECTING HIS MOST ENDANGERED CHILDREN...
"...AND BURNING DOWN THE OCCASIONAL CONDO.
"I WAS OUR MASTER'S FAVORITE SWORD...
"...SAVAGE AND PERFECT...
"...WHICH PUT ME IN THE IDEAL POSITION..."

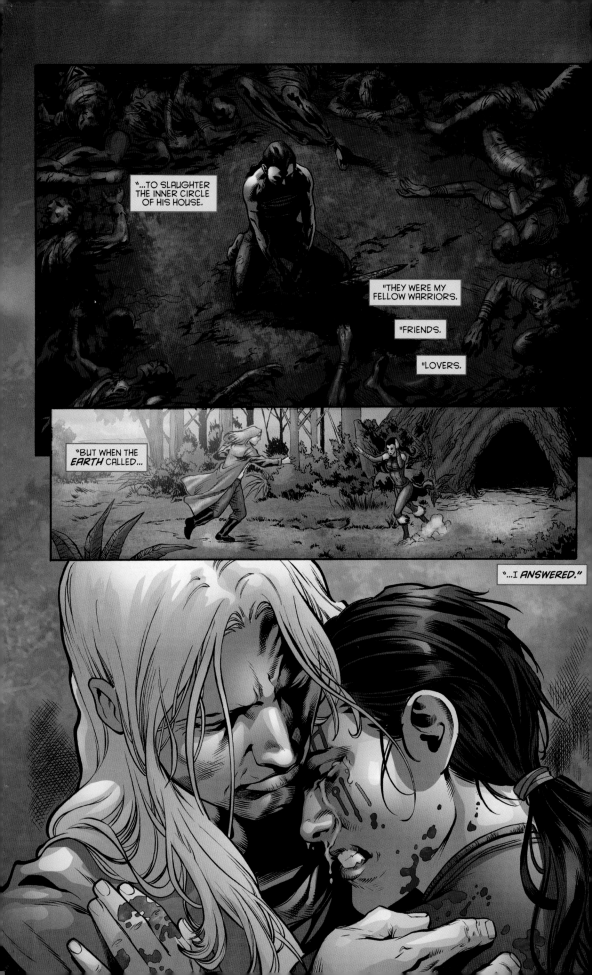

"...TO SLAUGHTER THE INNER CIRCLE OF HIS HOUSE.

"THEY WERE MY FELLOW WARRIORS.

"FRIENDS.

"LOVERS.

"BUT WHEN THE *EARTH* CALLED...

"...I *ANSWERED*."

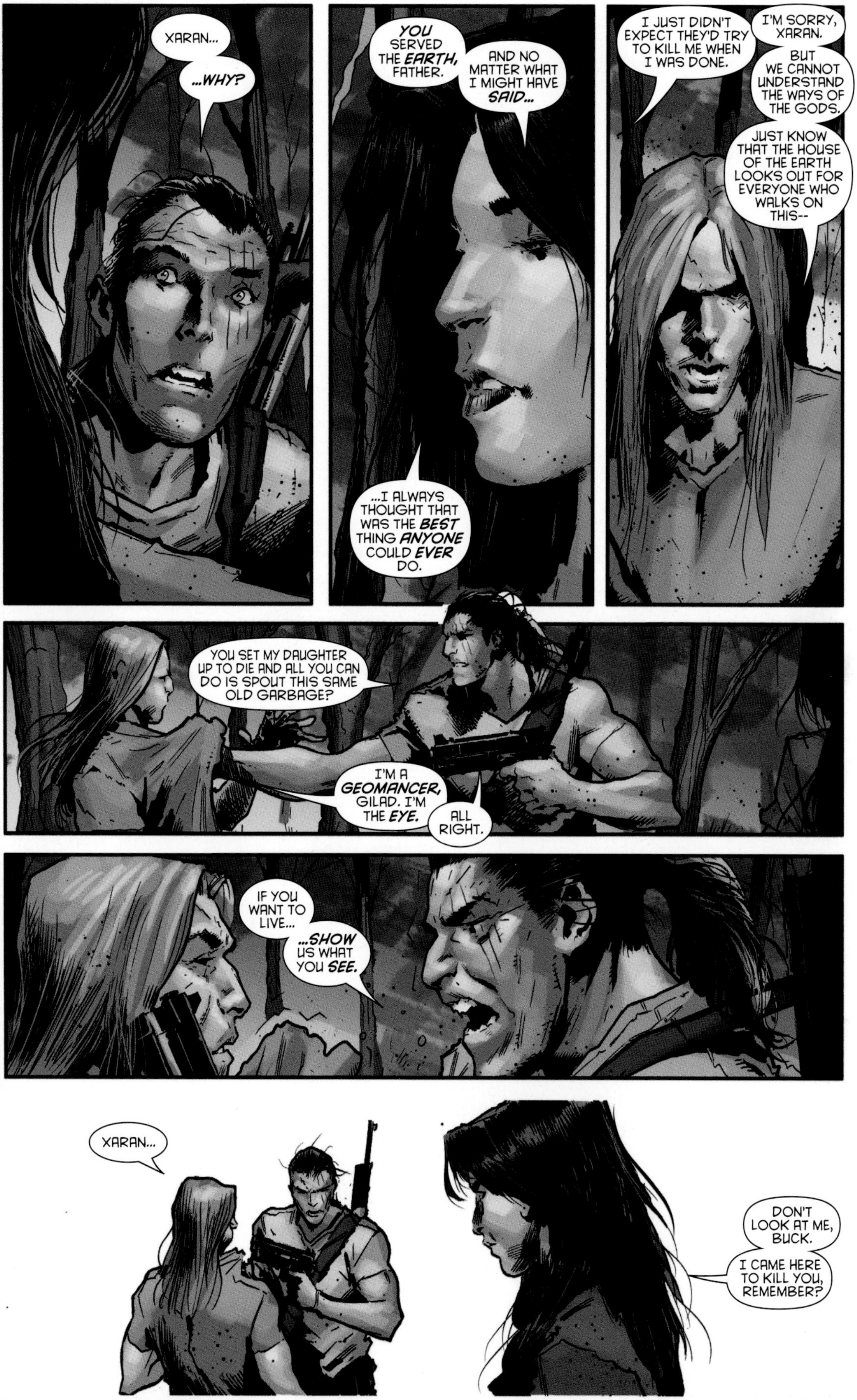
XARAN...
...WHY?
YOU SERVED THE EARTH, FATHER.
AND NO MATTER WHAT I MIGHT HAVE SAID...
...I ALWAYS THOUGHT THAT WAS THE BEST THING ANYONE COULD EVER DO.
I JUST DIDN'T EXPECT THEY'D TRY TO KILL ME WHEN I WAS DONE.
I'M SORRY, XARAN.
BUT WE CANNOT UNDERSTAND THE WAYS OF THE GODS.
JUST KNOW THAT THE HOUSE OF THE EARTH LOOKS OUT FOR EVERYONE WHO WALKS ON THIS--
YOU SET MY DAUGHTER UP TO DIE AND ALL YOU CAN DO IS SPOUT THIS SAME OLD GARBAGE?
I'M A GEOMANCER, GILAD. I'M THE EYE.
ALL RIGHT.
IF YOU WANT TO LIVE...
...SHOW US WHAT YOU SEE.
XARAN...
DON'T LOOK AT ME, BUCK.
I CAME HERE TO KILL YOU, REMEMBER?

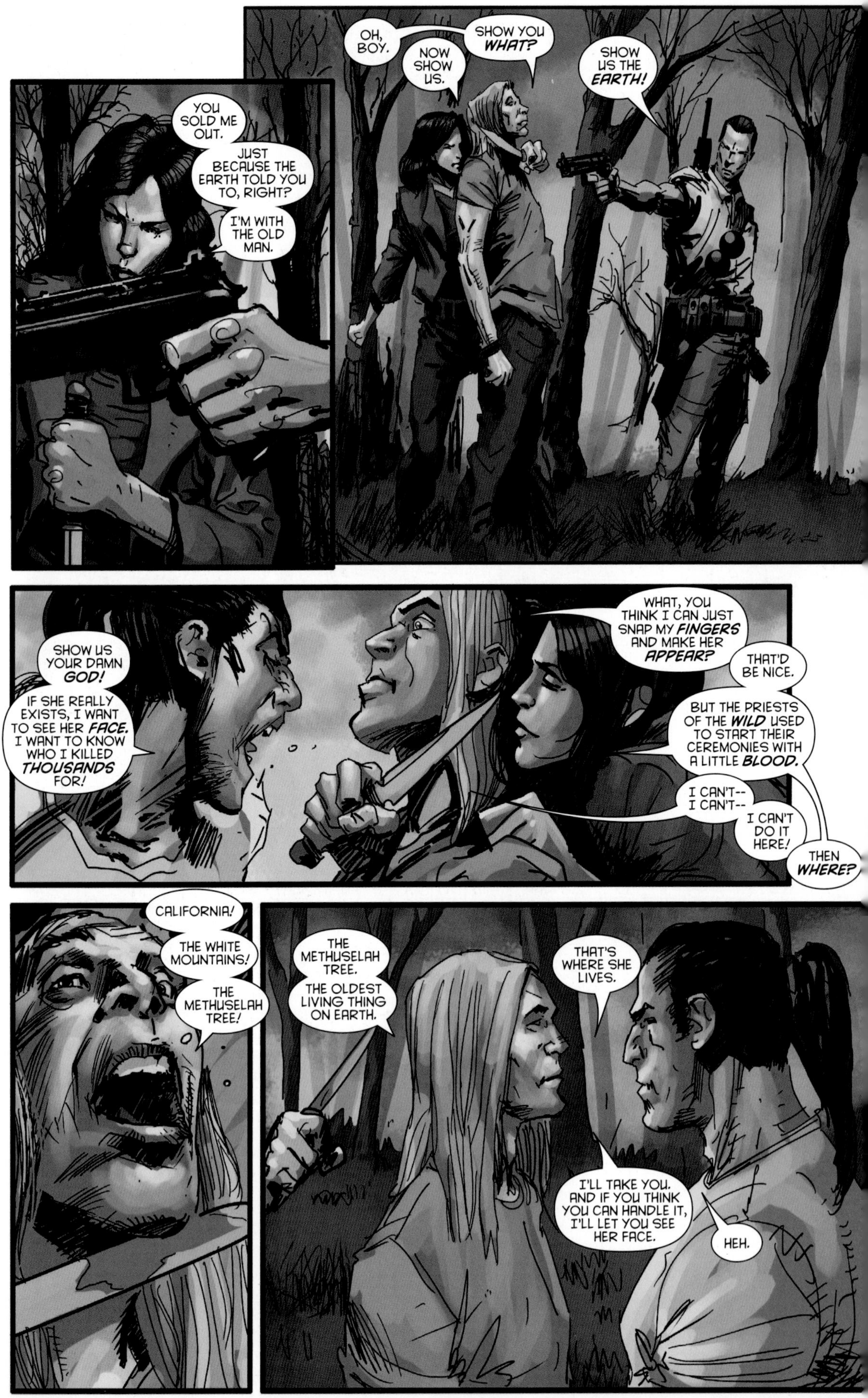
YOU SOLD ME OUT.
JUST BECAUSE THE EARTH TOLD YOU TO, RIGHT?
I'M WITH THE OLD MAN.
OH, BOY.
SHOW YOU *WHAT?*
NOW SHOW US.
SHOW US THE *EARTH!*
SHOW US YOUR DAMN *GOD!*
IF SHE REALLY EXISTS, I WANT TO SEE HER *FACE.* I WANT TO KNOW WHO I KILLED *THOUSANDS* FOR!
WHAT, YOU THINK I CAN JUST SNAP MY *FINGERS* AND MAKE HER *APPEAR?*
THAT'D BE NICE.
BUT THE PRIESTS OF THE *WILD* USED TO START THEIR CEREMONIES WITH A LITTLE *BLOOD.*
I CAN'T-- I CAN'T--
I CAN'T DO IT HERE!
THEN *WHERE?*
CALIFORNIA!
THE WHITE MOUNTAINS!
THE METHUSELAH TREE!
THE METHUSELAH TREE.
THE OLDEST LIVING THING ON EARTH.
THAT'S WHERE SHE LIVES.
I'LL TAKE YOU. AND IF YOU THINK YOU CAN HANDLE IT, I'LL LET YOU SEE HER FACE.
HEH.

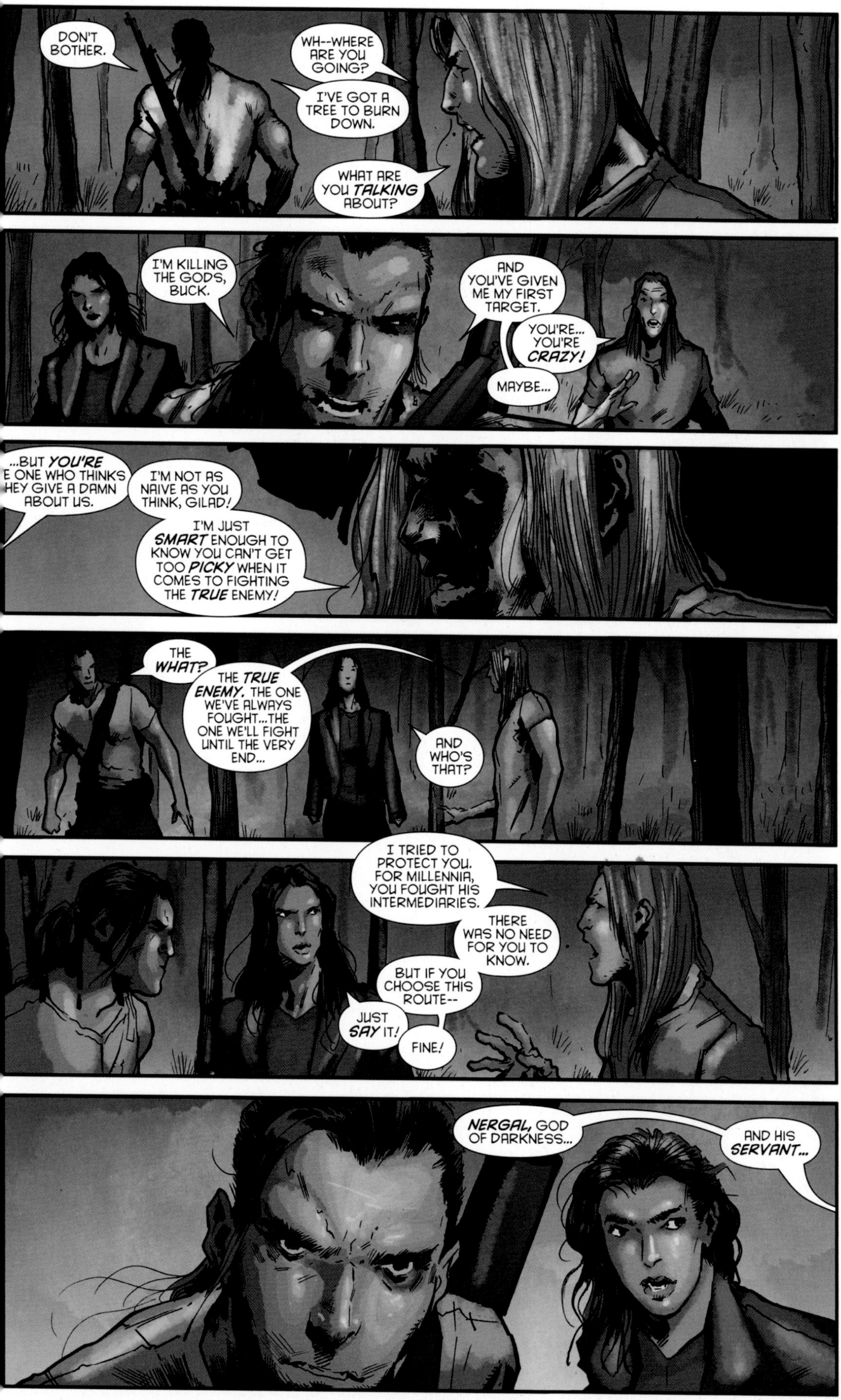
DON'T BOTHER.
WH--WHERE ARE YOU GOING?
I'VE GOT A TREE TO BURN DOWN.
WHAT ARE YOU TALKING ABOUT?
I'M KILLING THE GODS, BUCK.
AND YOU'VE GIVEN ME MY FIRST TARGET.
YOU'RE... YOU'RE CRAZY!
MAYBE...
...BUT YOU'RE E ONE WHO THINKS HEY GIVE A DAMN ABOUT US.
I'M NOT AS NAIVE AS YOU THINK, GILAD!
I'M JUST SMART ENOUGH TO KNOW YOU CAN'T GET TOO PICKY WHEN IT COMES TO FIGHTING THE TRUE ENEMY!
THE WHAT?
THE TRUE ENEMY. THE ONE WE'VE ALWAYS FOUGHT...THE ONE WE'LL FIGHT UNTIL THE VERY END...
AND WHO'S THAT?
I TRIED TO PROTECT YOU. FOR MILLENNIA, YOU FOUGHT HIS INTERMEDIARIES.
THERE WAS NO NEED FOR YOU TO KNOW.
BUT IF YOU CHOOSE THIS ROUTE--
JUST SAY IT!
FINE!
NERGAL, GOD OF DARKNESS...
AND HIS SERVANT...

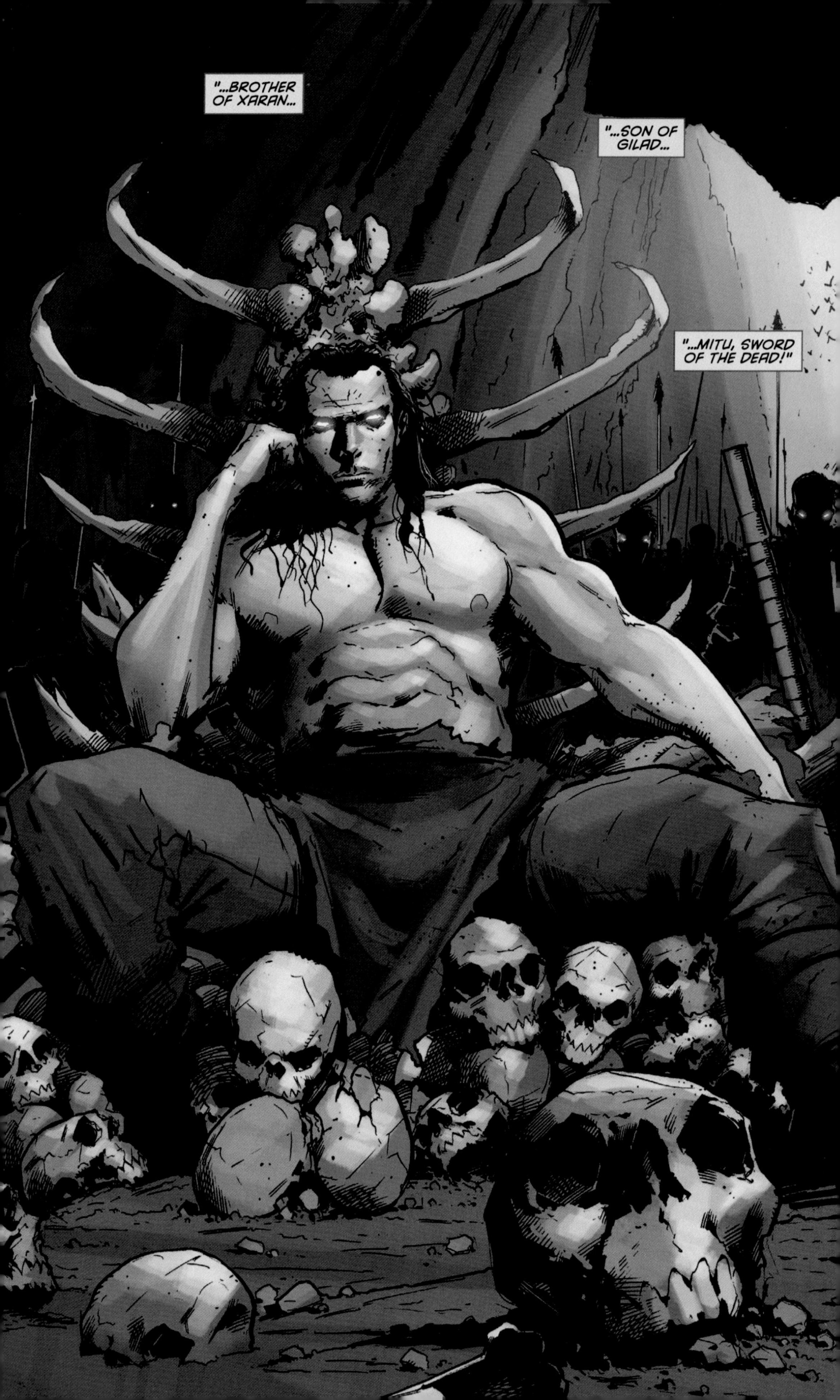
"...BROTHER
OF XARAN...
"...SON OF
GILAD...
"...MITU, SWORD
OF THE DEAD!"

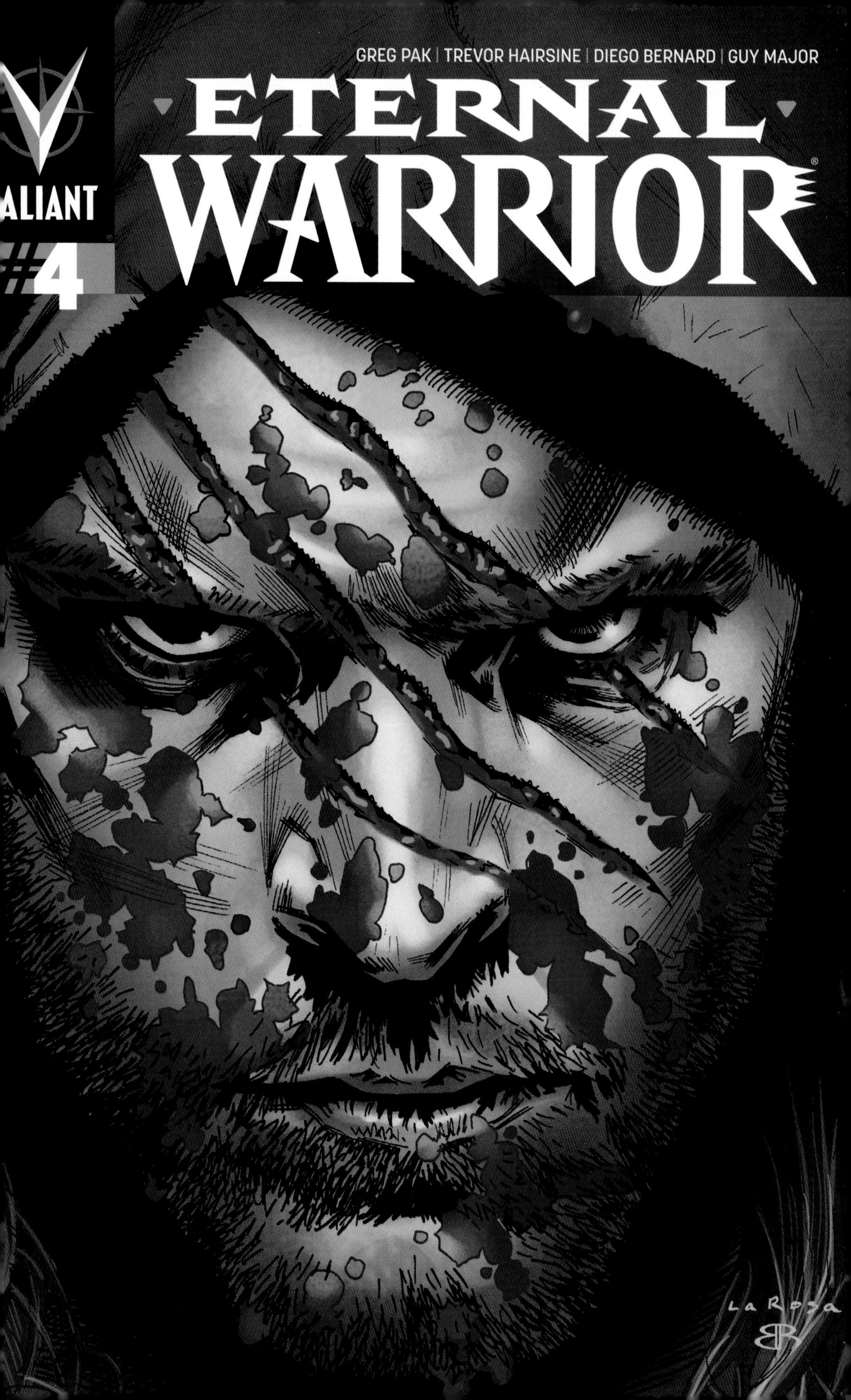
VALIANT
#4
GREG PAK | TREVOR HAIRSINE | DIEGO BERNARD | GUY MAJOR
ETERNAL
WARRIOR
La Rosa

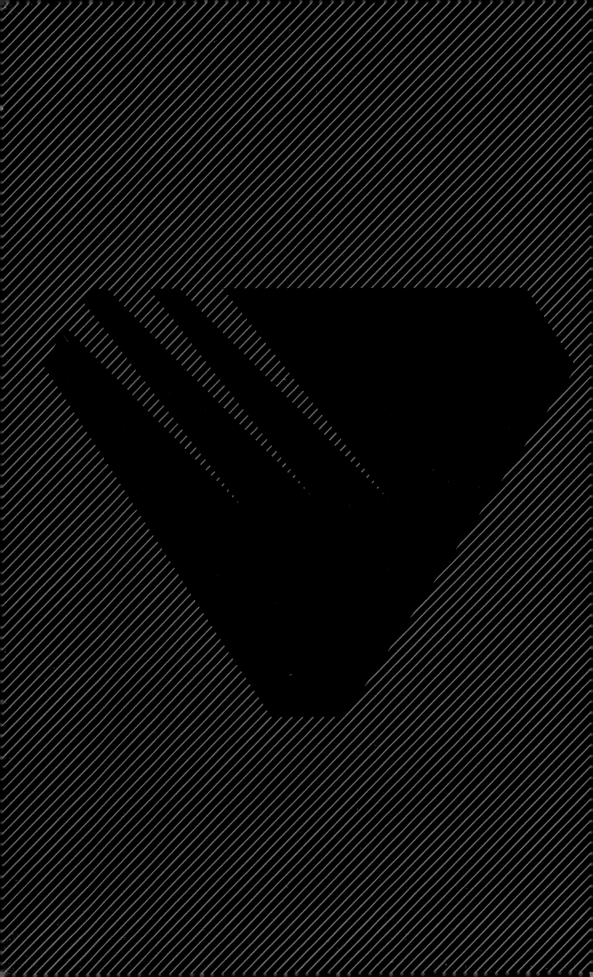

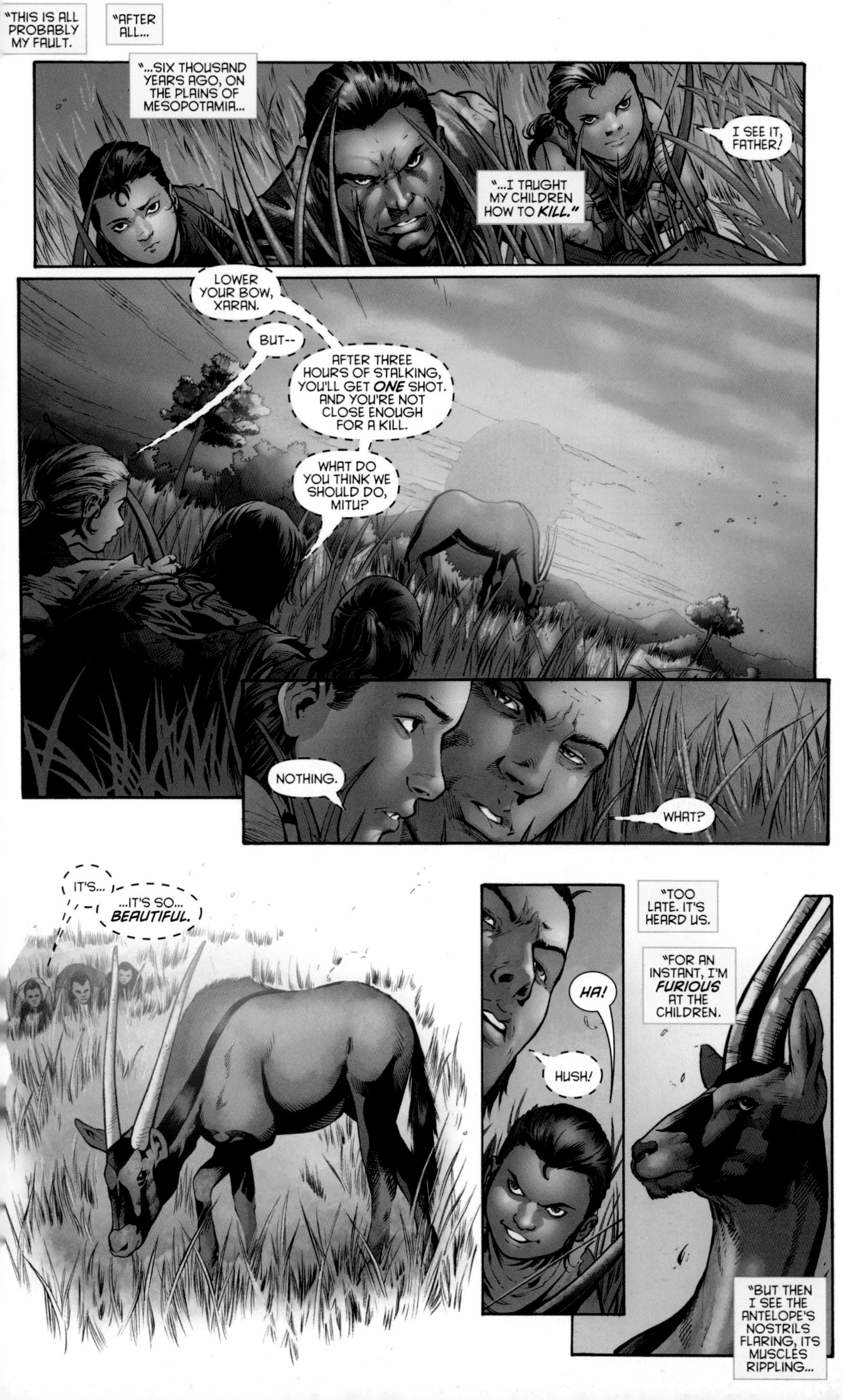
"THIS IS ALL PROBABLY MY FAULT.
"AFTER ALL...
"...SIX THOUSAND YEARS AGO, ON THE PLAINS OF MESOPOTAMIA...
"...I TAUGHT MY CHILDREN HOW TO KILL."
I SEE IT, FATHER!
LOWER YOUR BOW, XARAN.
BUT--
AFTER THREE HOURS OF STALKING, YOU'LL GET ONE SHOT. AND YOU'RE NOT CLOSE ENOUGH FOR A KILL.
WHAT DO YOU THINK WE SHOULD DO, MITU?
NOTHING.
WHAT?
IT'S...
...IT'S SO... BEAUTIFUL.
"TOO LATE. IT'S HEARD US.
"FOR AN INSTANT, I'M FURIOUS AT THE CHILDREN.
HA!
HUSH!
"BUT THEN I SEE THE ANTELOPE'S NOSTRILS FLARING, ITS MUSCLES RIPPLING...

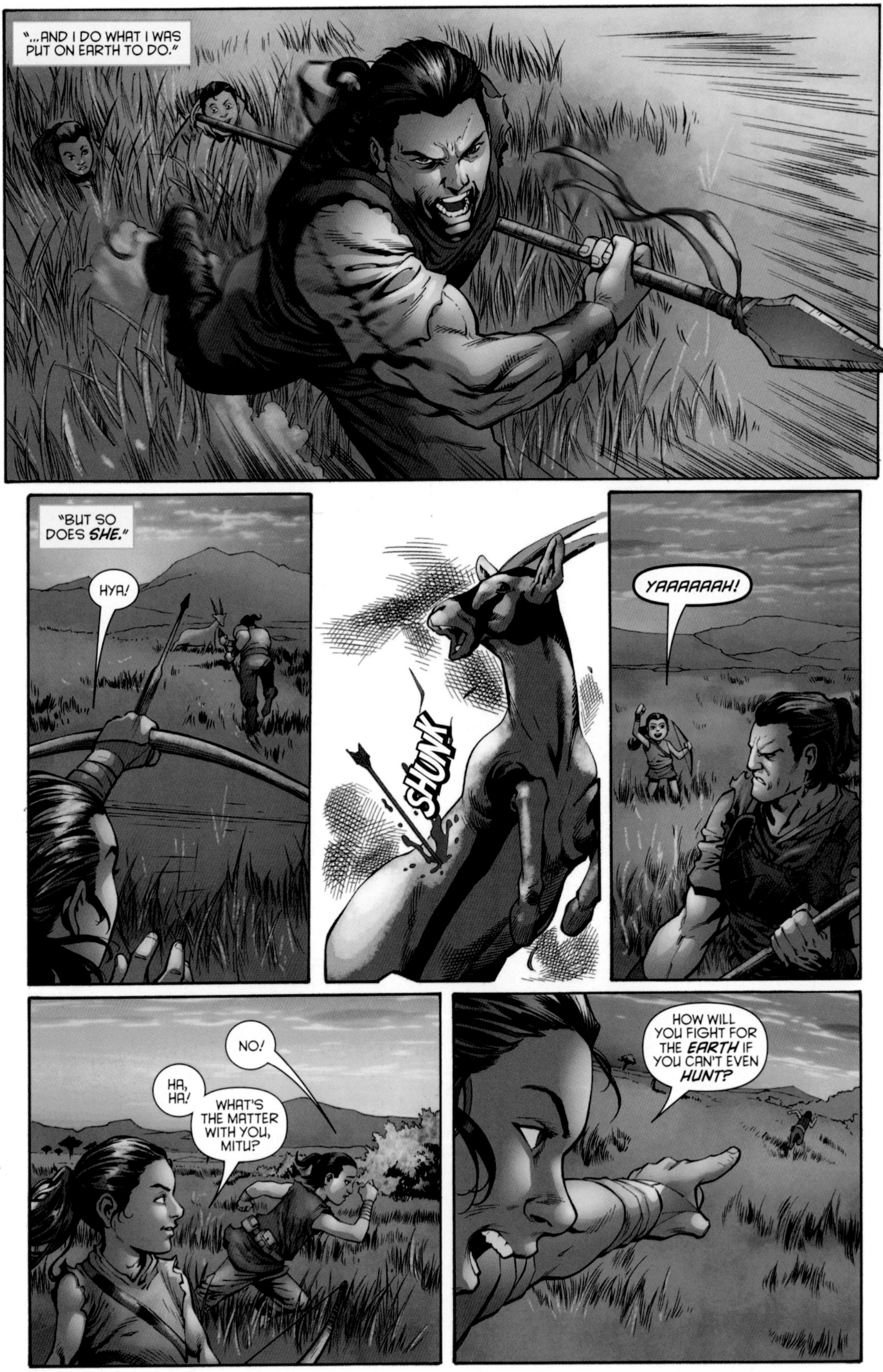
"...AND I DO WHAT I WAS PUT ON EARTH TO DO."
"BUT SO DOES SHE."
HYA!
SHUNK
YAAAAAAH!
NO!
HA, HA!
WHAT'S THE MATTER WITH YOU, MITU?
HOW WILL YOU FIGHT FOR THE EARTH IF YOU CAN'T EVEN HUNT?

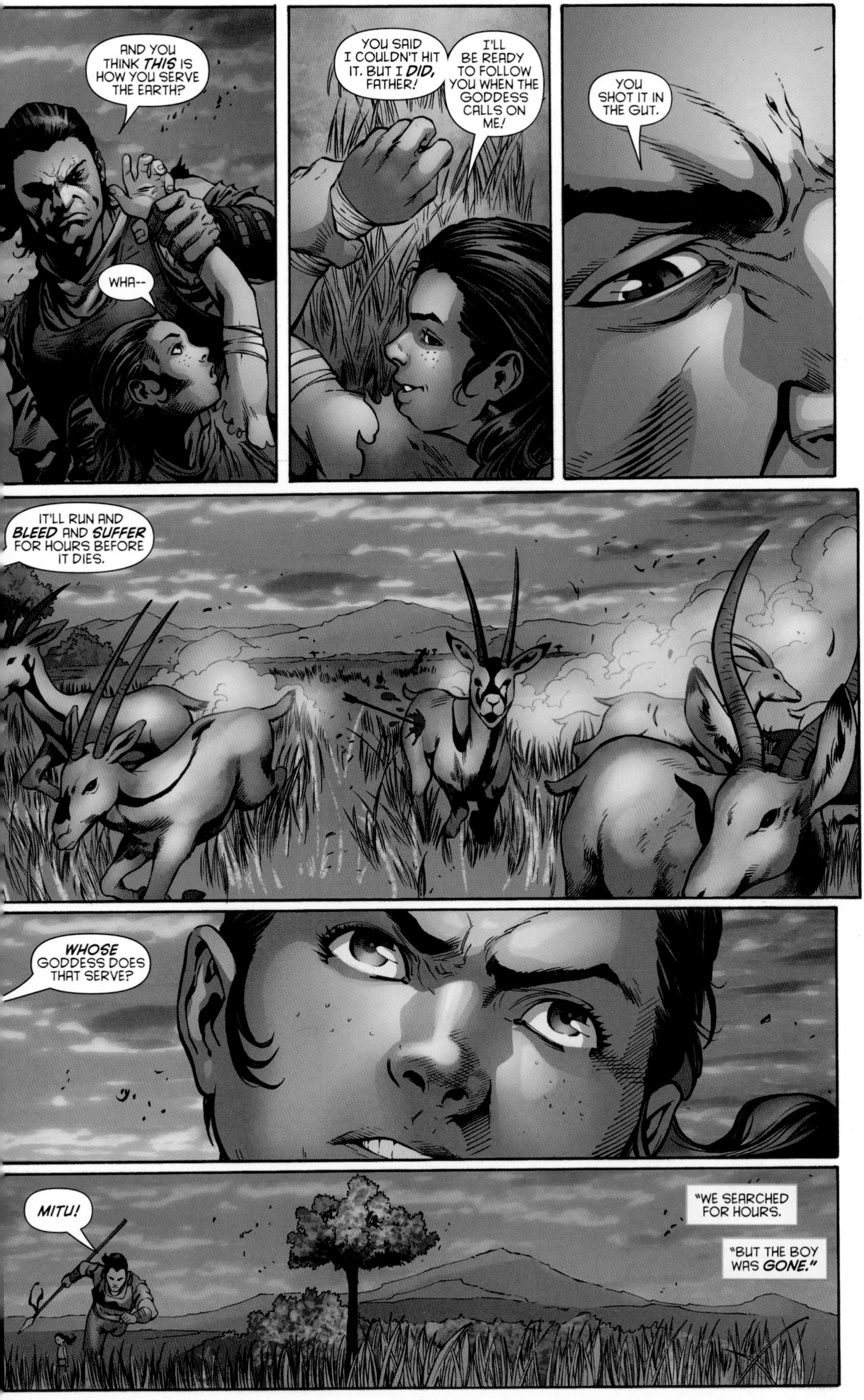
AND YOU THINK THIS IS HOW YOU SERVE THE EARTH?
WHA--
YOU SAID I COULDN'T HIT IT. BUT I DID, FATHER!
I'LL BE READY TO FOLLOW YOU WHEN THE GODDESS CALLS ON ME!
YOU SHOT IT IN THE GUT.
IT'LL RUN AND BLEED AND SUFFER FOR HOURS BEFORE IT DIES.
WHOSE GODDESS DOES THAT SERVE?
MITU!
"WE SEARCHED FOR HOURS.
"BUT THE BOY WAS GONE."

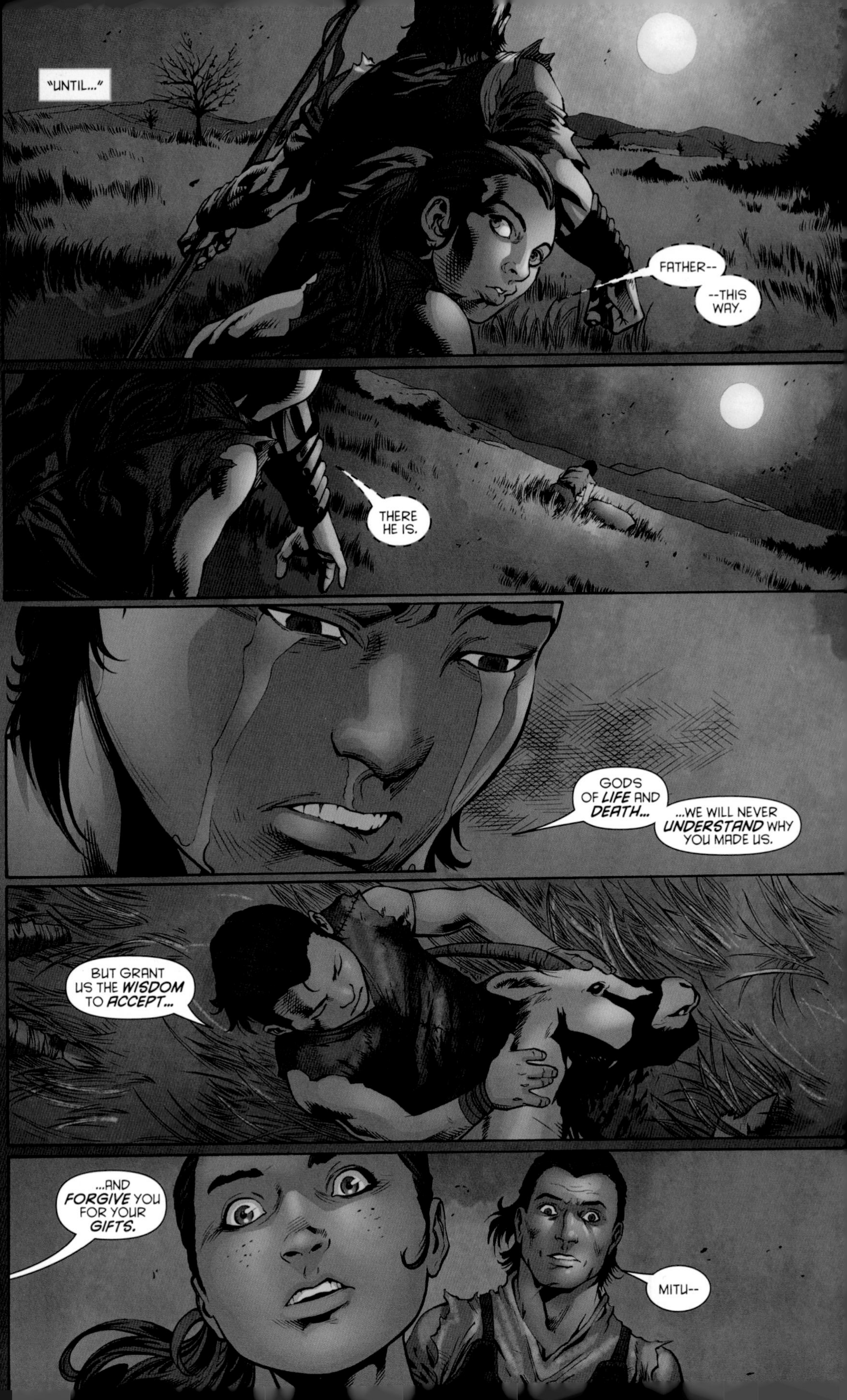
"UNTIL..."
FATHER--
--THIS WAY.
THERE HE IS.
GODS OF LIFE AND DEATH...
...WE WILL NEVER UNDERSTAND WHY YOU MADE US.
BUT GRANT US THE WISDOM TO ACCEPT...
...AND FORGIVE YOU FOR YOUR GIFTS.
MITU--

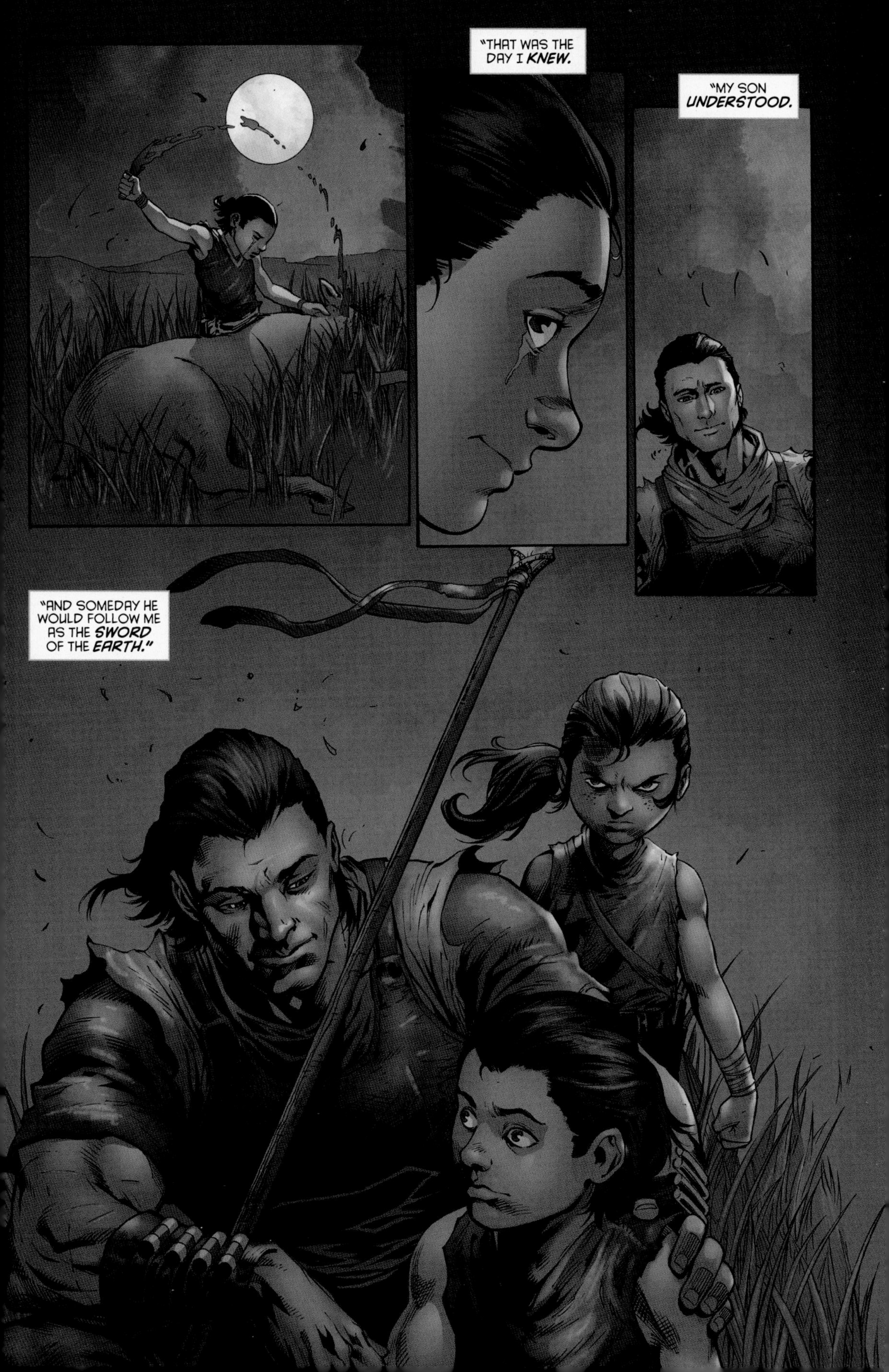
"THAT WAS THE DAY I KNEW.
"MY SON UNDERSTOOD.
"AND SOMEDAY HE WOULD FOLLOW ME AS THE SWORD OF THE EARTH."

TODAY.

AND NOW YOU TELL ME...

...HE'S THE **SWORD** OF THE **DEAD?**

YES.

HE FIGHTS FOR **NERGAL,** GOD OF **DARKNESS.**

THE **BLIGHT** AND THE **VOID.**

HE WAS NOT...

HE WAS NOT A CHILD WHO...

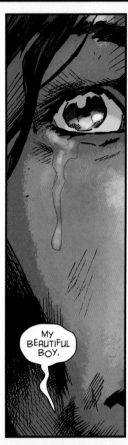

MY BEAUTIFUL BOY.

FATHER...

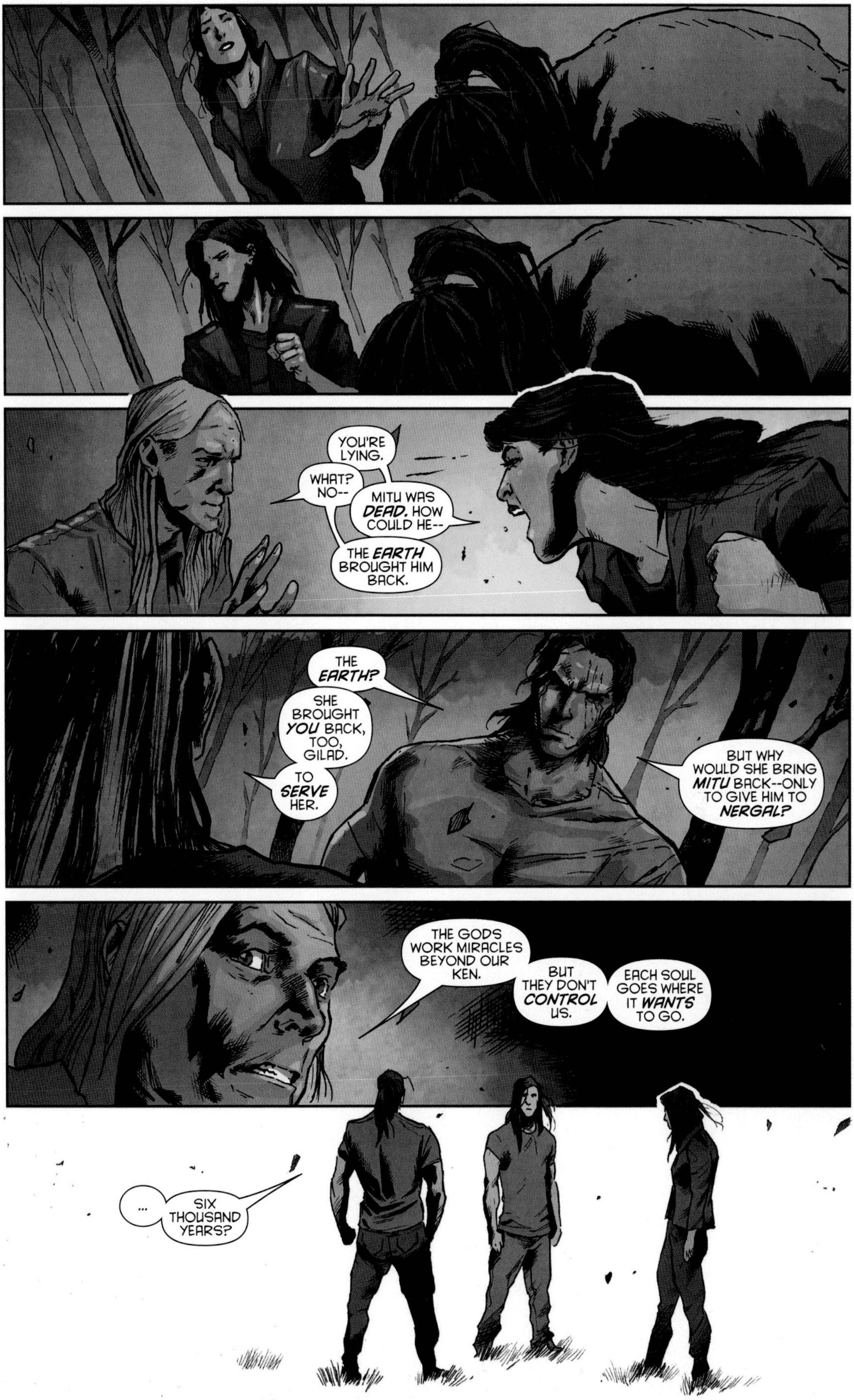
YOU'RE LYING.
WHAT? NO--
MITU WAS DEAD. HOW COULD HE--
THE EARTH BROUGHT HIM BACK.
THE EARTH?
SHE BROUGHT YOU BACK, TOO, GILAD.
TO SERVE HER.
BUT WHY WOULD SHE BRING MITU BACK--ONLY TO GIVE HIM TO NERGAL?
THE GODS WORK MIRACLES BEYOND OUR KEN.
BUT THEY DON'T CONTROL US.
EACH SOUL GOES WHERE IT WANTS TO GO.
... SIX THOUSAND YEARS?

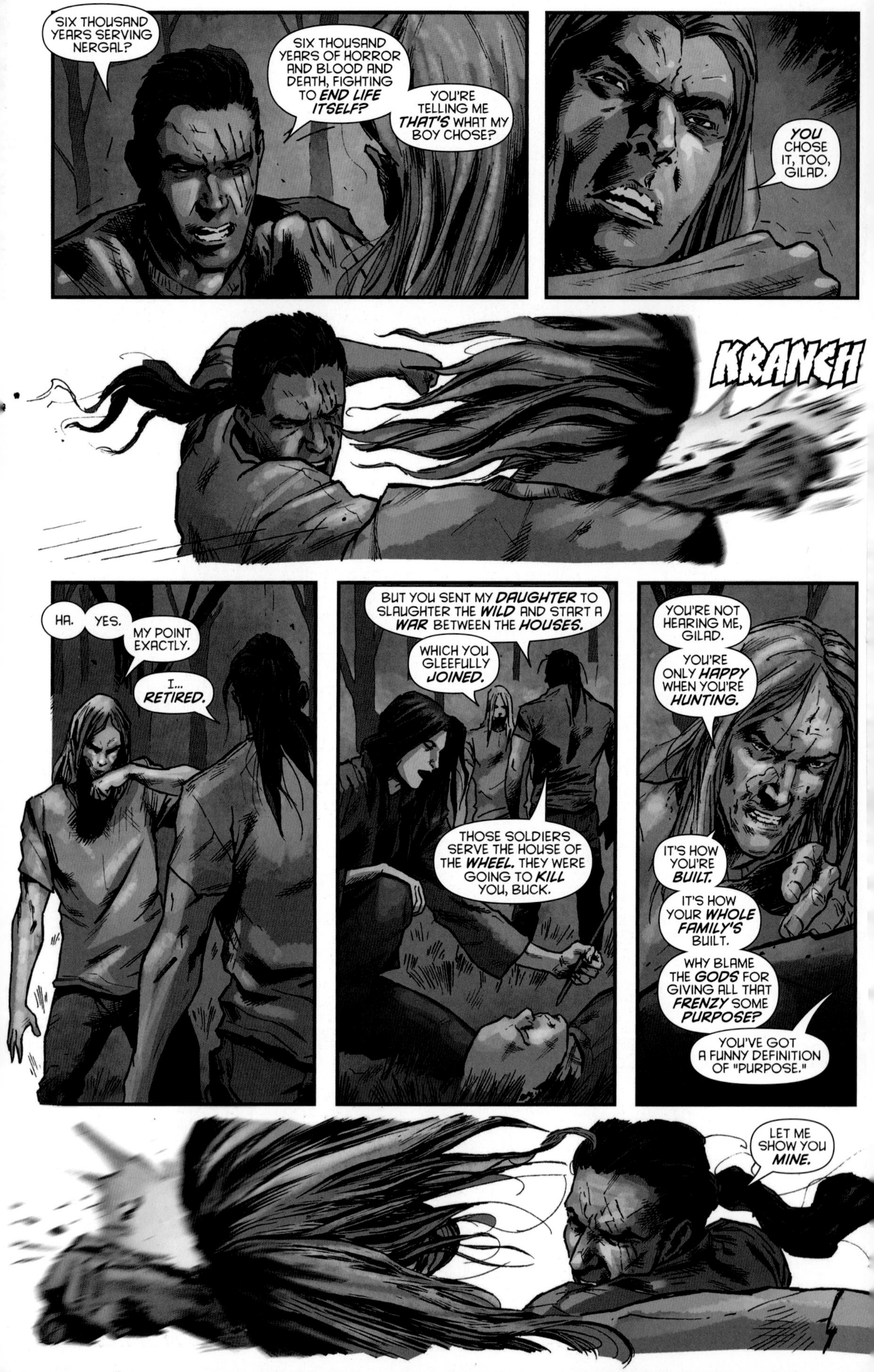
SIX THOUSAND YEARS SERVING NERGAL?
SIX THOUSAND YEARS OF HORROR AND BLOOD AND DEATH, FIGHTING TO END LIFE ITSELF?
YOU'RE TELLING ME THAT'S WHAT MY BOY CHOSE?
YOU CHOSE IT, TOO, GILAD.
KRANCH
HA.
YES.
MY POINT EXACTLY.
I... RETIRED.
BUT YOU SENT MY DAUGHTER TO SLAUGHTER THE WILD AND START A WAR BETWEEN THE HOUSES.
WHICH YOU GLEEFULLY JOINED.
THOSE SOLDIERS SERVE THE HOUSE OF THE WHEEL. THEY WERE GOING TO KILL YOU, BUCK.
YOU'RE NOT HEARING ME, GILAD.
YOU'RE ONLY HAPPY WHEN YOU'RE HUNTING.
IT'S HOW YOU'RE BUILT.
IT'S HOW YOUR WHOLE FAMILY'S BUILT.
WHY BLAME THE GODS FOR GIVING ALL THAT FRENZY SOME PURPOSE?
YOU'VE GOT A FUNNY DEFINITION OF "PURPOSE."
LET ME SHOW YOU MINE.

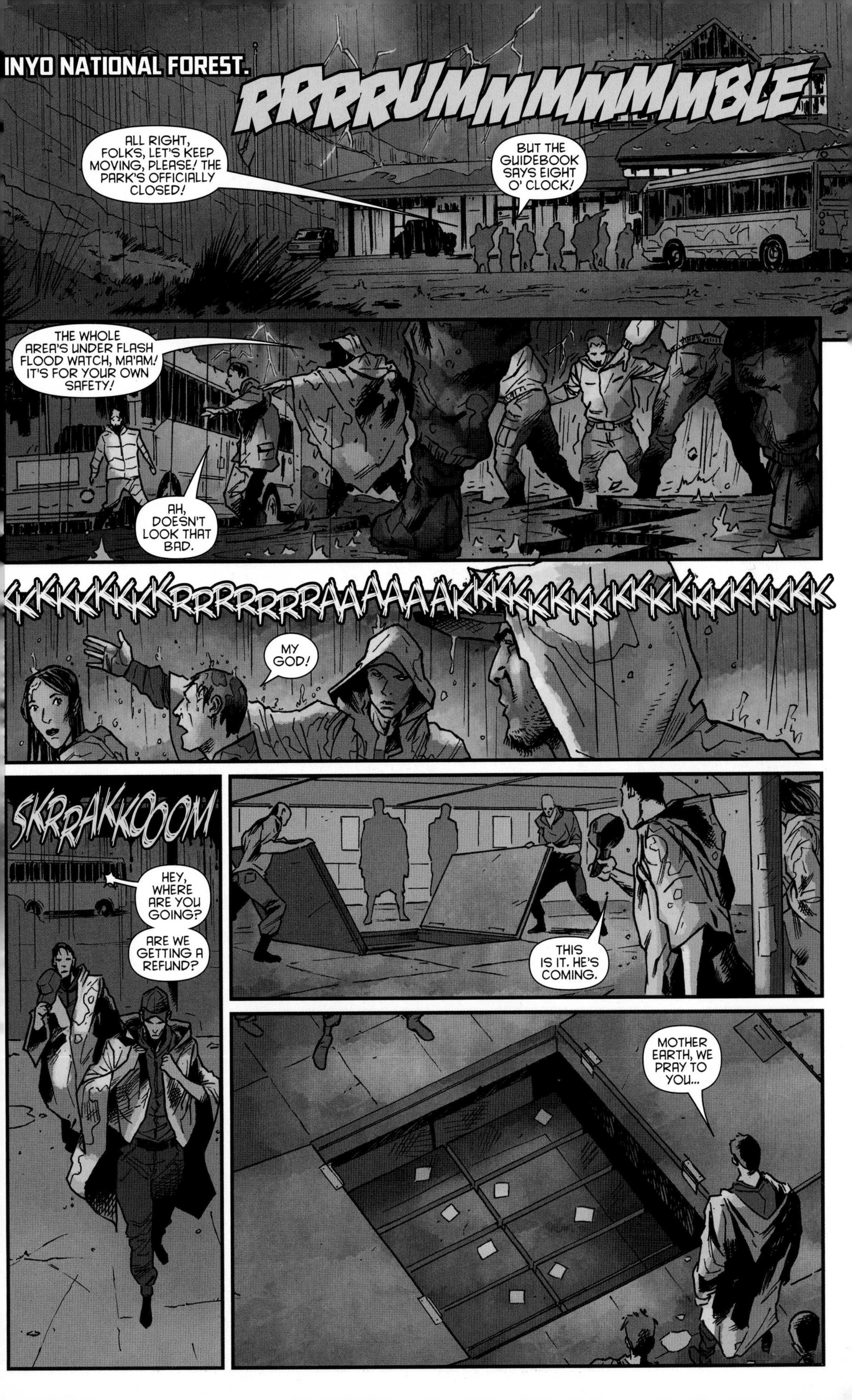
INYO NATIONAL FOREST.
RRRRUMMMMMMMBLE
ALL RIGHT, FOLKS, LET'S KEEP MOVING, PLEASE! THE PARK'S OFFICIALLY CLOSED!
BUT THE GUIDEBOOK SAYS EIGHT O' CLOCK!
THE WHOLE AREA'S UNDER FLASH FLOOD WATCH, MA'AM! IT'S FOR YOUR OWN SAFETY!
AH, DOESN'T LOOK THAT BAD.
KKKKKKKRRRRRRRRAAAAAKKKKKKKKKKKKKKKKKK
MY GOD!
SKRRAKKOOOM
HEY, WHERE ARE YOU GOING?
ARE WE GETTING A REFUND?
THIS IS IT. HE'S COMING.
MOTHER EARTH, WE PRAY TO YOU...

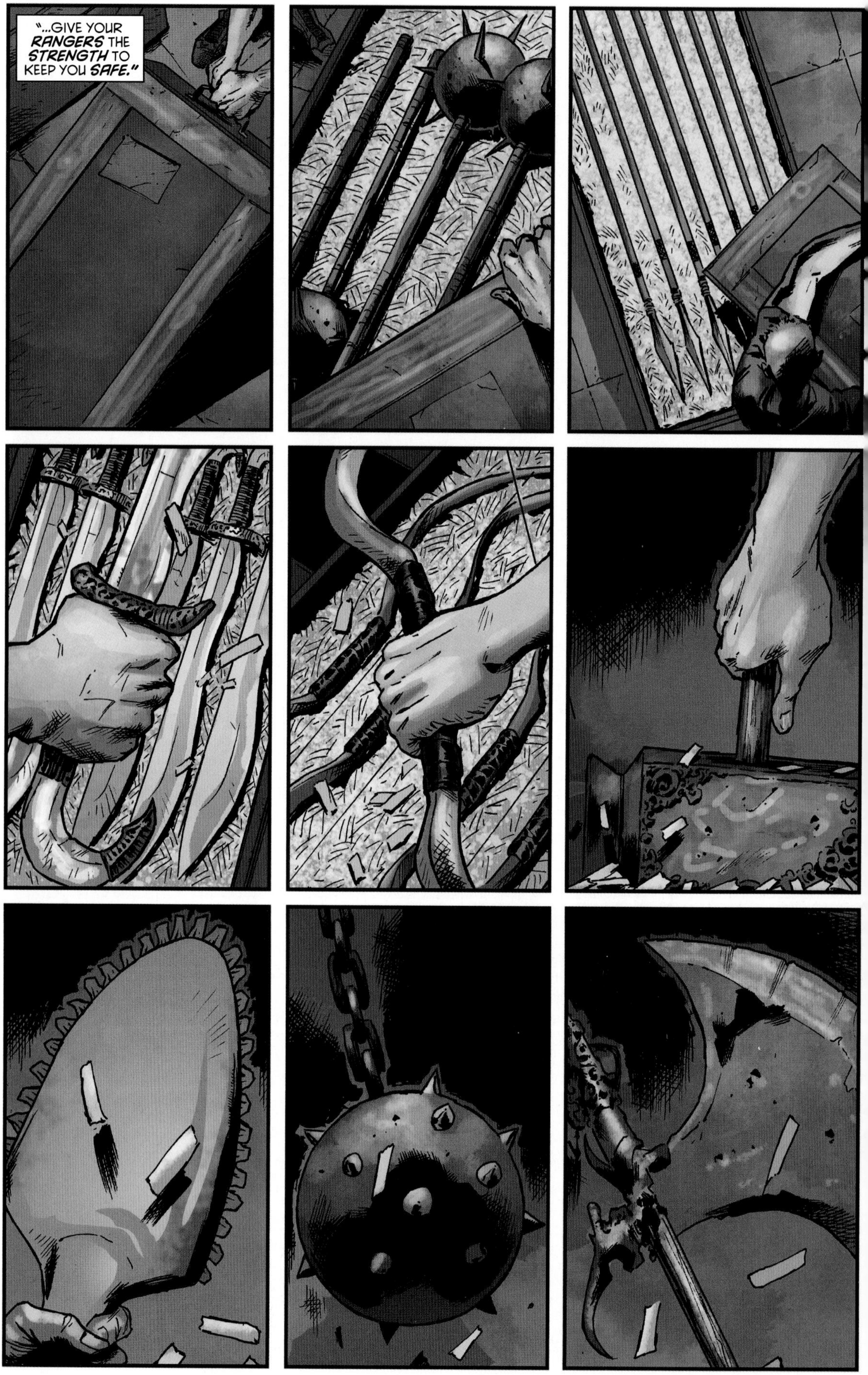
"...GIVE YOUR RANGERS THE STRENGTH TO KEEP YOU SAFE."

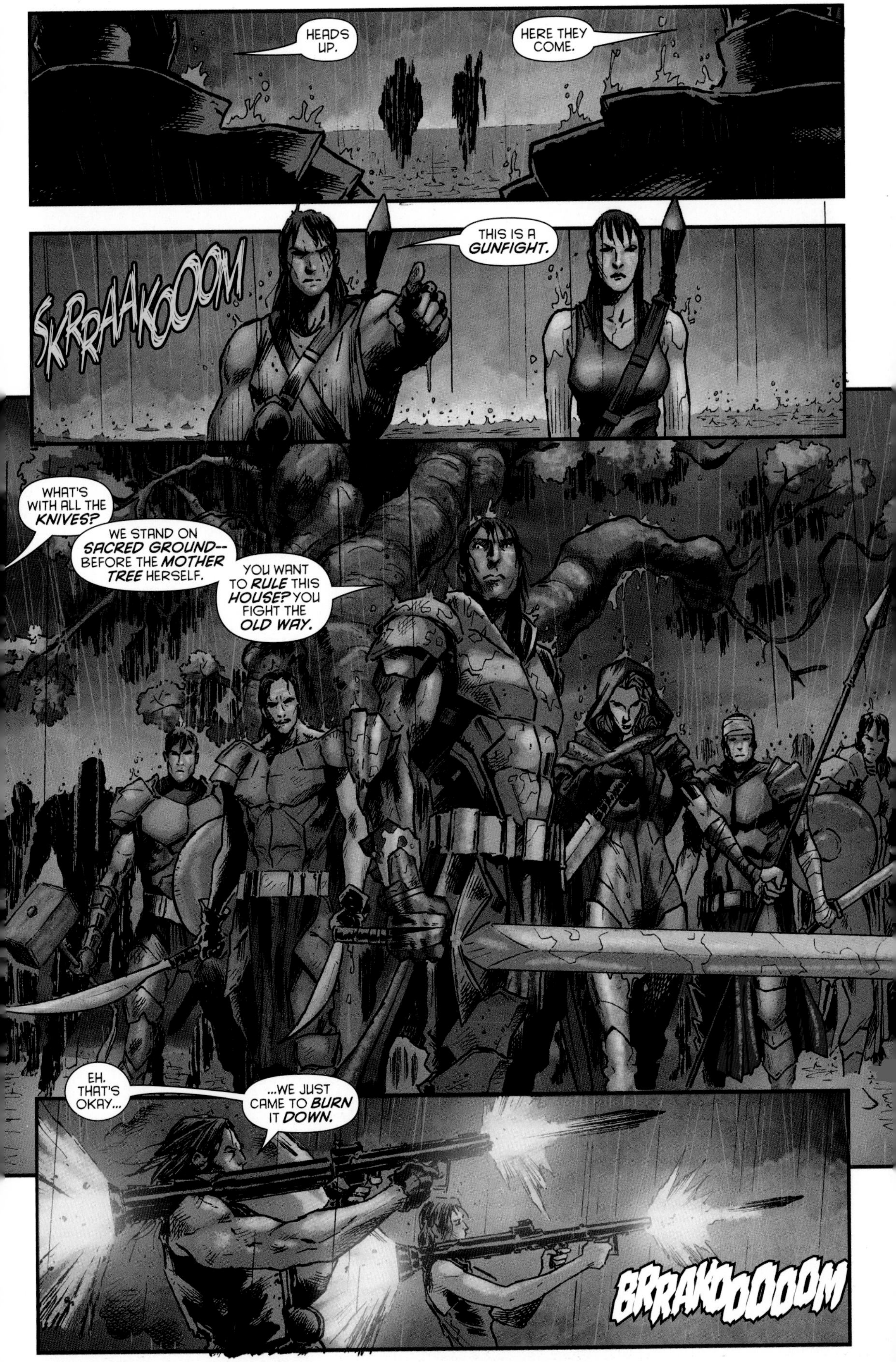
HEADS UP.
HERE THEY COME.
SKRRAAKOOOM
THIS IS A GUNFIGHT.
WHAT'S WITH ALL THE KNIVES?
WE STAND ON SACRED GROUND-- BEFORE THE MOTHER TREE HERSELF.
YOU WANT TO RULE THIS HOUSE? YOU FIGHT THE OLD WAY.
EH. THAT'S OKAY...
...WE JUST CAME TO BURN IT DOWN.
BRRAKOOOOOM

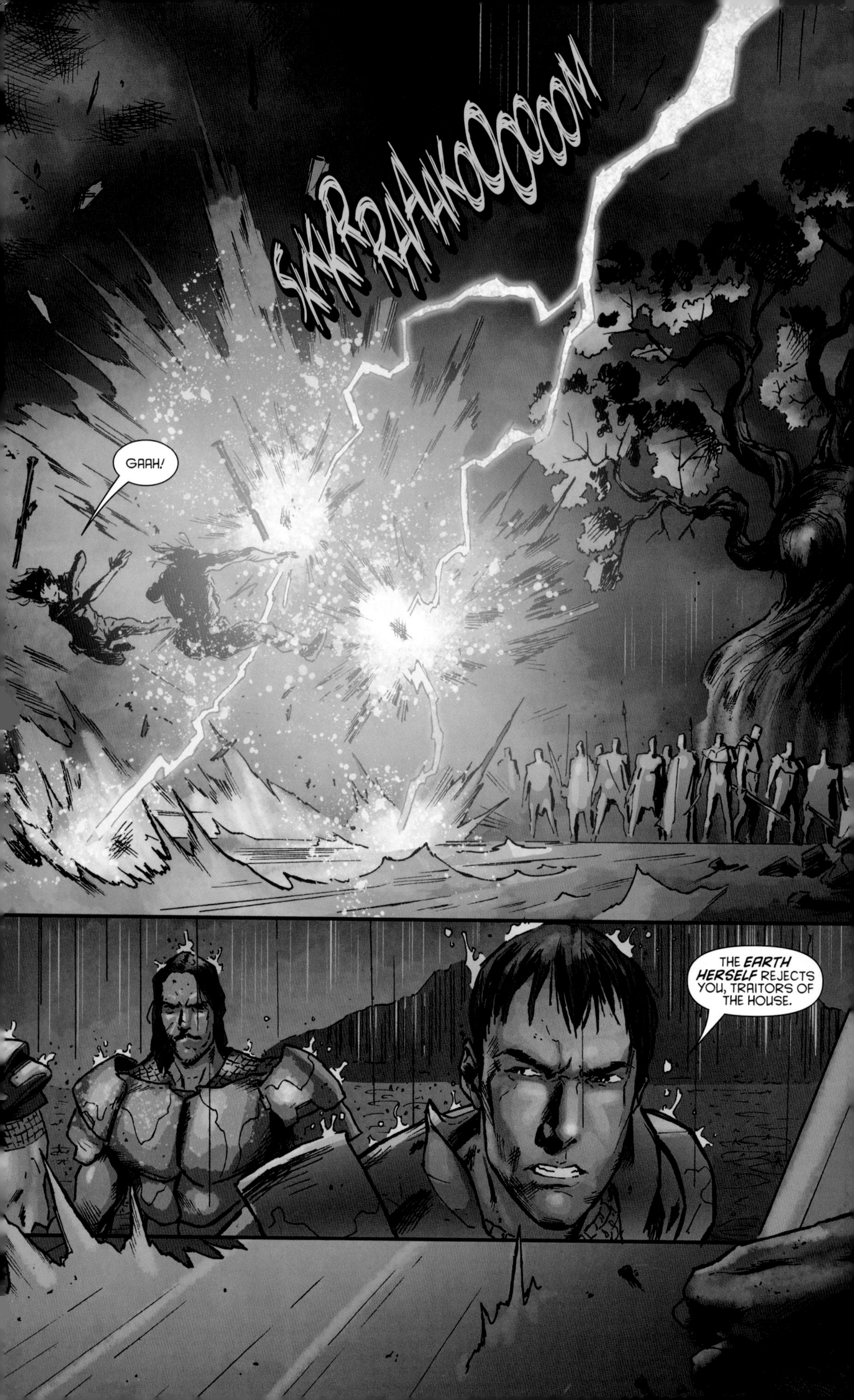
SKRRAAKOOOOOM
GAAH!
THE EARTH HERSELF REJECTS YOU, TRAITORS OF THE HOUSE.

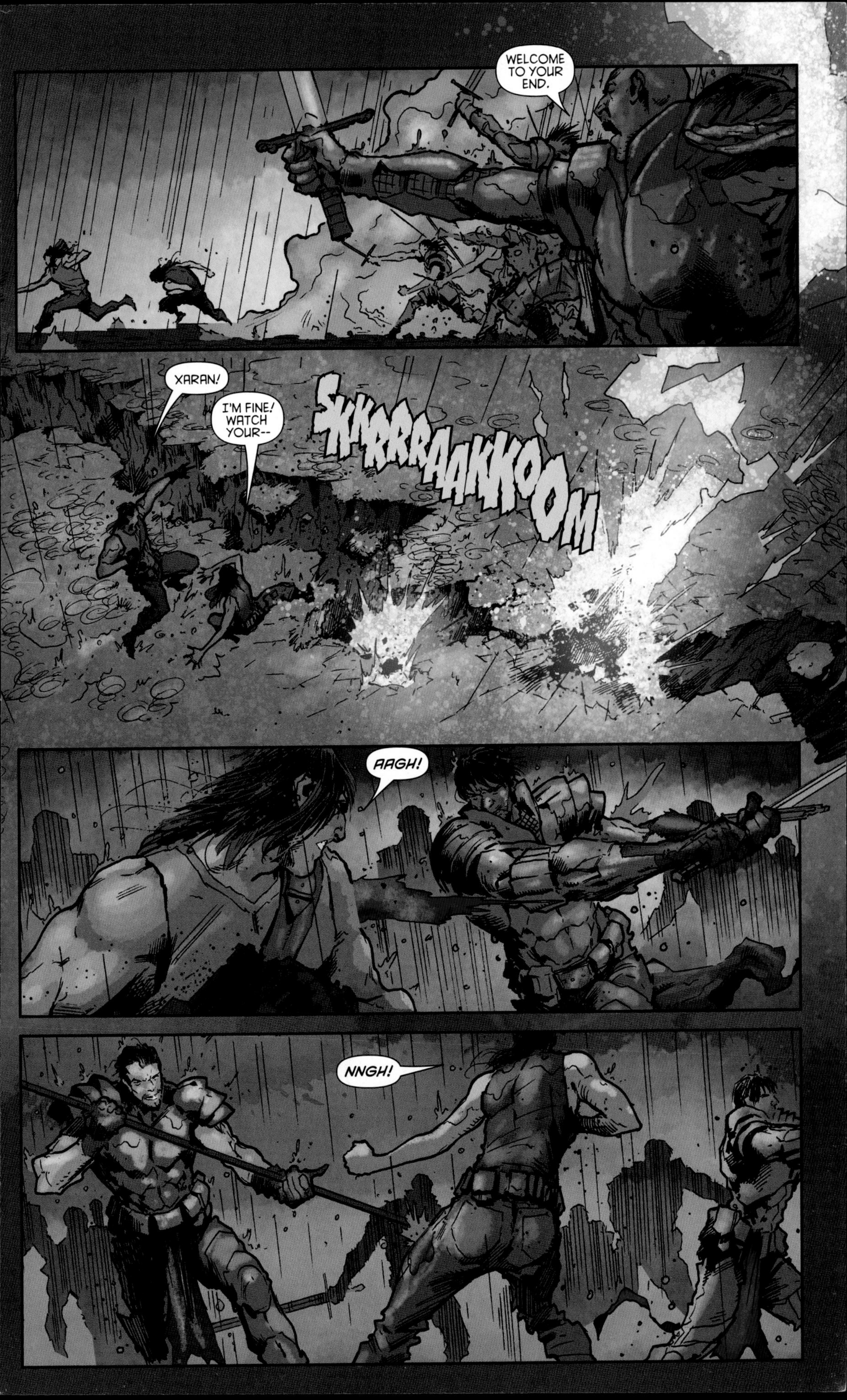
WELCOME TO YOUR END.
XARAN!
I'M FINE! WATCH YOUR--
SKKRRRAAKKOOM
AAGH!
NNGH!

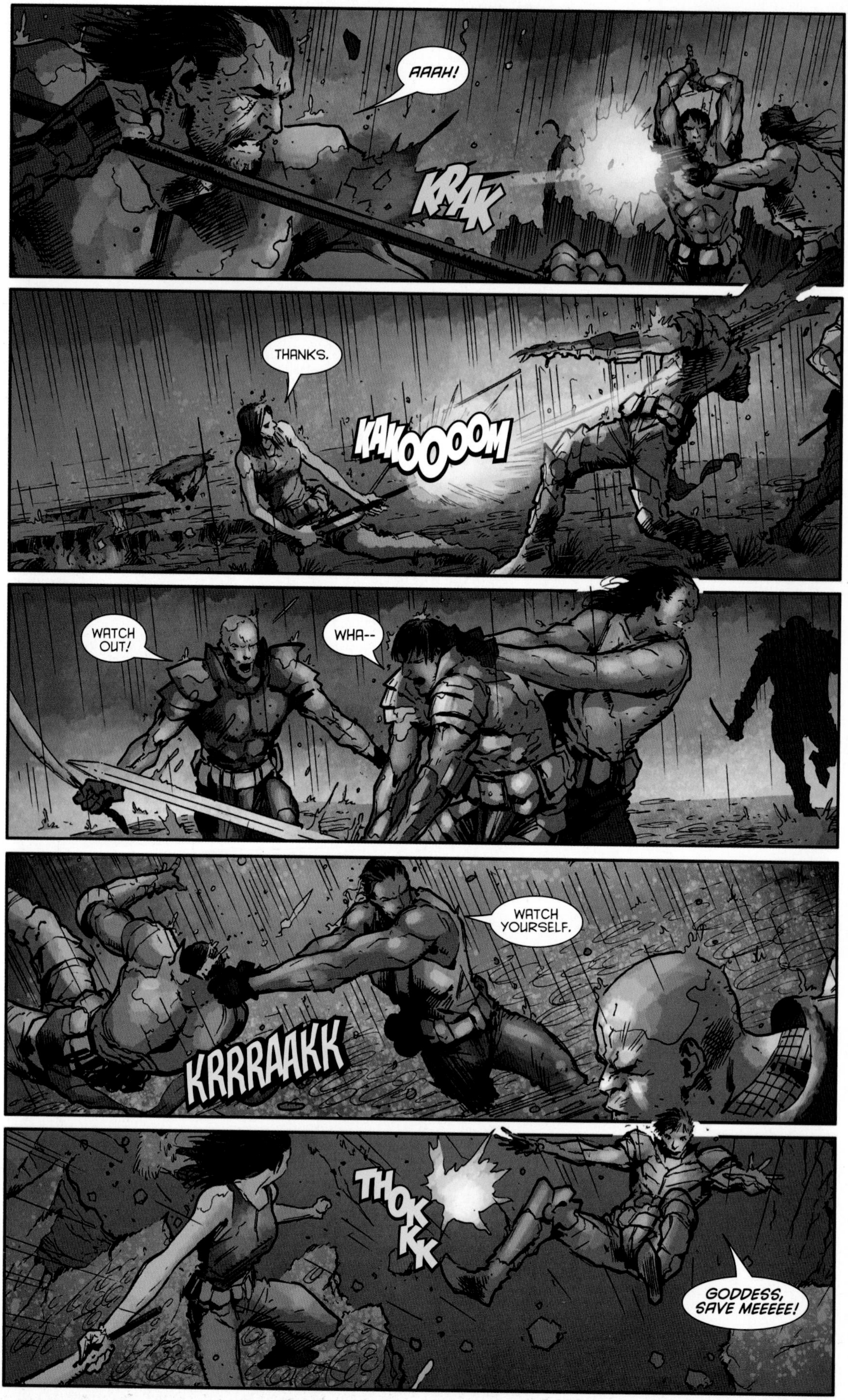
AAAH!
KRAK
THANKS.
KAKOOOOOM
WATCH OUT!
WHA--
WATCH YOURSELF.
KRRRAAKK
THOKKK
GODDESS, SAVE MEEEEE!

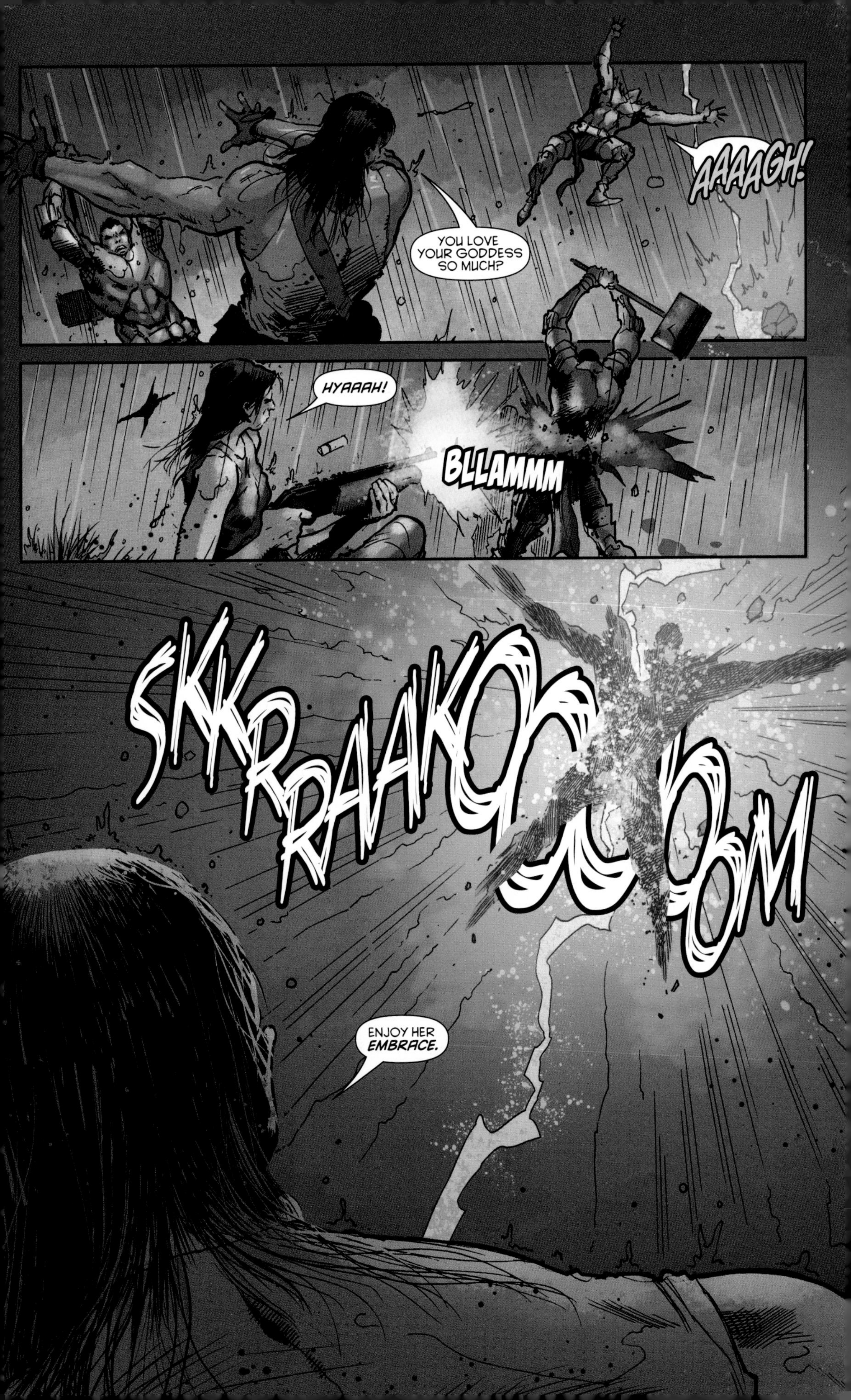
AAAAGH!
YOU LOVE YOUR GODDESS SO MUCH?
HYAAAH!
BLLAMMM
SKKRAAKOOOOOM
ENJOY HER *EMBRACE.*

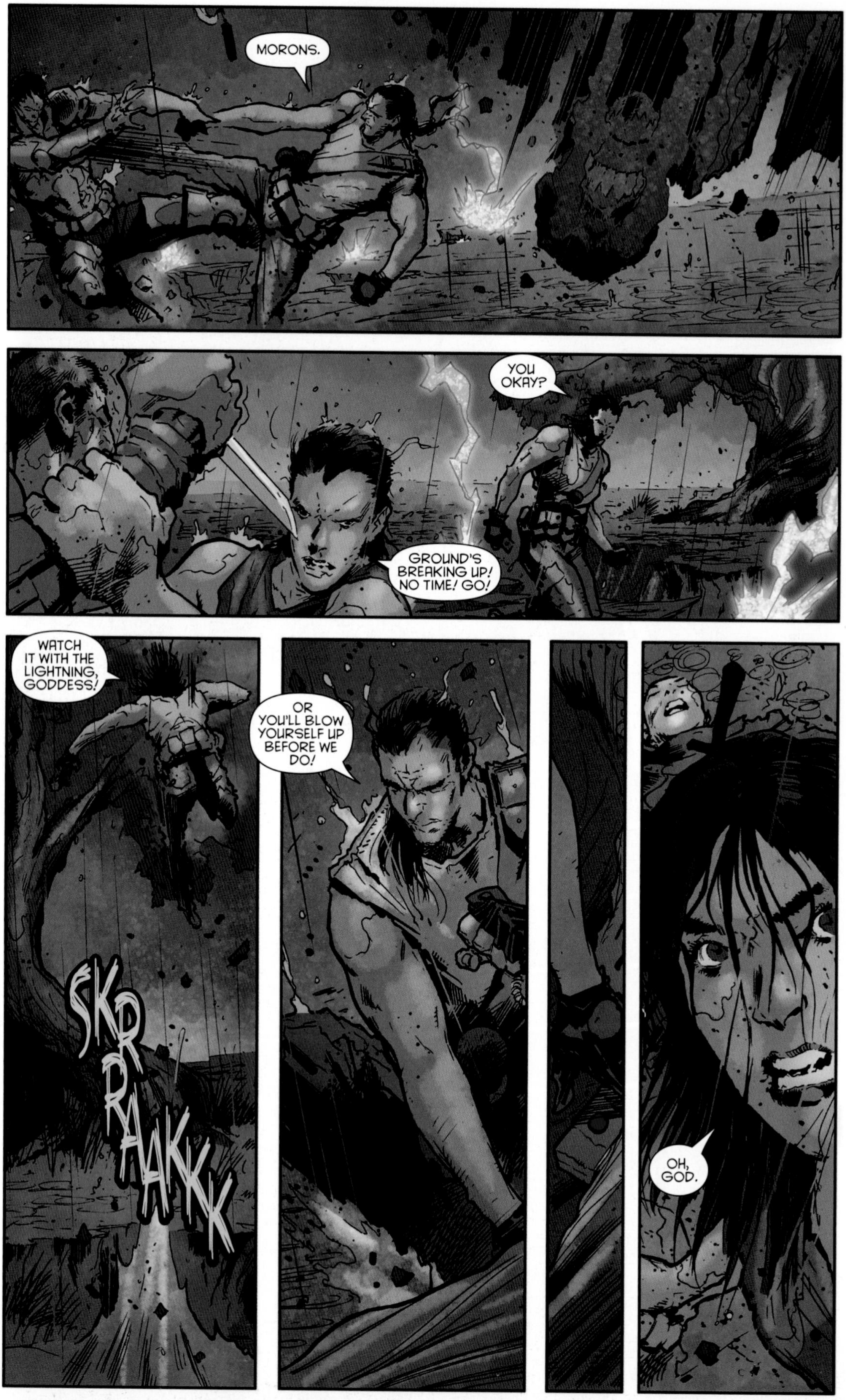
MORONS.
YOU OKAY?
GROUND'S BREAKING UP! NO TIME! GO!
WATCH IT WITH THE LIGHTNING, GODDESS!
SKRRAAKKK
OR YOU'LL BLOW YOURSELF UP BEFORE WE DO!
OH, GOD.

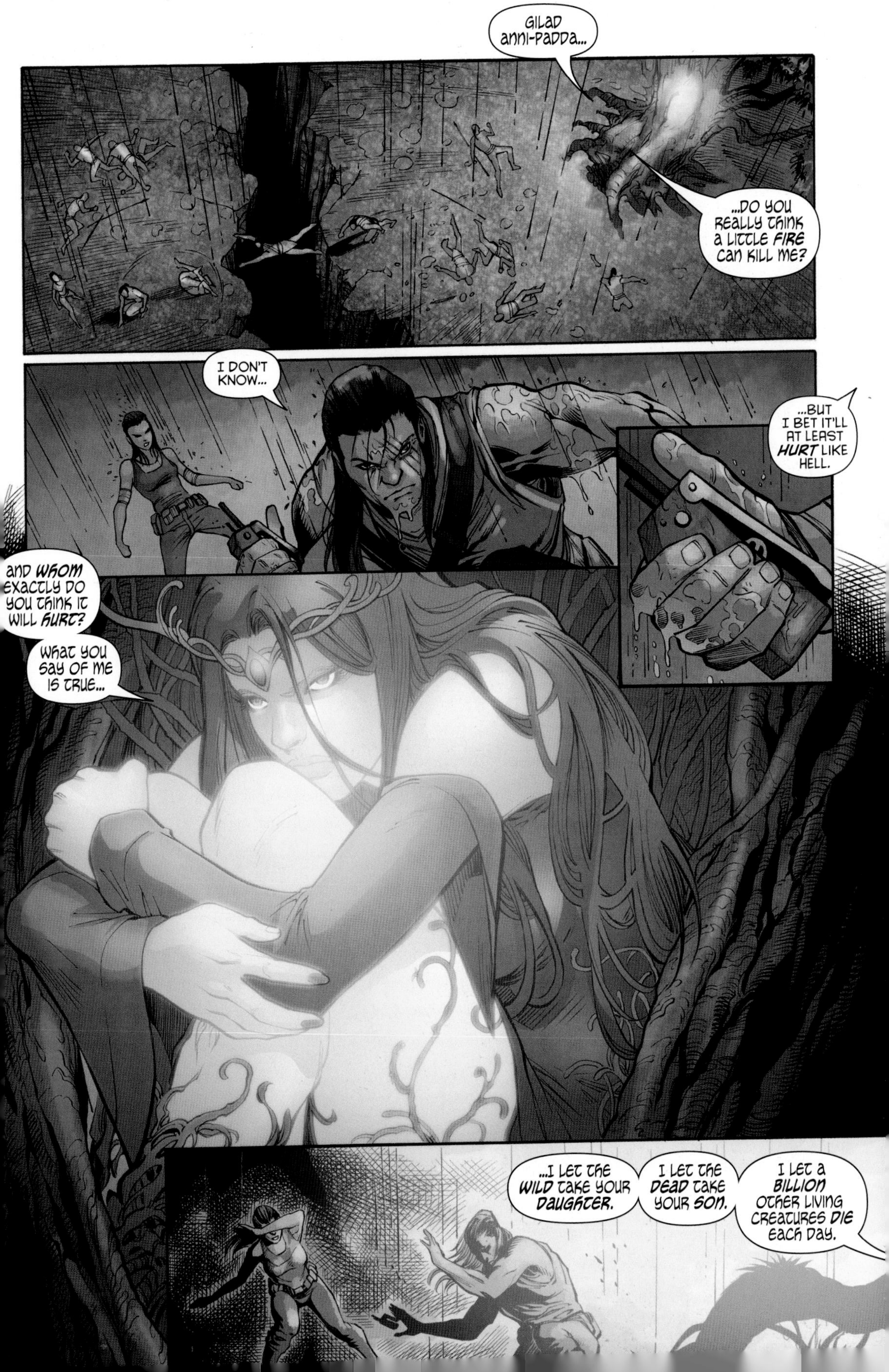
GILAD anni-padda...
...DO YOU REALLY THINK A LITTLE FIRE CAN KILL ME?
I DON'T KNOW...
...BUT I BET IT'LL AT LEAST HURT LIKE HELL.
AND WHOM EXACTLY DO YOU THINK IT WILL HURT?
WHAT YOU SAY OF ME IS TRUE...
...I LET THE WILD TAKE YOUR DAUGHTER.
I LET THE DEAD TAKE YOUR SON.
I LET A BILLION OTHER LIVING CREATURES DIE EACH DAY.

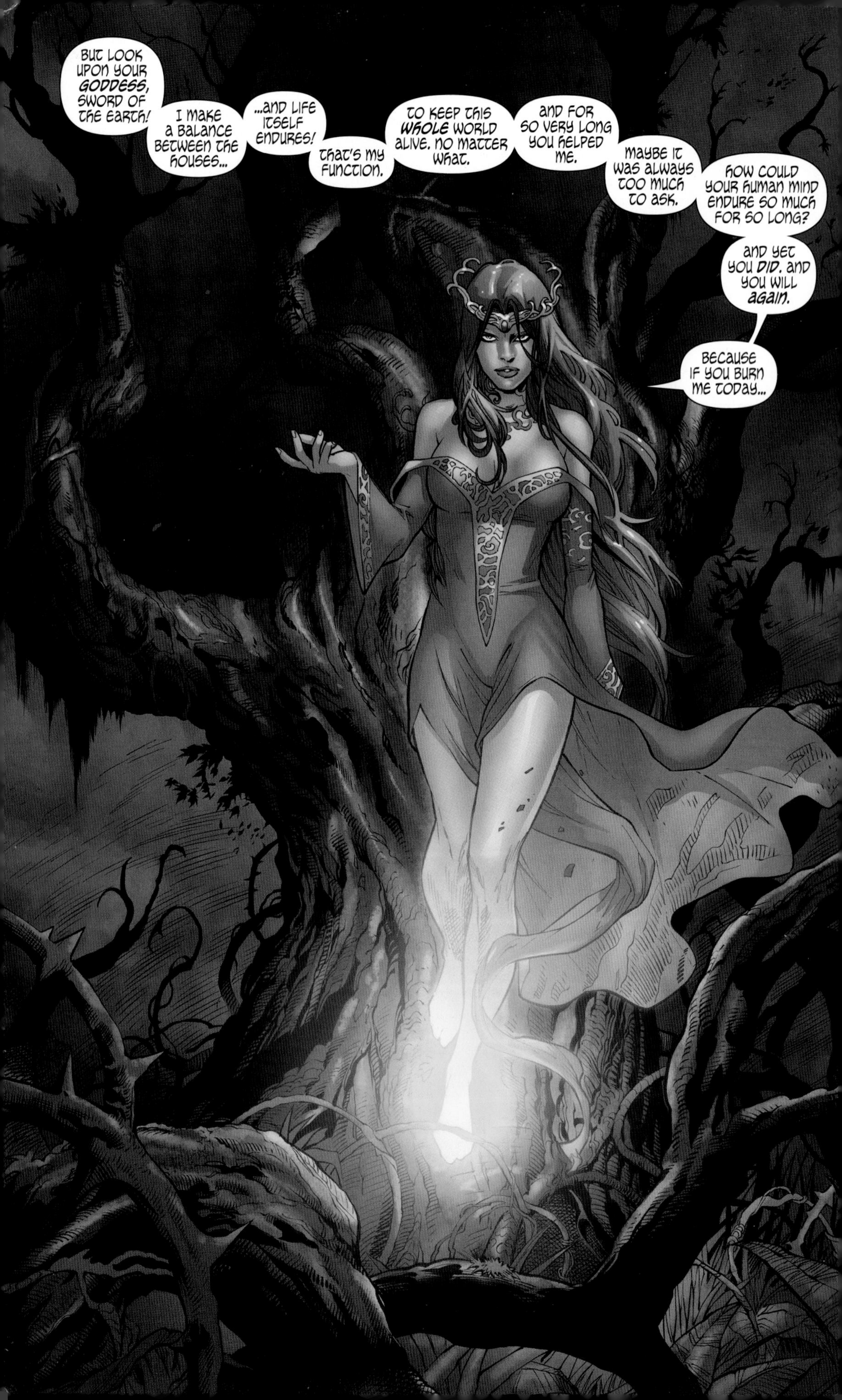
BUT LOOK UPON YOUR GODDESS, SWORD OF THE EARTH!
I MAKE A BALANCE BETWEEN THE HOUSES...
...AND LIFE ITSELF ENDURES!
THAT'S MY FUNCTION.
TO KEEP THIS WHOLE WORLD ALIVE. NO MATTER WHAT.
AND FOR SO VERY LONG YOU HELPED ME.
MAYBE IT WAS ALWAYS TOO MUCH TO ASK.
HOW COULD YOUR HUMAN MIND ENDURE SO MUCH FOR SO LONG?
AND YET YOU DID. AND YOU WILL AGAIN.
BECAUSE IF YOU BURN ME TODAY...

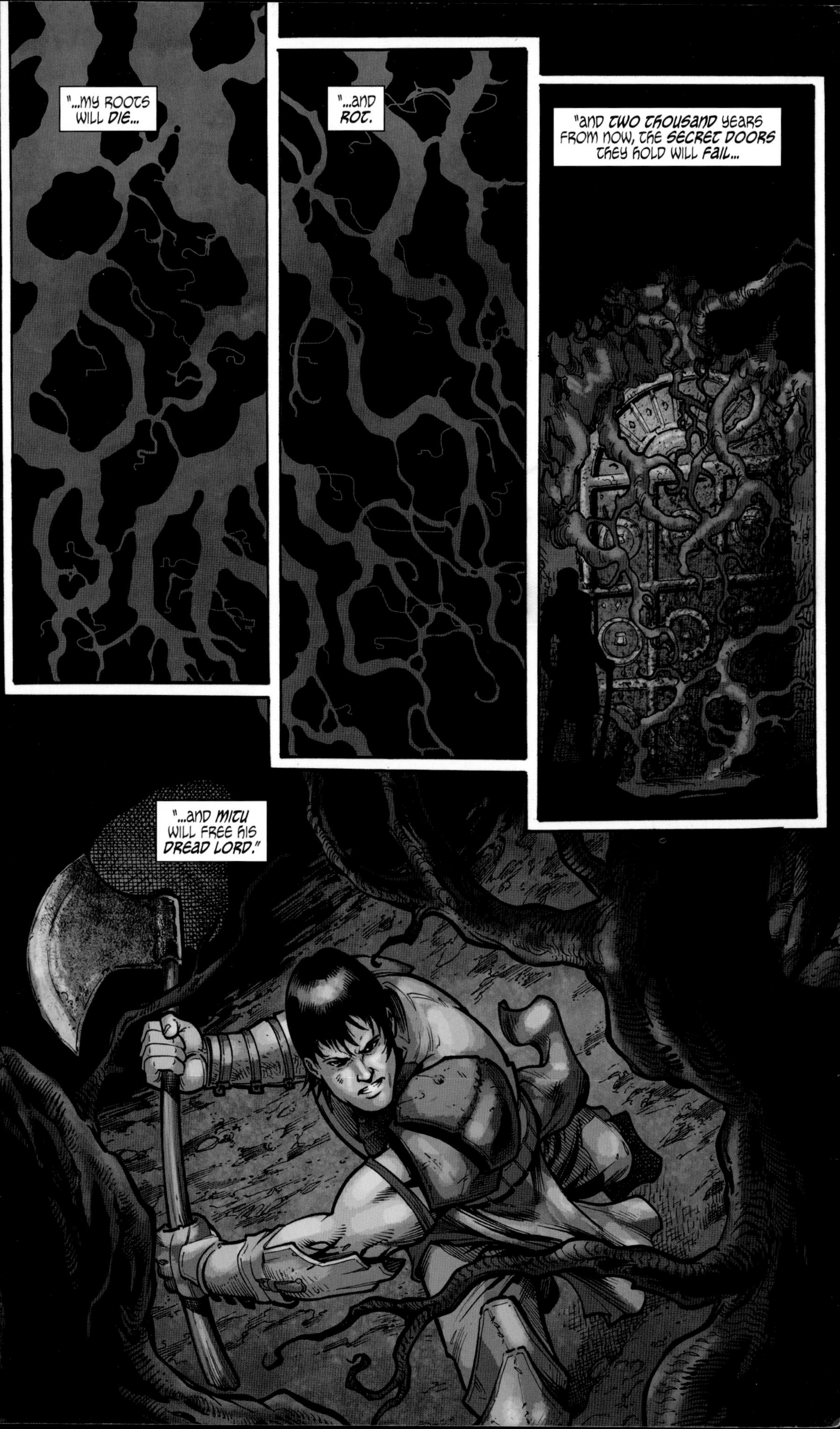
"...MY ROOTS WILL DIE...
"...AND ROT.
"AND TWO THOUSAND YEARS FROM NOW, THE SECRET DOORS THEY HOLD WILL FAIL...
"...AND MITU WILL FREE HIS DREAD LORD."

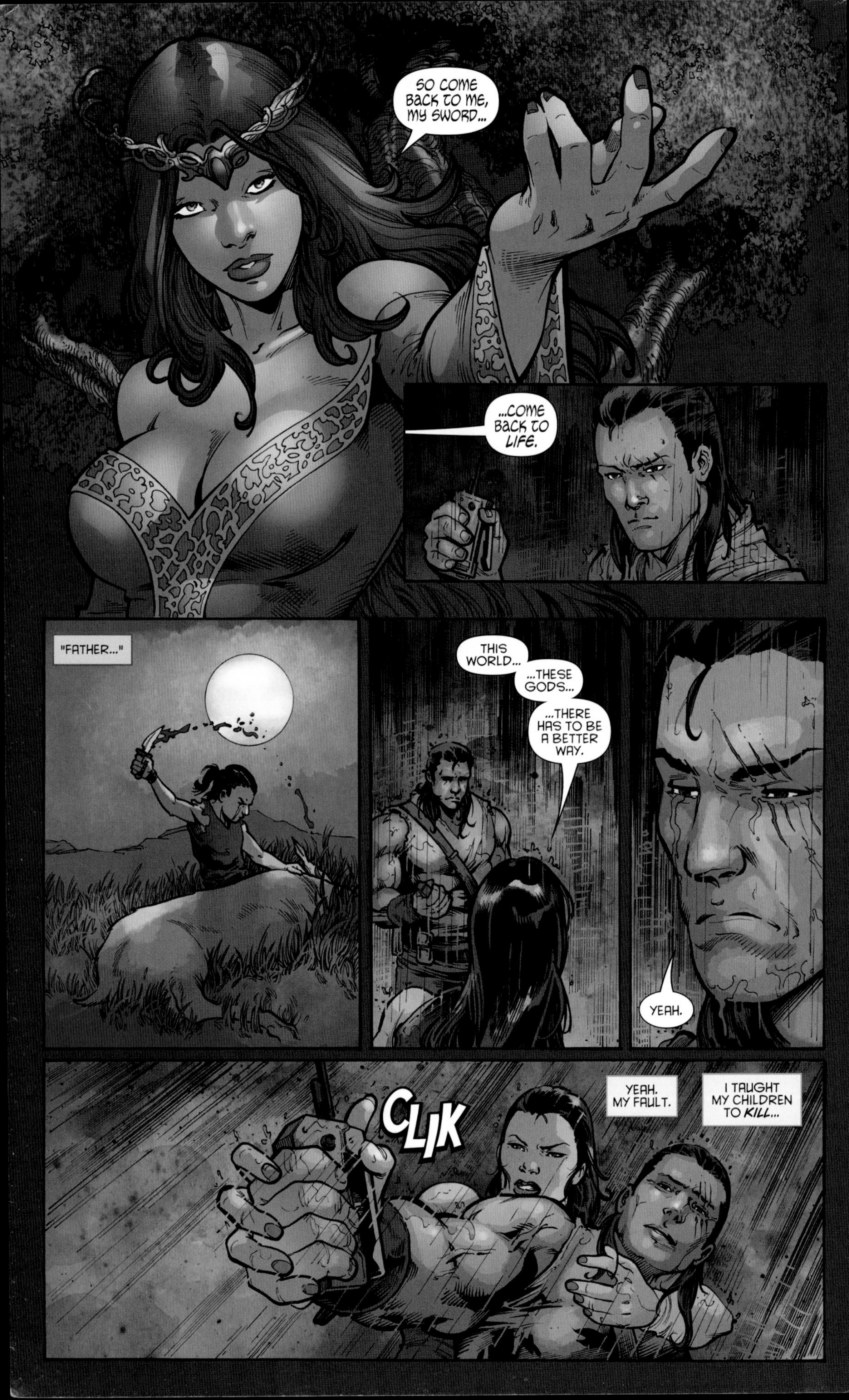
SO COME BACK TO ME, MY SWORD...
...COME BACK TO LIFE.
"FATHER..."
THIS WORLD...
...THESE GODS...
...THERE HAS TO BE A BETTER WAY.
YEAH.
CLIK
YEAH. MY FAULT.
I TAUGHT MY CHILDREN TO KILL...

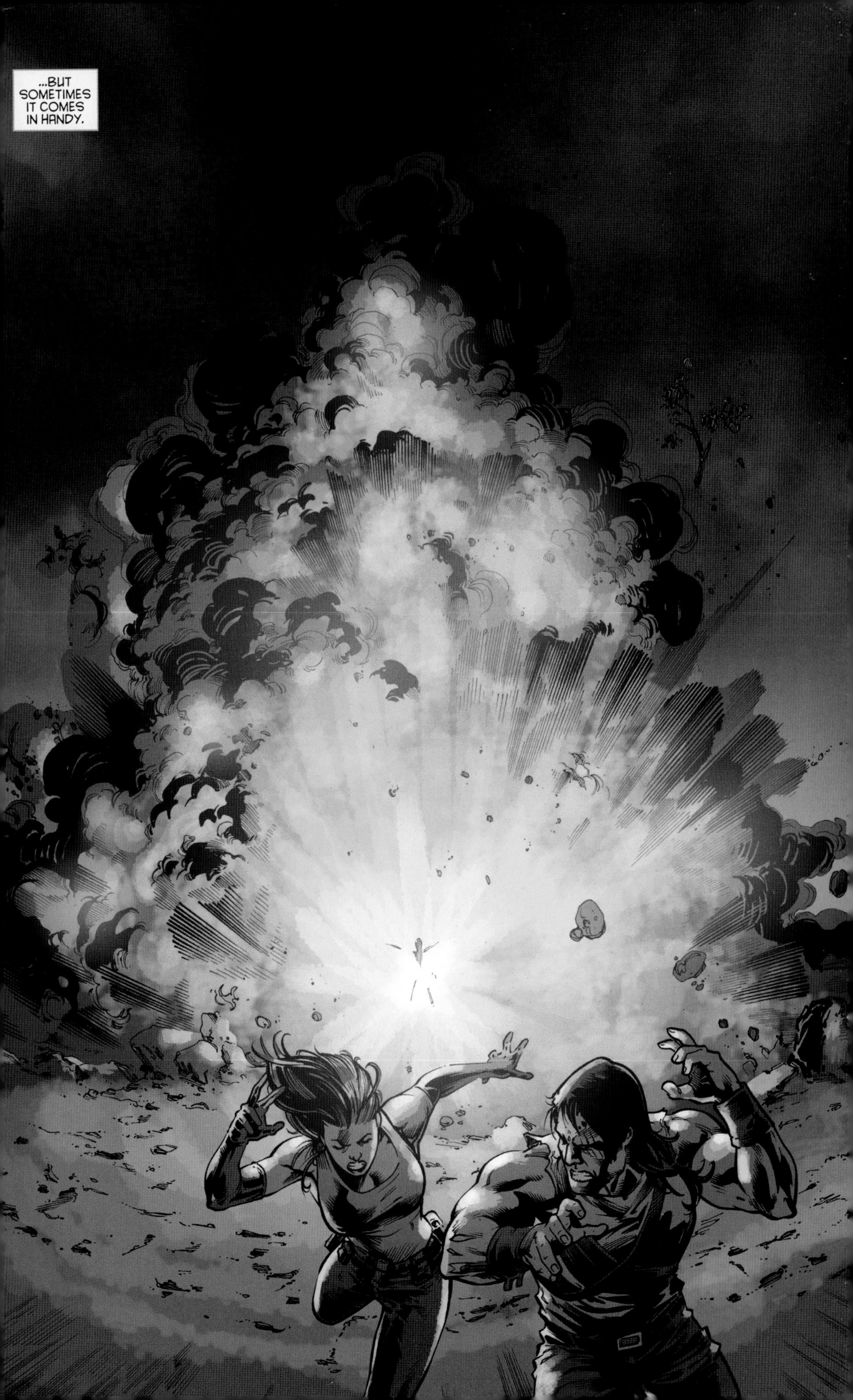
...BUT SOMETIMES IT COMES IN HANDY.

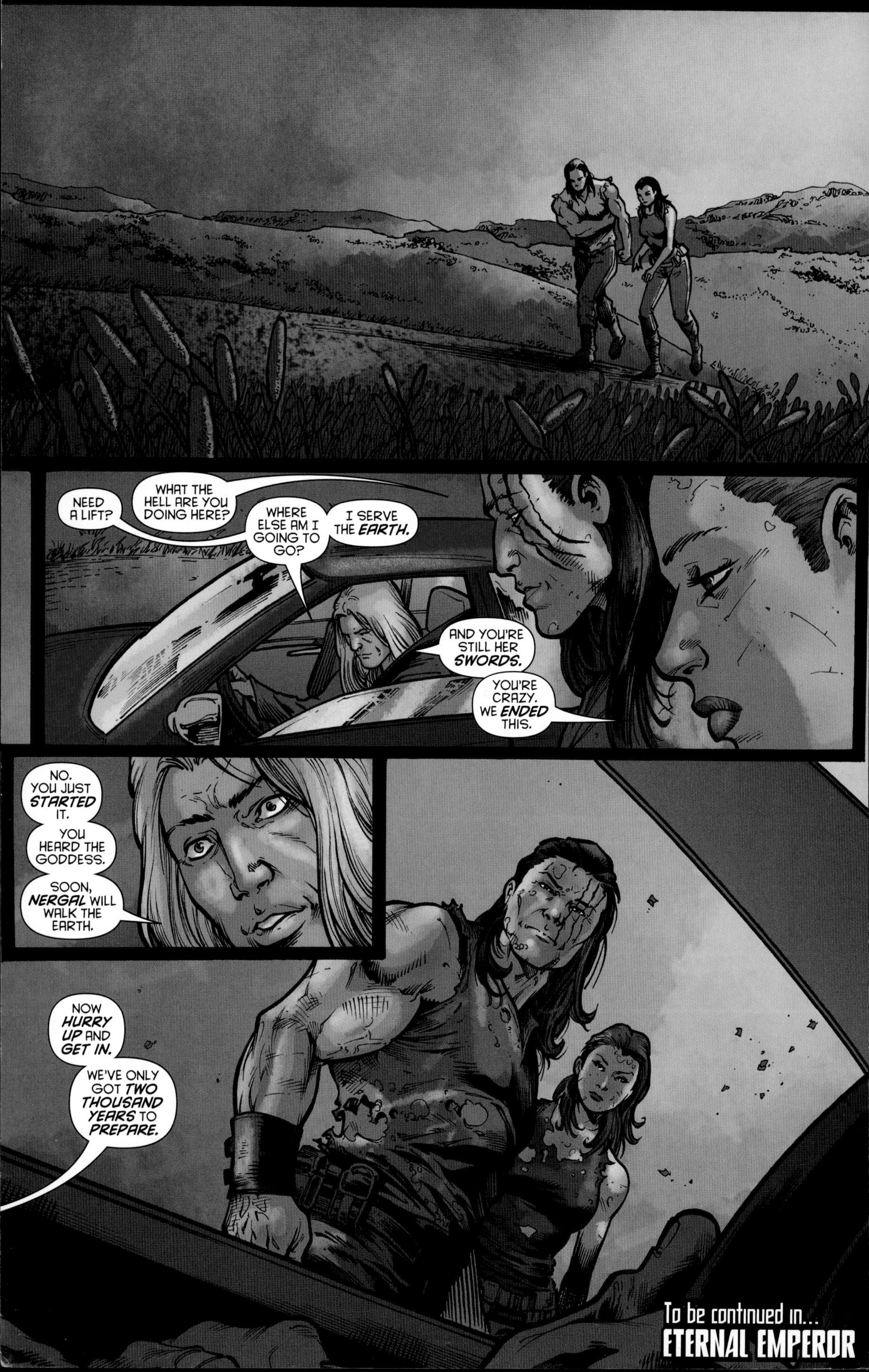
NEED A LIFT?
WHAT THE HELL ARE YOU DOING HERE?
WHERE ELSE AM I GOING TO GO?
I SERVE THE EARTH.
AND YOU'RE STILL HER SWORDS.
YOU'RE CRAZY. WE ENDED THIS.
NO. YOU JUST STARTED IT.
YOU HEARD THE GODDESS.
SOON, NERGAL WILL WALK THE EARTH.
NOW HURRY UP AND GET IN.
WE'VE ONLY GOT TWO THOUSAND YEARS TO PREPARE.
To be continued in...
ETERNAL EMPEROR

GALLERY

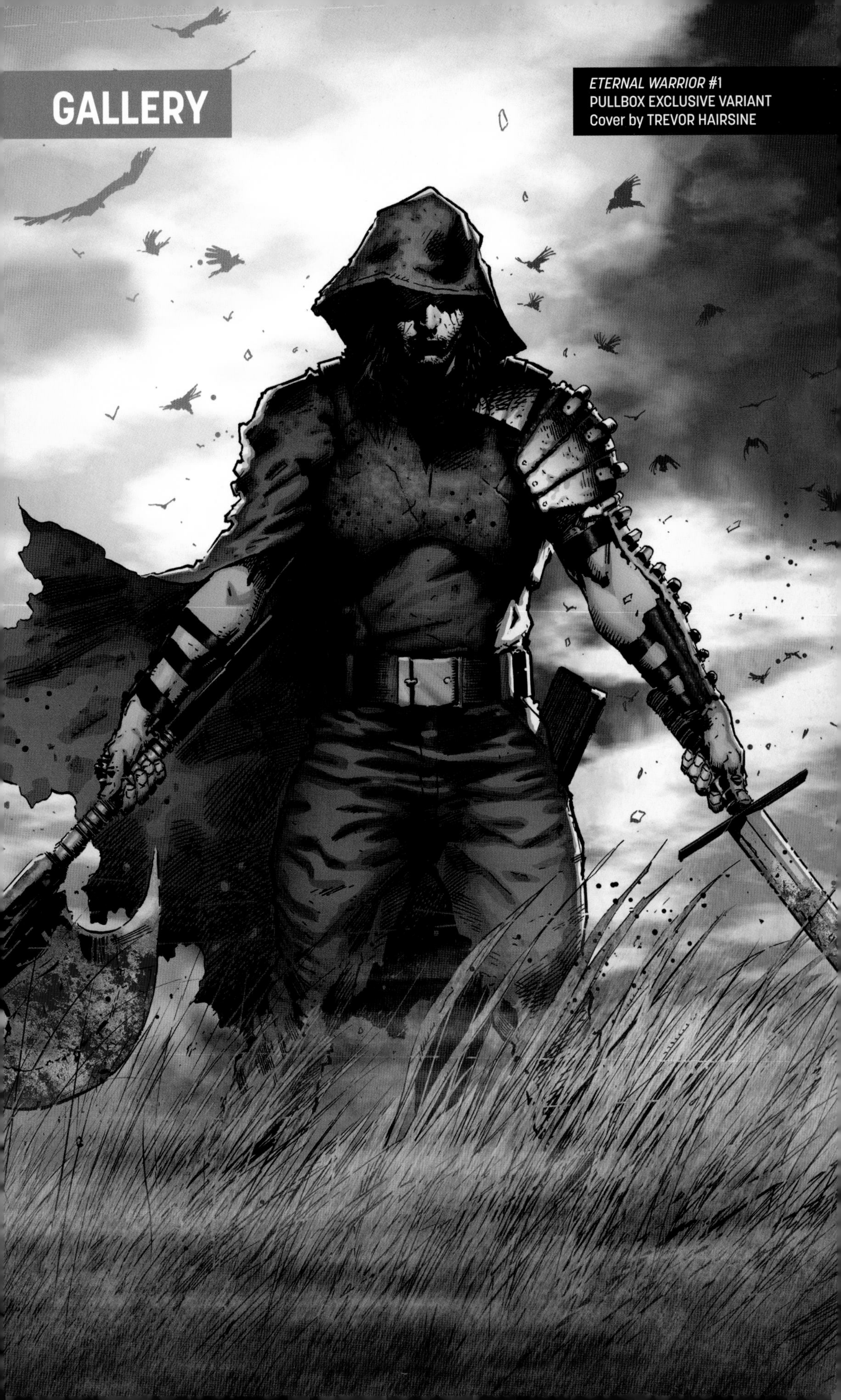

ETERNAL WARRIOR #1
PULLBOX EXCLUSIVE VARIANT
Cover by TREVOR HAIRSINE

ETERNAL WARRIOR #1 VARIANT
Cover by DAVE BULLOCK

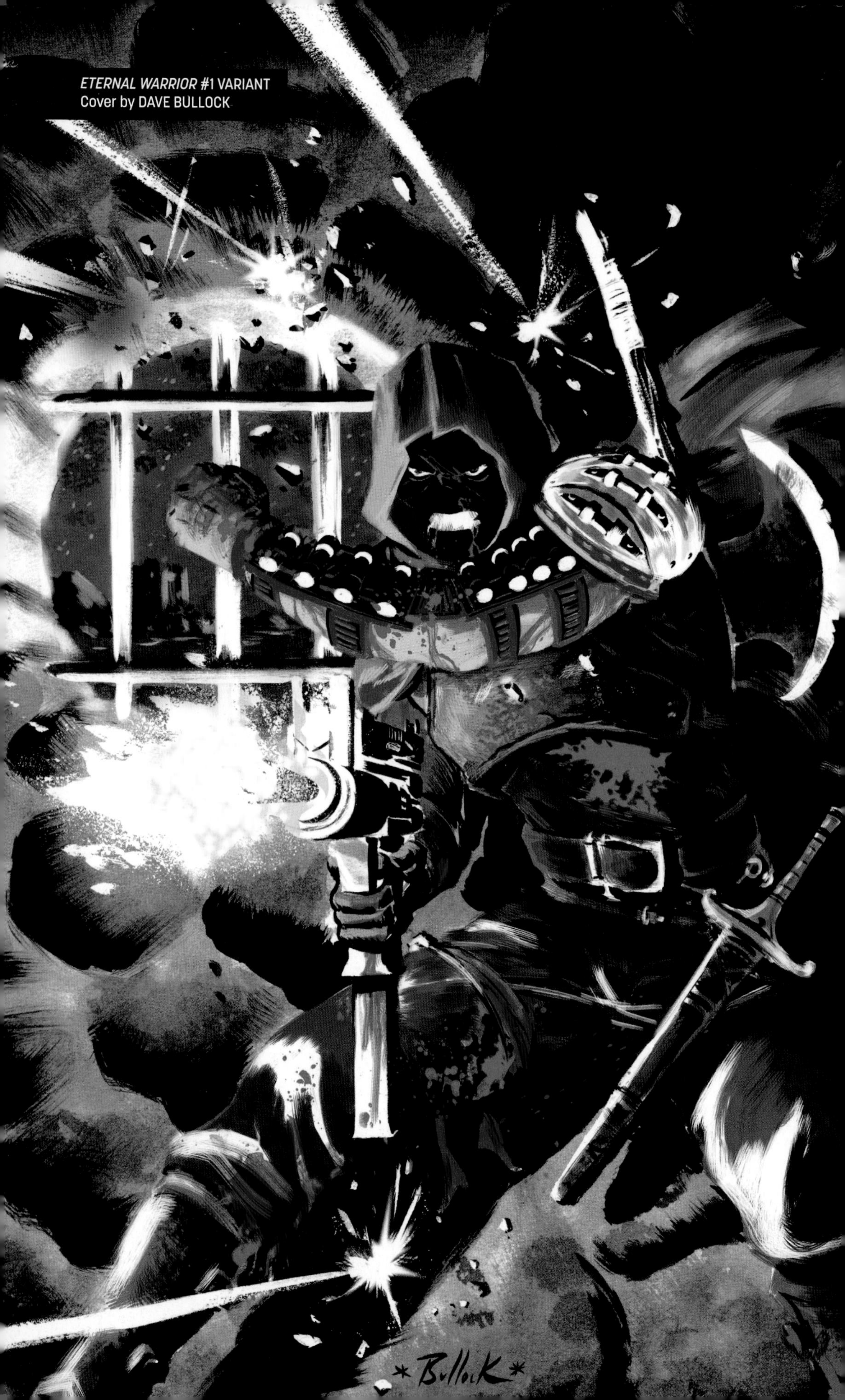
Bullock

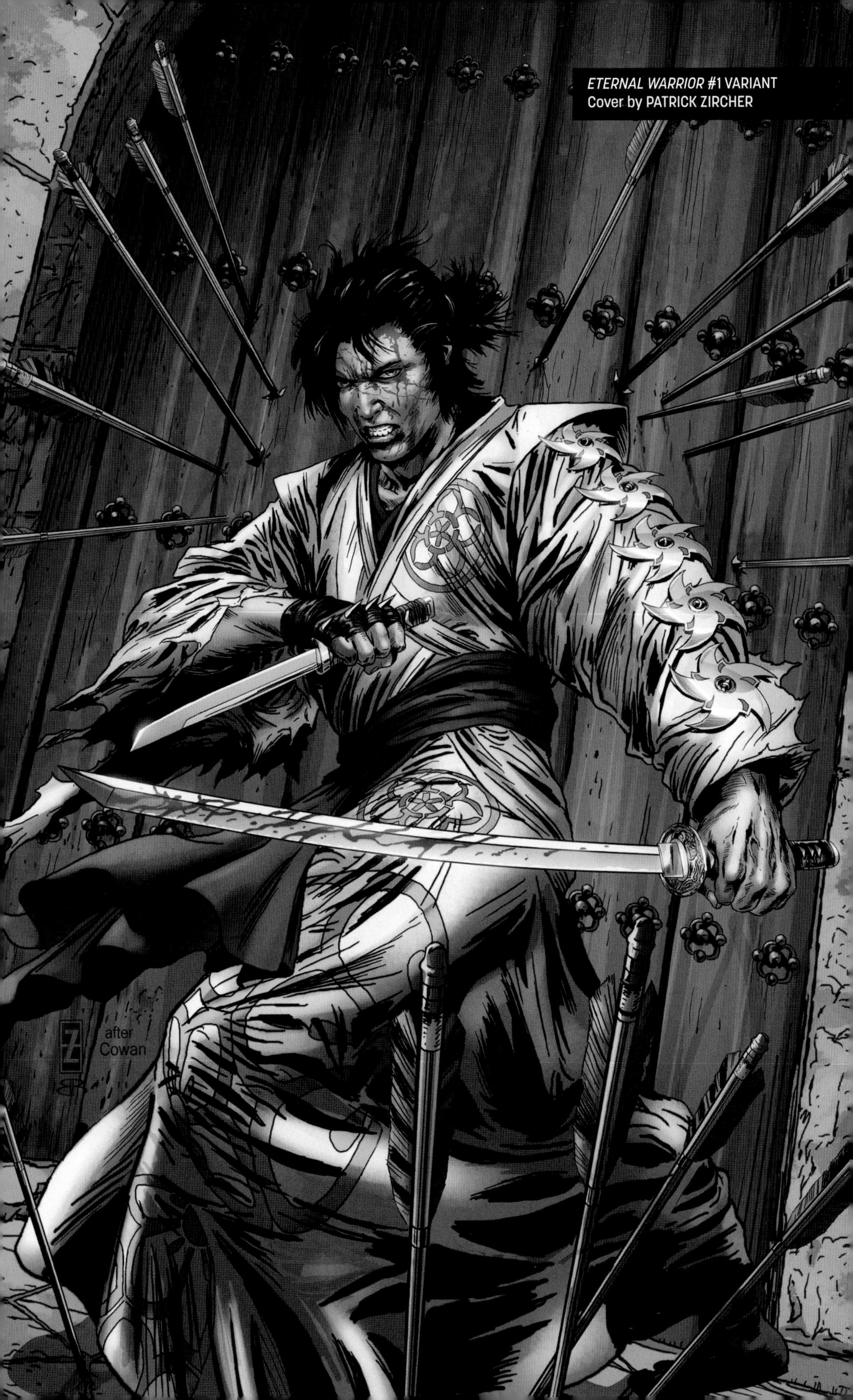
after
Cowan
ETERNAL WARRIOR #1 VARIANT
Cover by PATRICK ZIRCHER

ETERNAL WARRIOR #2 VALIANT
8-BIT LEVEL TWO VARIANT
Cover by DONOVAN SANTIAGO

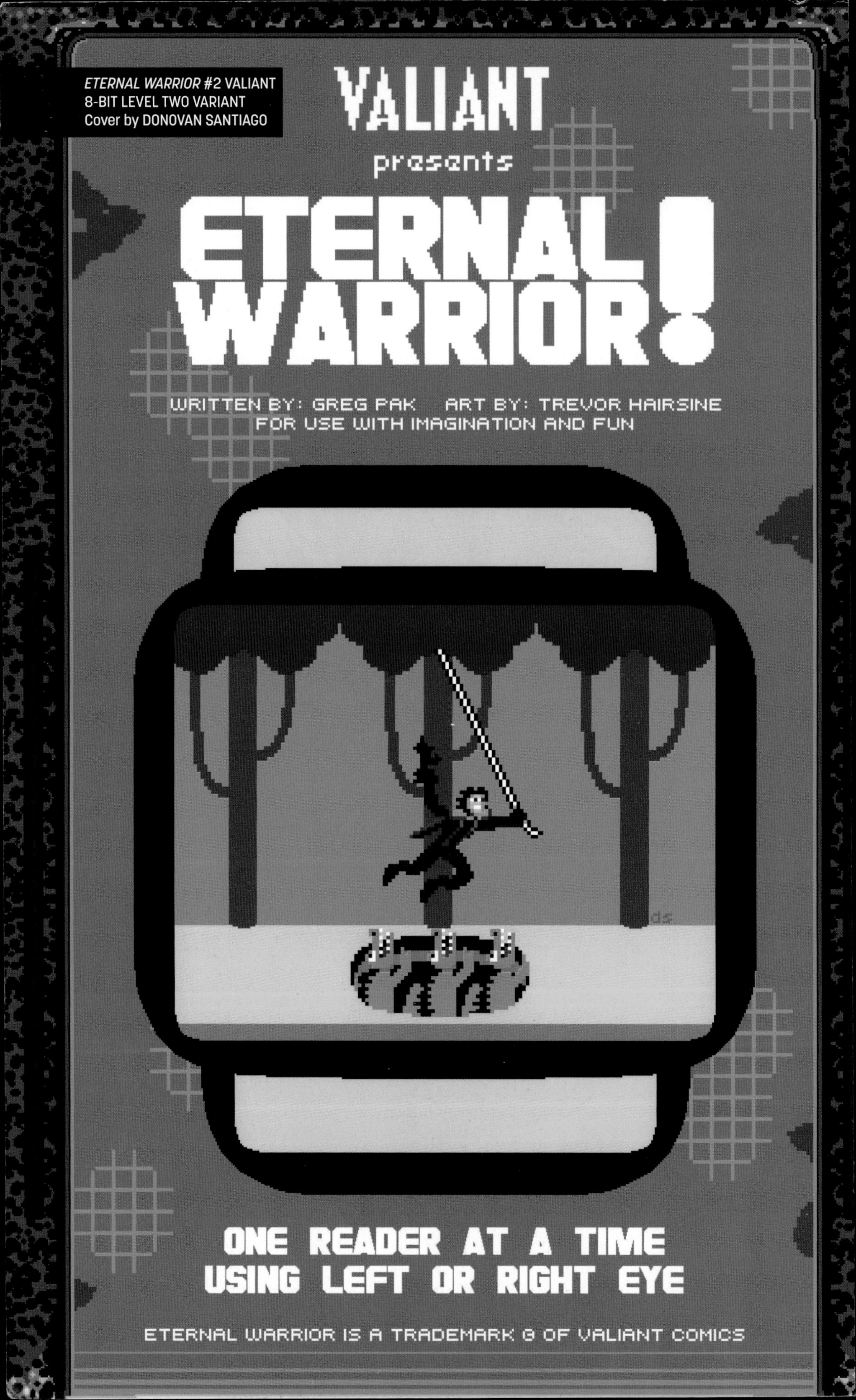

VALIANT
presents
ETERNAL WARRIOR!
WRITTEN BY: GREG PAK ART BY: TREVOR HAIRSINE
FOR USE WITH IMAGINATION AND FUN
ONE READER AT A TIME
USING LEFT OR RIGHT EYE
ETERNAL WARRIOR IS A TRADEMARK © OF VALIANT COMICS

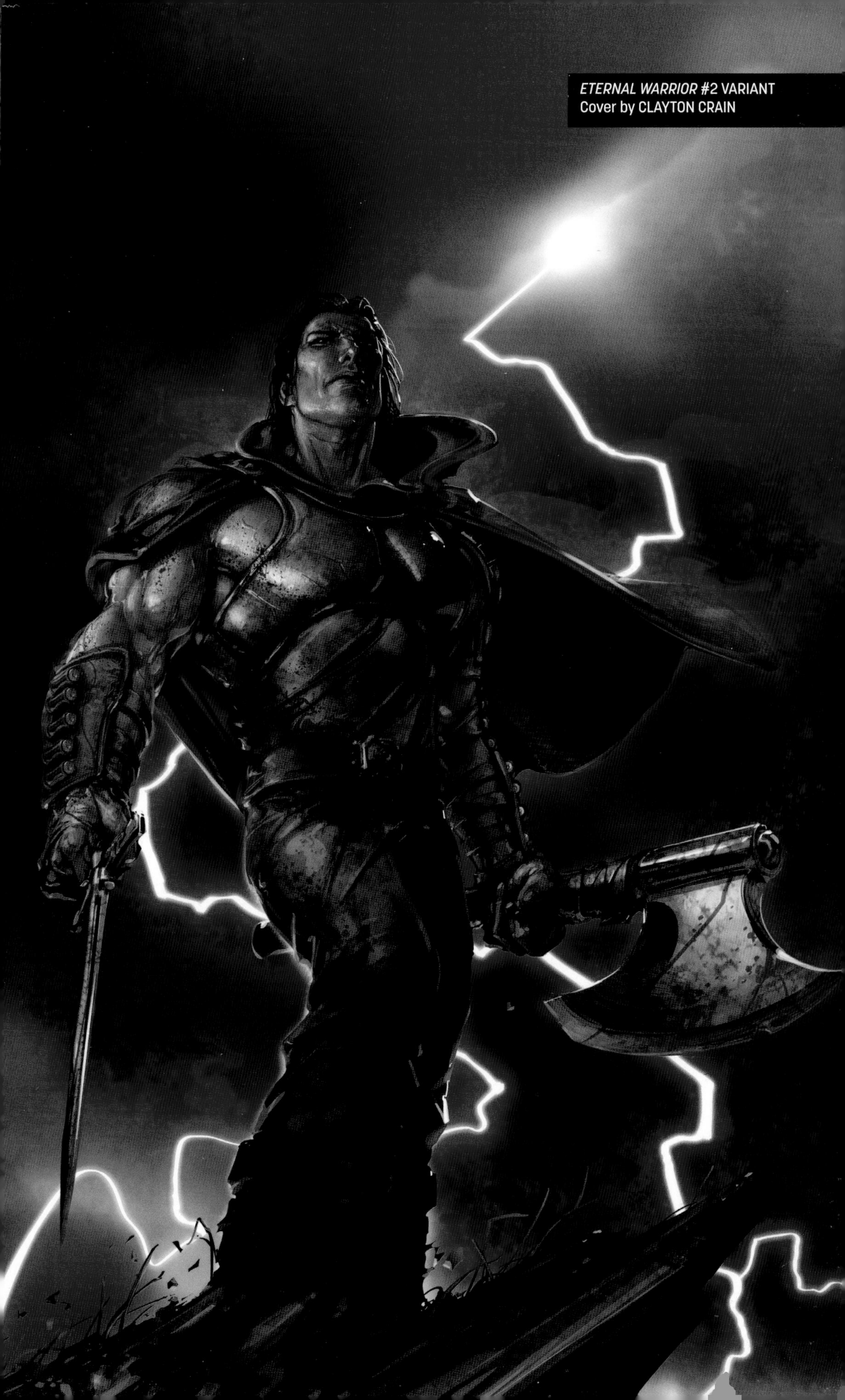

ETERNAL WARRIOR #2 VARIANT
Cover by CLAYTON CRAIN

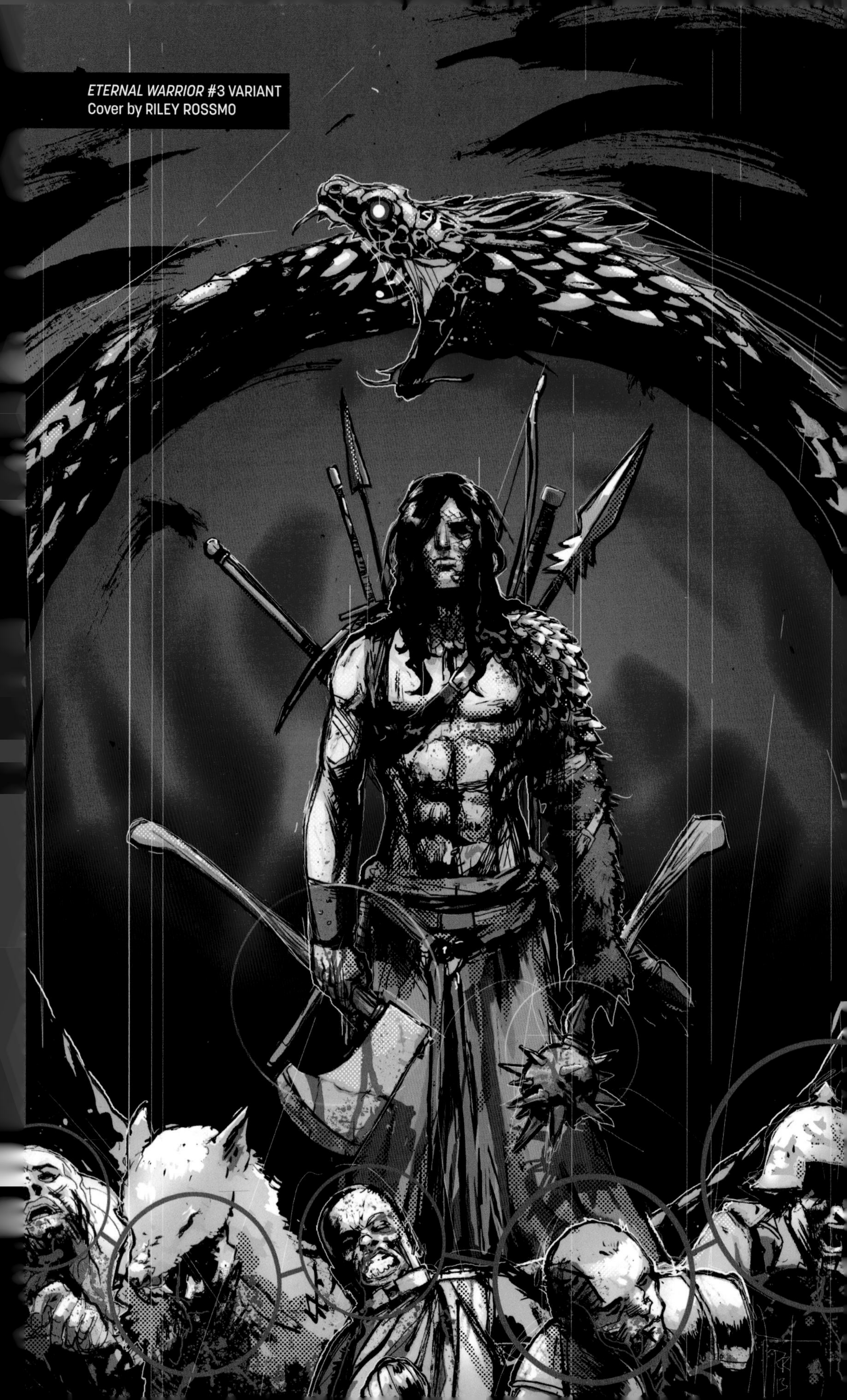

ETERNAL WARRIOR #3 VARIANT
Cover by RILEY ROSSMO

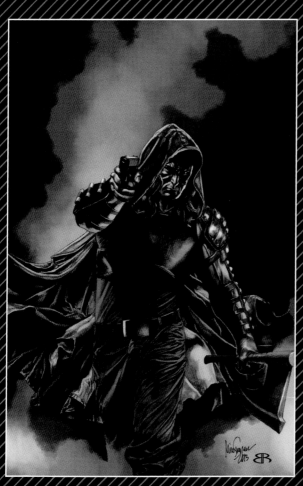

ETERNAL WARRIOR #4 VARIANT
Cover by MICO SUAYAN

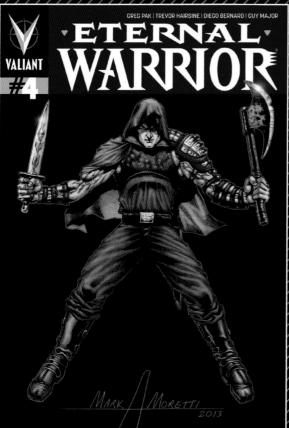

VALIANT
GREG PAK | TREVOR HAIRSINE | DIEGO BERNARD | GUY MAJOR
ETERNAL
WARRIOR
#4
MARK A MORETTI
2013

ETERNAL WARRIOR #4
VALIANT SIGNATURE SERIES VARIANT
Cover by MARK MORETTI

ETERNAL WARRIOR #1, p. 4
Art by TREVOR HAIRSINE

ETERNAL WARRIOR #1, p. 5
Art by TREVOR HAIRSINE

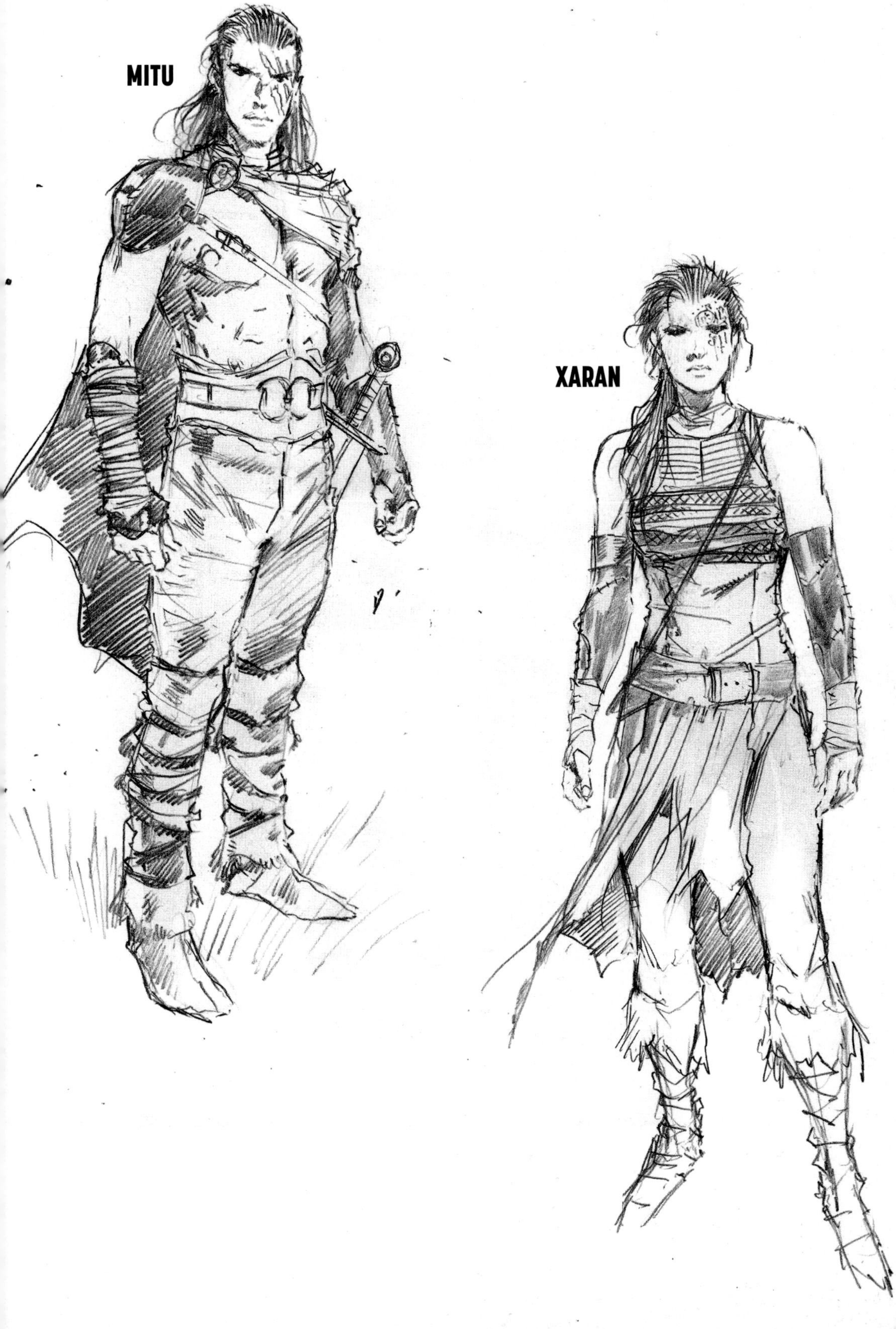
MITU
XARAN

VALIANT COLLECTIONS

TRADE PAPERBACKS

**X-O MANOWAR VOL. 1:
BY THE SWORD**

**X-O MANOWAR VOL. 2:
ENTER NINJAK**

**X-O MANOWAR VOL. 3:
PLANET DEATH**

**HARBINGER VOL. 1:
OMEGA RISING**

**BLOODSHOT VOL. 3:
HARBINGER WARS**

**ARCHER & ARMSTRONG VOL. 1:
THE MICHELANGELO CODE**

**ARCHER & ARMSTRONG VOL. 2:
WRATH OF THE ETERNAL WARRIOR**

**ARCHER & ARMSTRONG VOL. 3:
FAR FARAWAY**

DELUXE EDITIONS

X-O MANOWAR DELUXE EDITION BOOK 1

HARBINGER DELUXE EDITION BOOK 1

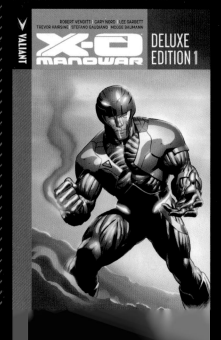

THE STORY STARTS HERE.

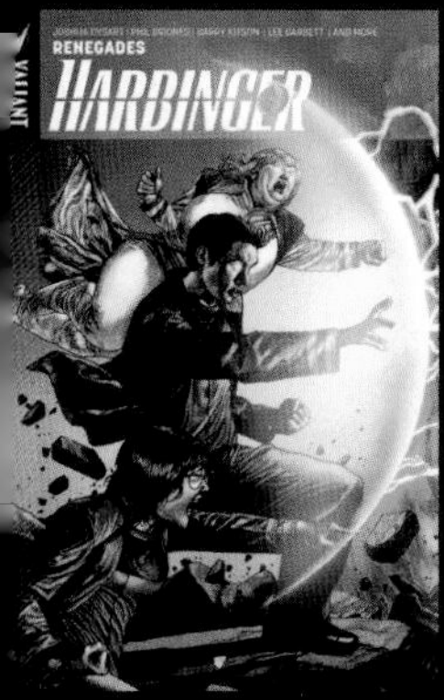
VALIANT
RENEGADES
HARBINGER

ARBINGER VOL. 2:
ENEGADES

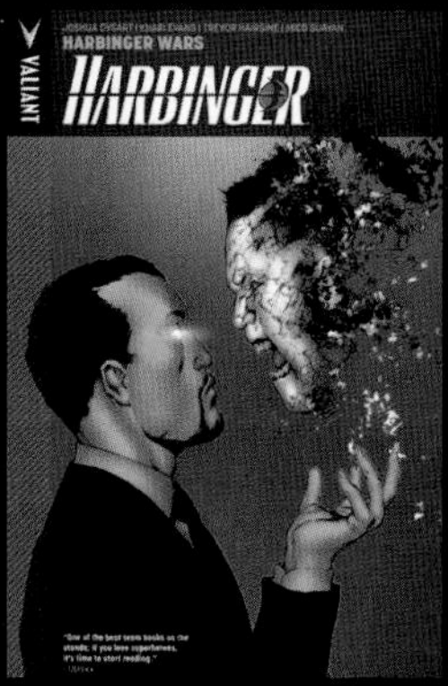
VALIANT
HARBINGER WARS
HARBINGER

HARBINGER VOL. 3:
HARBINGER WARS

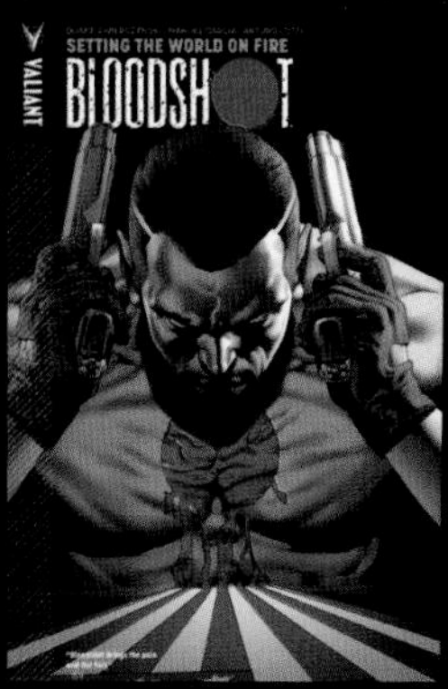
VALIANT
SETTING THE WORLD ON FIRE
BLOODSHOT

BLOODSHOT VOL. 1:
SETTING THE WORLD ON FIRE

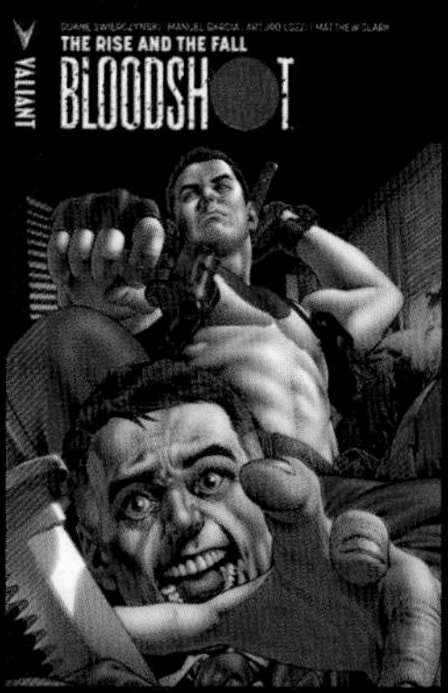
VALIANT
THE RISE AND THE FALL
BLOODSHOT

BLOODSHOT VOL. 2:
THE RISE AND THE FALL

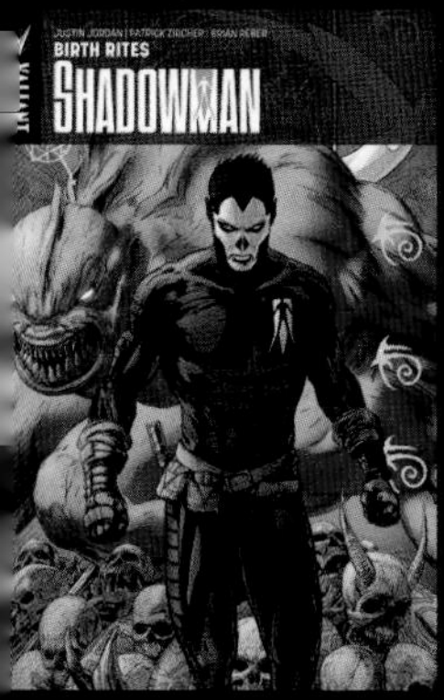
BIRTH RITES
SHADOWMAN

HADOWMAN VOL. 1:
IRTH RITES

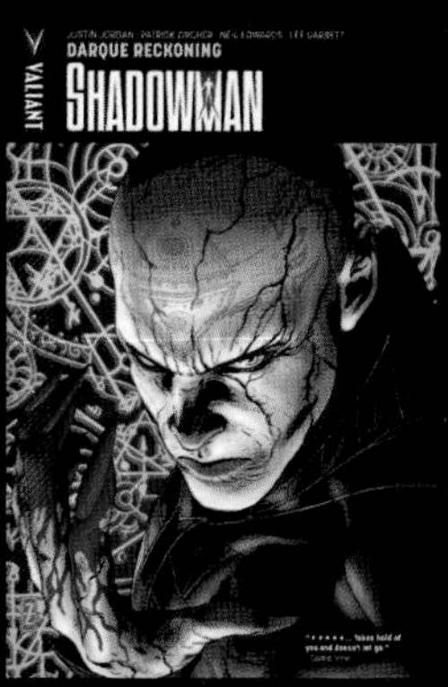
VALIANT
DARQUE RECKONING
SHADOWMAN

SHADOWMAN VOL. 2:
DARQUE RECKONING

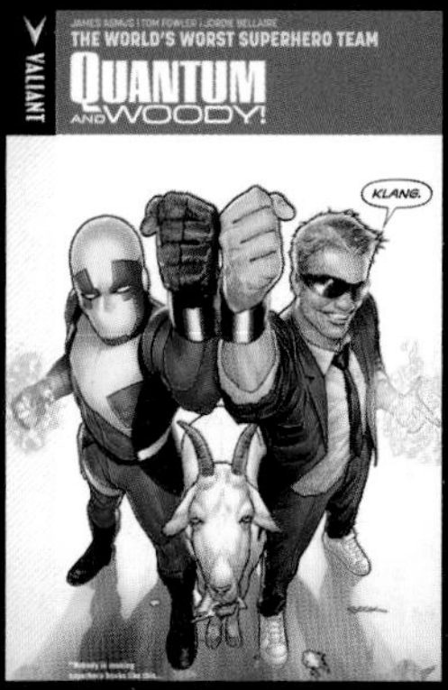
VALIANT
THE WORLD'S WORST SUPERHERO TEAM
QUANTUM AND WOODY!
KLANG.

QUANTUM AND WOODY VOL. 1:
THE WORLD'S WORST
SUPERHERO TEAM

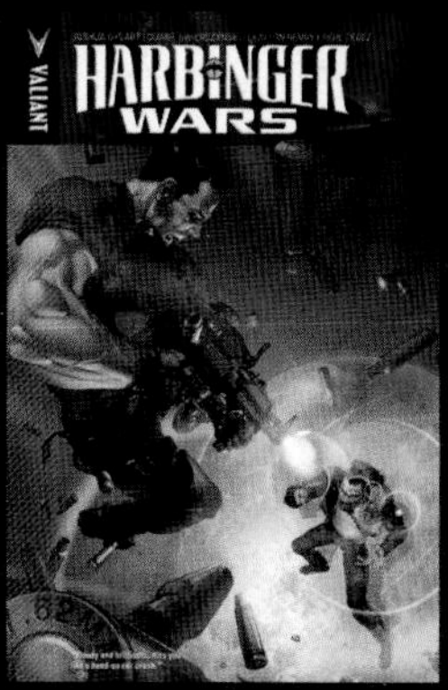
VALIANT
HARBINGER
WARS

HARBINGER WARS

ALIANT MASTERS

ALIANT MASTERS: BLOODSHOT VOL. 1:
LOOD OF THE MACHINE

VALIANT MASTERS: NINJAK VOL. 1:
BLACK WATER

VALIANT MASTERS: SHADOWMAN VOL. 1:
SPIRITS WITHIN

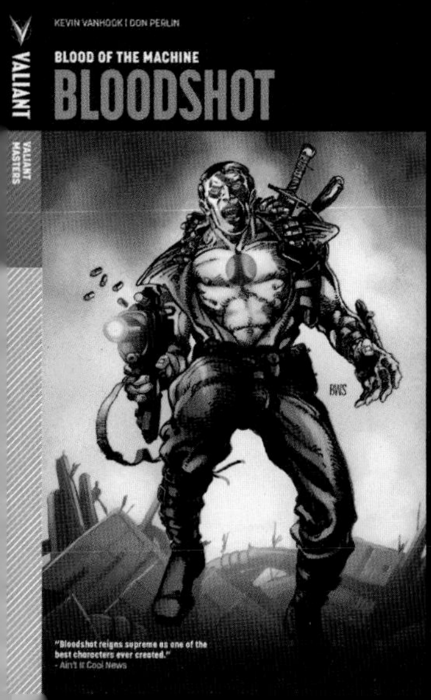
KEVIN VANHOOK | DON PERLIN
VALIANT
BLOOD OF THE MACHINE
BLOODSHOT
VALIANT MASTERS
"Bloodshot reigns supreme as one of the best characters ever created."
- Ain't It Cool News

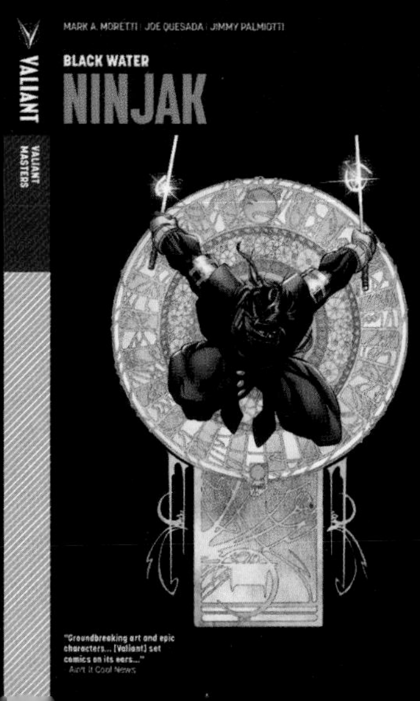
MARK A. MORETTI | JOE QUESADA | JIMMY PALMIOTTI
VALIANT
BLACK WATER
NINJAK
VALIANT MASTERS
"Groundbreaking art and epic characters... [Valiant] set comics on its ears..."
- Ain't It Cool News

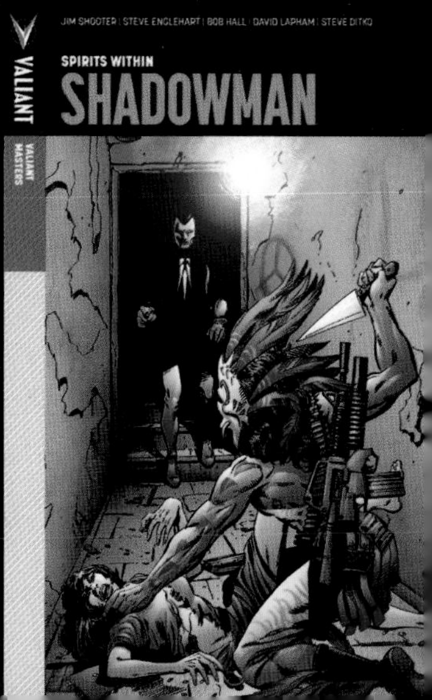
JIM SHOOTER | STEVE ENGLEHART | BOB HALL | DAVID LAPHAM | STEVE DITKO
VALIANT
SPIRITS WITHIN
SHADOWMAN
VALIANT MASTERS

VALIANT

ETERNAL WARRIOR

VOLUME TWO: ETERNAL EMPEROR

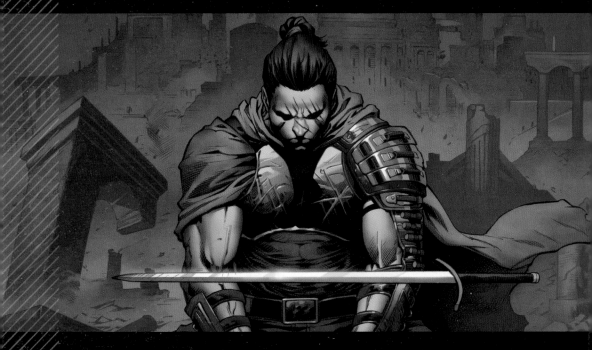

THE COMING OF...4001 A.D.!

Two thousand years from today, the planet has been transformed by science, technology...and war. The centuries have not been kind to the Earth's own undying warrior - but a battle that could change everything is just beginning right here in the 21st century. Find out where the roots of humanity's last stand will begin as a transformed Gilad Anni-Padda fights the forces of final extinction and protects a tattered remnant of humanity on a ravaged continent.

Collecting ETERNAL WARRIOR #5-8, the Fist and Steel's battle continues right here as New York Times best-selling writer Greg Pak (*Batman/Superman*) and rising star Robert Gill build a bridge to the year 4001... and unearth a brand-new era for the heroes of the Valiant Universe.

GREG PAK | ROBERT GILL
ETERNAL EMPEROR
ETERNAL WARRIOR
VALIANT

TRADE PAPERBACK
ISBN: 978-1-939346-29-2

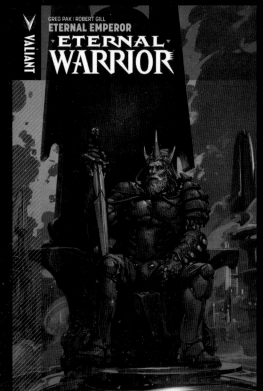